CW00392909

A Glimpsed-at Reality

A priest's diary of life and meaning
in Lockdown and beyond

Susan Bedford

A Glimpsed-at Reality

A priest's diary of life and meaning in Lockdown and beyond

Susan Bedford

Pendlebury Press Limited
20 May Road
Swinton
Manchester
M27 5FR
U.K.

Copyright © 2023 Susan Bedford

All rights reserved.

ISBN: 978-1-9999846-8-7

CONTENTS

Acknowledgements

A huge thanks to all the dogs, people and places that have inspired me, who and which enrich my life, especially those who have crept in to this book, and a special thank you to Ann Sansom, co-director, editor and tutor of The Poetry Business, for her poetry wisdom and support, and to The Right Reverend Dr Tim Ellis, retired Bishop of Grantham and now Assistant Bishop in the Diocese of Sheffield, for his gentle encouragement.

FOREWORD

"This is a collection of life's gems: Susan's mixture of prose and poetry is an exercise in mindfulness and the knowledge that beauty, wisdom and meaning are to be found in the routine encounters and experiences of an 'ordinary' life. These reflections raise the everyday occurrences to become 'extraordinary'. Read it and be delighted!"

The Right Reverend Dr Tim Ellis, Assistant Bishop in the Diocese of Sheffield

INTRODUCTION

Out of the blue my friend Ann Sansom gave me Maitreyabandhu's beautiful, absorbing and thrilling *A Cezanne Haibun* * I was then inspired, putting it boldly, to write a haibun of my own, *A Town Fields Haibun*. This was followed by *A Red Path Haibun*.

A haibun is a Japanese literary form which combines prose and haiku poems, and frequently includes memoir, diary, travel, and images of the natural world.

Strictly speaking a haiku poem is three lines long, the first line five syllables, the second seven, and the third five, but it doesn't have to be that. Many poems in these two haibuns are far from haiku.

Town Fields and the Red Path are places where I walk my dogs, and so my daily natural world.

These haibuns are a reflective diary in prose and poems from November 2019 - October 2022.

* Published 2019 by SmithIDoorstop Books
The Poetry Business, Campo House, 54 Campo Lane
Sheffield S1 2EG https://poetrybusiness.co.uk

A TOWN FIELDS HAIBUN

PART 1

21 DAYS

All Saints' Day 2019

The same walk as Monday, only then the late afternoon October sun shone directly on to the green-gold leaves, against an azure sky. I told my Painter and Decorator about it. We got on to talking about the colour red. He told me that red attracts and then repels, and that's why red is used in fast food outlets, because it brings people in, but soon they've had enough of it, and want to leave.

Today damp clogs the ground. The day seems to be in a waiting room, long overdue having its name called out.

At home the two dogs sleep, the walk having taken it out of them. I wish I could do that: put the washing out, have a nap, take a service, have a nap, exert myself over a few emails, nap.

Autumn colours
like Harris tweed
on Town Fields

All Souls' Day

This morning's walk was hurried because my cousin, co -executor, was going to ring.

An assortment of dogs, sniffing, and running at sitting gulls, who fly and sit again a little further away, apart from one, who I think may be ill, because it doesn't fly off. Then at last it does, as if calculating just how much energy needs to be expended, as if it is on a smart meter.

Cut and left grass sticks to my wellie boots. The tarmac paths are strewn with gold. In my sermon tonight I will mention the thin line between heaven and earth and how the living and departed are bound together in a communion of prayer. Not everyone believes that.

My cousin rings, frustrated by another incompetence of the bank. After that, the house has a silence I could drink. When my cousin arrives I'll put the kettle on.

Morning thunder in November. Different sized raindrops on the window, caught by the glass on their way down, where now they lodge, looking stuck.

On the radio more about Brexit
A macaroni cheese in the oven
Wet roof tiles opposite.

All Saints' Sunday

Rods of morning sunbeams, highlighted by the incense, slant through the clerestory windows. The music soars. The ancient liturgy is recited.

Dew-saturated grass this morning. On a colder day it would have been frost. Baby-blue sky with sparse white cloud.

Sometimes you meet dogs you know, but today there were new ones, a spaniel bringing back its Frisbee.

A friend and I go to a neighbour's house. He hasn't been seen in Marks and Spencer's for three weeks. He shuffles to the door. Apparently, he now has carers. I resolve to call round more.

It's nearly dark at half past four now, and a few stray explosions are let off. On Saturday night the house shook. One of my dogs is deaf. The other one seemed happy enough with Liza Tarbuck on Radio 2.

I asked a man outside church this morning not to speak to his dog so harshly. He didn't reply, but when he went off, he spoke to it more reasonably. I wonder if this is on his mind like it is on mine?

Faure said of his Requiem that in it he sees death as a happy deliverance rather than a fearful experience. The Minster choir sing it. The tenor soloist is clear and true.

That last week before your expected death
the closing down
that slow ride
where you think there's nowhere else to go
then there is
like writing a conclusion
pausing, writing, and putting in the full stop.

Monday 4 November

Today would have been my mother's birthday, and the date I was expected to be born, except I arrived eight weeks early and had to have an emergency baptism. I wonder if I was never able to let God go after that. Or God me. At Morning Prayer I thank my mother. I can do that now.

A heavy white-grey dampness shrouds the morning. Eddi, my younger dog, and Stanley, another Miniature Schnauzer, chase on the Field. Stanley's owner tells me Stanley is a thief. Yesterday he leapt up and took a Yorkshire Pudding from the table, then came downstairs with a five pack of Kit-Kats from the wardrobe. The perspective on this long straight path delights me, each golden tree adjusting its position to converge.

Eight gulls who were lined up on the goal post fly off when a dog approaches them. They've not worked out that a dog could never get them up there. If just one worked it out the others would know through the morphogenetic field, according to Rupert Sheldrake, like those monkeys who learnt how to use a tool from others across the world.

My hairdresser's partner wishes me a Happy Christmas.

One break of clouds
holds warm white light,
the rest calling it a day.

Lights click on
curtains close.
Cars park up.

I have been put on Vitamin D,
my body's ability to manufacture it
in the presence of sunlight
compromised.

I heard on the radio
that we don't know enough about the sun.

Or anything, for that matter.

A bird calls out something
as it flits by the window.

Tuesday 5 November

My train to Leeds is delayed for half an hour. A fatality
at Grantham. The station is fuller than usual. People
look at the boards and saunter with hot drinks,
consulting their phones. That person's family and
friends will be devastated. Worse if they're not. I say
to the woman issuing tickets how sorry I am, and then,
like them, I carry on with my day.

I come home to hear that 38kg of frozen dog food
has been delivered today instead of tomorrow, with
the freezer still defrosting, and that the boiler has
rattled and overheated itself to a standstill. There's an

engineer now tinkering with it, but he pronounces it dead by the time he leaves.

In Debenhams today my friend and I looked at a polar bear ornament. He might have remembered our old joke, as I did, but I didn't mention it in case he didn't.

Wednesday 6 November

The house where I grew up sometimes had ice on the inside of the windows, and sometimes wet sheets on the airier taking all the heat from the fire. I think of this now our central heating has broken down.

The first time I encountered central heating was at Ann's, aged thirteen. The absolute pleasure of a warm bathroom. Her parents also had a tiled kitchen, a wall mounted gas fire and Fingal's Cave on an LP. Ann is one of the people from those days I'd like to see again. Today's walk in the rain, less gulls and dogs. More leaves every shade of gold, parachuting down. I wonder how many leaves there are on the ground, which reminds me of Psalm 139: *How weighty to me are your thoughts, O God. How vast is the sum of them. I try to count them. They are more than the sand; I come to the end — I am still with you.*

I would like to know the number of leaves, except more are falling by the second.

Is the tree still them, or has it already moved on, consolidating itself for next Spring?

I don't miss my hair when I've had it cut.

My elderly dog with dementia walks a long way in small circles when left to herself.

The washing machine now leaks and has been repaired with a patch from a bicycle repair kit.

Thursday 7 November

Strewn glazed gold now obliterates the path. Cold rain slants behind my glasses to hit my eye. Wide tree trunks have tree pools, moats. Seb, an Italian Spinone, gets his favourite drinks from those. Today on the Field there's Stanley and his owner, a woman with two whippets in macs and me and my dogs.

I review my vinyl records to assess which to take for professional cleaning, having gunged some up fifty years ago with a spray. An old friend remembers that I used to clean them with a velvet cloth. I tell her that the place I've taken them has an impressive machine, and that I leave them there, but I imagine, once I've left, they just take out a velvet cloth.

My records are a photographic slice of around ten years of my life, with the way I felt then now back in full technicolour - or technicolor.

The garden flashed by this year after the first longed-for snow drop. The winter is such a long wait for the cherry blossom, and then once the garden starts the bulbs and shrubs rattle through, the perennials come and go, a bit of garden work happens and then it's over, all hunkering down, blown, sodden, like someone who should have gone hours ago.

Friday 8 November

There are floods in Doncaster.

An environmental speaker I heard two years ago told us that eventually Doncaster will be completely under water. As I travel to York and pass all the flooded fields it feels like it could be soon. A few black birds sit on an unexpected pond. The rivers want no more. A power station chugs out water vapour. The ground is weary with it all. The sun comes out, and more rain clouds are forming.

Thursday 14 November

Rain. Many people in Bentley Toll bar are flooded. Floods are coming to that area more frequently now.

We have eleven years to go before climate change is irreversible. Sorrow fills my heart.

Today I had a letter and pictures from The Dogs Trust showing a dog they rescued that had been thrown away with the rubbish.

The leaves on the paths are trodden down now. They've given of their best. Some leaves cling on, gungy green.

I feel extraordinarily fortunate to have a warm house again.

I am told of a toy collection that is being organised for children in families with flooded homes. I imagine the children's delight, and their parents having to grin and bear Christmas.

Friday 15 November

I am surprised, though I shouldn't be, by how grief makes one behave. With some money I have been left from my Aunt I buy a new vacuum cleaner, which needs charging, which Linda offers to do. It doesn't get charged, and the longer it doesn't the more upset I feel. My Aunt looks at me from the cover page of her poetry collection. I didn't miss her much at first. Reading her diaries, I realised I didn't really know her as much as I could. Now the cleaner, the first thing I have bought with her money, has taken on a ridiculous importance.

The bank sinks to a new low in its catalogue of incompetence and we executors are issued with a cheque book, but the bank has not put the funds into the account, so had we issued cheques the beneficiaries would have found that their cheques bounced. Fortunately, going on experience, we didn't believe the bank when they assured us that the funds were there.

On the walk today a large brown dog charges full pelt towards Eddi. They attempt to play, but the brown dog is too rough. It quickly rolls her on her back, and I shout its owners to call their dog, which they do, so Eddi is put on her lead until we have got away from it. We meet Peppi and her people. The daughter, a sixth-former, is having lessons with her class on how to hide if an intruder gets into the school. Peppi, a Lab, ambles along, loosely keeping an eye on them, but not bothered if they go out of sight.

Maitreyabandhu wrote twenty-one days of haibun and haiku, and I could do no better than follow him. Today is my tenth day.

Saturday 16 November

Today we remember Margaret Queen of Scotland, philanthropist, Reformer of the Church, who died this day 1093. It is said of her that she was a woman of prayer and good works, who founded many monasteries. From what I read about her she was also a theologian, although, being a woman, not described as such.

Scotland is a good place to think about God.

Arran

Sleeping Warrior
Fallen Rocks
the whisky distillery

Arran candles
The Laughing Stone
The Apostles.

An otter at Pirnmill
sheep on the beach
The King's Cave.

Monday 18 November

Bendy rays of sun wobble on the water, while on the bottom of the swimming pool the pattern is of a shifting giraffe.

Tuesday 19 November

St Hilda's day, also known as St Hild, who was influential and a great educator in the 600s. My theological college was named after her.
Monasticism continues in the background, the Religious praying for the world through every day and night. We would be in a worse place without them.

The voice of prayer is never silent, the hymn says

The brothers and sisters,
when we're not there,
go in to the chapel,
and go in to the chapel.

Wednesday 20 November

On the radio there is a conversation about antimatter, and the interviewer asks if a bomb could be made of it.

Leaves are on the paths, so you can't tell where the grass stops and where the path begins. We meet a new dog today, who is also one year old. Our dogs chase, having the time of their lives. As a dog you know straight away what to do with another dog: You look, chase, and come away. Job done.

I write a letter to a friend. We have talked about Leonard Cohen for nearly fifty years.

I think of Maitreyabandhu in his ruined cottage, and his opportunity for thinking about Cezanne and his work, which makes me think of my friend Anne, where I first saw a Cezanne print. Like for Anne, colour to me is vital. It gives me a hit. In a service I am preparing for artists, I am going to mention one of my favourite paintings, *The Dunes of Perrow* by the Russian Expressionist painter Alexej Jawlensky, who died in 1941. Of his work he said, 'The pictures were the product of an overwhelming inner ecstasy'. You can't complain about that.

The Doncaster Rubies had a week at Lumb Bank this year, thanks to the wonderful Ann and Peter Sansom, of The Poetry Business. We wrote, looked, shared time, listened to Louise. It is a time treasured.

I am aware that I am two thirds through my twenty-one-day haibun. It's about Thursday on a week's holiday, when you're starting to think about what you'd really like to do before you leave.

I have no plans. The next seven days will be as they will be.

Lumb Bank

In the summer, the light.
We write, walk
and listen.

Green
Mesembryanthemums clump in a pot,
a black and white photograph is taken.

Monday 25 November

A grey film lies over the day, like a cataract.
Then it rains.

A grumpy engineer comes to repair the leaking washing machine.
Afterwards it still leaks.

Everything is about water
I continue with my service for artists.

Today on the Field paths lies a coppery leafy mush. The black-barked trees can do nothing but wait. The Field is sodden. My young dog is not held back, and runs about. Two people with muzzled German Shepherds walk by.

We have The Festival of Light at the Minster, the soundscape is loud and my ears feels sensitive after it, as if they want to pop and relax.

I cheer up listening to *Sorry I Haven't a Clue*.

Tuesday 26 November

Lights in the street where I live wish everyone a Merry Christmas, while in the Christian calendar we are gearing up for the start of our New Year, Advent, with Christmas nearly a month away. In fact, a month today will be Boxing Day, or St Stephen's Day, if you prefer.

I'm looking forward to the shortest day, because every day after that will be a teeny-weeny bit lighter.

One of our neighbour's dogs has died. I've known her for most of her life. I write a card to put through her owners' door, then on the last dog walk of the day I bump into them and we talk.

Christmas to come is seeping in and I am thinking of books my great nieces might like.

My elderly dog, Phoebe, now fifteen and four months, is getting worse, so we adjust, not letting her dementia get the better of her, or us.

The walk today was functional, Tuesday being a day of juggling to fit everything in. The Vicar is on BBC1 talking about the Festival of Light and welcoming people.

Climate change

irreversible in eleven years.
We know exactly what to do,
a bit like healthy eating.

Ostrich like -
after Sylvia Plath -

happiest in the sand
Feet to the stars, and dumb skulled.

Saturday 30 November

After singing Handel's Messiah in the Minster, which
was not so much singing as being carried inside a St
Ives-style wave of sound, the singer next to me said, 'I
want heaven to be like this', and I said, 'This, and a
couple of dogs and I'll be fine'. She readily agreed. We
presumed God.

Sometimes one Amen isn't enough,
and so the Amens glide, circle and climb over one
another
like puppies in a basket

so you can't tell where one begins and one ends,
rising up and up
so you can't distinguish between what is singing and
what is being them.

Advent Sunday

A gear shift. A lot of from darkness to light, and turning our thoughts to the last things. So we're in penitential purple.

Leading the service, I see the booklet that's been on my screen come to life on paper, words, choral music and movement, and I look at the congregation in candlelight, making of it whatever they do.

Merry Christmas lights in our street welcome us home. With twenty-four days to go how do they keep the momentum going, I wonder, to The Big Day? When Christmas starts at 11.30pm on 24 December, for me that's soon enough.

It's Christmas card cold,
with a melting gold sunrise
and air like walking into a steel sheet.

It wouldn't surprise me if it snowed,
and we had to dig a path for the dogs,
who would ignore it.

Dogs like snow,
like children like sand,
ice balls forming on their legs,
dog socks not acceptable.

Tuesday 3 December

The faintest pink strewn across the palest blue sky and I am compelled to gaze at it. It requires sheep on a snow-covered field, like a Christmas card, but makes do with the college and some Victorian terraces, and an Aldi.

We were introduced to the new bishop, a woman. A lifetime away from when there were no such thing as women priests.

I went to a party for elderly people who are being supported to continue living at home. A woman told me that her mother had married at the Minster. So many people I speak to have the church interweaving and connecting with their lives.

I was given a lift home in the Civic Mayor's car. I worked with her driver over thirty years ago, in the building which was formerly the hospital, which the Mayor also remembers, so we talk about the old days. I used to love, on the upstairs corridor, the magnificent aspidistra. I wonder what happened to it? The ceilings had majestic ornate coving. If you were wheeled under it on a trolley, you would temporarily have your mind taken off your procedure. The building was demolished overnight. Now it's a Job Centre Plus.

If I place the plant in good compost,
in its preferred light,
with its preferred amount of drainage and water
it might reward me with leaves, flowers, growth.

If I don't, if I don't look on it as a thing of beauty,
if I don't feel glad for its new leaf,
its shiny green,

if I couldn't care less,
what could it do?

Wednesday 4 December

The cold bulbs love. I plant Purple Lady, White
Dream and Princess Irene tulips, and imagine they are
happy.

On the Field the sorry leaf mush is frozen. Many
dogs in coats. Eddi looks for a chase, body language
indicating a yes or a no, and then they're off, the thrill
of running in circles.

The car now is now beyond repair, so we choose
another.

I put my cookery books back how they were before
the new boiler was fitted, when they had to be moved
for new pipes, and think I'll consult them more,
choose something different. I have thought this before.

Cold damp soil,
lovely worms burrowing away from me,
knowing a world I don't.

Planting bulbs late,
little green shoots already showing,
the bulb a mother, a meal and a home.

I realise I have one day left. It's Friday night, where you spend the holiday money you've got left on a special meal in the place you've had in mind all week.

Thursday 5 December

I celebrate Holy Communion, in words of 1662, then later watch bereaved people stream forward, each to light a red candle for their loved one, leaving a sea of red candles that look like a lit up half a pomegranate.

Wind wraps and unwraps the Field, matted old leaves stick to the paths. When I take the dogs out for their last walk before bed the Field would be a place I would never go. I did once go to the Field in the dark, but in that dark you can't wait to leave.

A TOWN FIELDS HAIBUN

PART 2

24 DAYS

Saturday 14 December

Four days ago, my beautiful elderly dog Phoebe died, aged fifteen and five months. She had a gentle, peaceful death in my arms, at the vet's. I blessed her, commended her to God, and let her go from this life with my love.

Phoebe's ashes

When I die, put Phoebe with me.
Although she's gone ahead -
every speckled hair,
paws smelling like warm mown grass,
Mountain Goat -
we will go as ash together.

Thursday 26 December - St Stephen's Day

After a marathon of services and carols, greeting, with the other clergy, hundreds of people, today I am not at church. I am reading *Bantam*, a Christmas present, which whoosh's me back to Scottish beaches, substantial pastel - coloured stone cottages and village shops. And loss, our universal experience. The grim grind of it.

Eddi runs on grass and mud, the ground wet, flagging and resigned.

While walking I meet a woman who is blind, accompanied by a woman I take to be her daughter, but not Glade, her black Labrador Guide Dog.

Glade too has died, and now this woman isn't allowed another Guide Dog because she is too old. She's stuck now.

Sunday 19 January 2020

Surfacing after a virus, I notice pink blossom out on the Viburnam, which makes me think of Kath and her tended garden with the Pilkingtons' glass rocks. Shoots are poking out through the soil, and I rejoice.

Sunday 16 February. Second Sunday before Lent

Surfacing once more after another episode of the virus… Rain is hurling itself at the windows, bashing them. I am grateful to be inside and warm. At Choral Evensong today the preacher talked about the beauty of the Lake District, and I
pictured it in my mind's eye, then thought of Appleby and all the other places currently flooded.

At church

Someone hymn-spotting for her funeral,
a woman delighted at her forthcoming Confirmation,
a man who's plucked up courage,

someone who's decided to come because he's hedging his bets,
one looking for meaning, who asks me what I believe,
a woman who's settled in,
some new people who don't speak much English,
who watch intently.

The front garden

Narcissi have appeared,
nothing one minute, then the next.

Colour.
Vulnerable.
Longed for.

Monday 17 February

Eddi has her first run on the Field for three weeks, as she's been in season. She ran in circles with an elderly dog. The wind is cold, but the evenings are lighter.

Sunday 23 February

I find a way of getting *The Road Not Taken* into a sermon, and always feel pleased when a poem makes an appearance.

I notice the balustrades shaped like bamboo in St George House, which I had never noticed before, pointed out as an original feature by Dan Cruickshank. The door knocker has broken and has been replaced by a bell.

St George's House

There once was a door in Donny
That announced the cheery and bonny
But it wasn't all knocking
It witnessed scenes shocking
And gave way for chimes ding- a- donging

Thursday 3 March

I gave a talk about St Benedict, which everyone liked. I like Benedict, his emphasis on listening, and the Benedictine way of staying in one place and doing and being all you can from there.

Saturday 21 March

The nation is in the grip of isolation against the nearing creep of the Coronavirus. The Minster is closed, except for clergy. However, behind the scenes clergy, church wardens and staff are working. The Director of Music is posting on- line our choir singing, organ recitals, and so on. In a predictive text sentence, he refers to 'the plainsong peppers'. I don't know what was meant instead of 'peppers' but it prompted from me:

The Plainsong Peppers

Each Office to the chapel they go
To chant to the Lord high and low
Their capsicum song
Heard all the day long
The Plainsong Courgettes a no no

We're all now social-distancing or self-isolating to try
to keep at bay the Coronavirus. In an effort to shop
less I am going to be planting seeds.

Leatherette

This morning sowing lettuce, listening to birds,
whose identity I don't know,
but I know all about the Woodcock,
after this morning's broadcast, and its high eye.

Now listening to *Night at the Opera*
which I first heard on my brother's headphones
on the leatherette chair,

which I marked on its first day
with a cigarette burn.

Lettuce maybe a life-saver now,
if all my townspeople continue to sweep all life-
sustaining supplies off the shelves,
storing tins of tomatoes in the bathroom cupboard,

not so bothered, I imagine, about leatherette,
unlike my parents.

Monday 23 March

6.10 a.m. Town Field: a gift for the soul

Crunchy clumps of frosted grass.

Above the grass a deep layer of mist,
visible and invisible.

Above that black trees silhouettes

and in the south east the brilliant white with yellow
just- risen sun.

The scene unworldly

not seeming transitory

but when the two dog-walkers, and me and Eddi,
the three runners,
and the man in a high-vis jacket taking a photo -
all silently social-distancing -
have given way to other dog-walkers,
people taking a short-cut,
and cyclists,

the Field will look how it always does,
this almost private glimpse of what the Field gets up
to
before it is claimed by the day.

Tuesday 24 March

On the Field today a man, as aware as the rest us
presumably of the new rules, allowed his dog to run
up to me, and then he came to get it, brushing me as
he picked it up. I came home, put my clothes in the
wash and had a shower, which I had planned to do
anyway.

Wednesday 8 April

We are three weeks into the national and international
restrictions regarding the Coronavirus. Right at the
beginning of this a friend wrote to me and said she'd
always believed it would be a virus that would kill us,
not a bomb.

Now the clergy are celebrating the Eucharist at
home, on behalf of the congregation, who have been
provided with a booklet to follow at home. I find this
to be an unbelievably powerful and moving
experience. The first time I did it I could hardly get
through it. I seem to have adjusted now.

Yesterday I laid out all the Stations of the Cross in the rooms of my house, and Linda, Eddi and I walked them.

I am phoning our Minster community, along with others, weekly. Some people's situations are very worrying. We are putting something on the Minster website for Easter. A very different Holy Week and Easter.

Today 08/04/20

Like a summer's day,
people on the Field,

all the right distance apart.

Dogs run,
we get to walk,
post a few Easter cards

pray for those stuck in flats with kids,
finding out how you become eligible for the foodbank,

those for whom life was bad enough as it was.

Thursday 23 April - St George's Day

St George's Day

Walking round, it's like how it used to be on a
Sunday,
nothing open, and nobody about,
like being on a summer silent retreat,
other people there, but avoiding one another

personally engaged with our own heads -
eyes on a leaf and all its intricacy, or on nothing.

The dogs haven't fully got the idea
still running up to each other on the Field

but then coming back quicker
because we're not with them -

owners having found a space and moved into it,
like in junior school music to movement.

So, we pray about and to St George
regarded as someone who triumphed over evil

doing good deeds known only to God,
by the power of love,

and go out at eight to clap the NHS,
wave, or call across the street.

Sunday 26 April

As everything eventually makes its way into a poem

when, in a poem, will the wood pigeon appear,
the one, standing on the kitchen roof and positioning
its head
this way and that, as in an aerobic warm-up,
momentarily peering in at me
through the dining room window,
making what it does of me
sipping a glass of merlot on my tartan M&S sofa -
years older than most people's sofas,
one cushion patched after Phoebe tore it
in her enthusiasm to scrape and scratch a bed,

the bird and me held in the same frame,
the same garden available,
though from different perspectives,
the same trees observed,
though different access,
the same birdsong listened to,
though different translations,

me in lockdown
thinking about the books I might read,
and the things I might think about
the wood pigeon
flying off.

Everyone now seems to have settled in to this lockdown, the new way of shopping, the opportunity to prune a bush or paint the front gates, the increased use of *what's app* and the newly acquired *Zoom*. Friends are sending little videos of singing toilet rolls or people unfurling out of paintings, and I find myself smiling at them long after I've watched them. More people are watching the clergy on the website than come to church, though whether they're there for the duration I don't know.

The meaning of the Eucharist, for here and now, for not here, for not now, is on my mind, plus the expectations of the ill on God.

Wednesday 29 April

Geoff rang, Would I come and get Nancy? Dave was just about finished doing a repair in the bathroom, and so we went on 'an emergency journey'. She was by then with a neighbour, Geoff waiting for an ambulance. I was handed the end of the lead, at the appropriate distance, and so put her in the car, sitting with her in the back, as we drove home. I rang Geoff to tell him we had the passenger on board.

Saturday 9 May

I decided to have a poetry workshop on my own, picking some poems at random to read, think a little about, then write my own. These poems came out of it:

Canzone: The new priory and chapel

Here is the narrow stone paved path that leads to the
new gate,
where you stop for breath in front of the new chapel,
a paved path round it, inside white and light
where you sit to gaze and pray

each person adding their silent words to the others,
the air thick with words, like alphabet spaghetti soup.
You could watch the words bump and spread like
dodgems,
many the same, overlapping, some stopping for
breath.

Here is the wooden door opposite the new gate,
heavy and solid
with a paved path leading up to it, keeping in and
out.
A man is sawing wood in his workshop opposite the
new gate,
and from time to time stops to gaze,

takes his planks over, and a door takes shape,
which he leans against the stone wall,
white and light. Weighing it up, he goes back for
nails
then saws again in his workshop.
People walk in and out in silence, a Sister pushing a
trolley of laundry,

another receiving a delivery, the engine of the van
distinct,
each person adding their steps to all the others on the
paved path
footprints overlapping, or one on another, stacking
up like the built-up shoe
of the boy who'd had polio, with the built-up shoe
and the caliper

this particular place on the paving a frequently
trodden spot
of sacred footfall. Someone gazes out towards the
wood
that has been carefully managed and planted,
full of years, with a path going up the side of it, and
says words of prayer.

Giant's Graveyard

As all the walks books mention it
we feel obliged to go

paths for serious walkers
who do this all the time

a waterfall half way up
and another walker

Katie in the rucksack.

We puff our way to the summit,
the Giant's Graveyard,

A pile of rocks.

Lockdown

To, and After, George Crabbe

If desolate your bleak sad verse leaves me
Which I can only just imagine's real,
I think today of all those parted, lone
Of those in flats or those who have no home
No sunny garden to in this lockdown tend
No Zoom phone call with a nearby friend.
In every age there's something to endure
That affects us all, but worst of all the poor.
Whether infirmity or conflict, people alive today
Come up with ways to manage - they have to
anyway.
Furloughed workers fret their jobs will go
Kids, for all their work, no grades to show,
But in a way people are more caring
And if they've got something you need, more
sharing.

Out after Lockdown

After Pearse Hutchinson

In the first country,
what you must do when the women have stopped
lamenting
is gather everyone together, but social distance,
and wait. If you are near a leaf, you can look at it

or listen to the blackbird's song,
but the blackbird is not essential.
Anything can happen.

In the second country,
when the dog walks the circumference of the garden
to check if everything is in its usual place,
you must place an Arran pebble in the water,
one from Fallen Rocks,
put a postcard in the letter box,
look at some guillemots just beyond the shore.

In the third country, should you ever get there,
you can collect water, plug in to electricity,
put the table and chairs out,
sit on your patch of grass in the shade of the van,
this little bit of sky like no other.

Places for crying

after Sian Hughes

The den with the shiny earth floor,
cool and dark,
ours then claimed as theirs

the steep path with grass steps
to the top lane
with its hawthorn guard of honour

the bridge,
the place of revelation
and carved initials.

I did go back, but it was overgrown,
inaccessible
not a real place,

nor the field -
with its the gentle pink grass,
the dyke

or later those people,
the French vocabulary,
the records taken backwards and forwards to
Tooting,

the socialist radicalist lesbian feminist house in
Dulwich
with shirts hanging over backs of chairs,
and the framed 3D velvet breast,

places as good as any to cry in
even if I were to start.

The Dressing Room

A chair in front of a shelf and mirror,
a clothes rail, her suitcase.

She glances at the mirror and the time.
In the corridor a piano is playing.

She hangs up her red dress,
begins the sirens and arpeggios

as if for the first time,
bringing in *giggle and surprise*

trying to think only of one note
going smoothly into the next

from a speaker in the room
a voice says *Miss Summerfield, fifteen minutes.*

She puts on the dress,
applies exaggerated eyeliner

smiles at no-one,
and head up glides to the stage door.

Wednesday 20 May

In a phone call Geoff tells me Nancy is no longer a
foster dog, she is mine. I have all sorts of feelings. I am
thrilled because I love her, Eddi loves having her here,

and Linda loves her and sees her as a solution to me
not wanting a second dog further down the line. I am
sad for Geoff, because he loves her too, but knows he
can't manage her now. He tells me he knows she is
happy with me. I send him lots of videos and
photographs of her.

Nancy

In my experience when you get a new dog
for a week, or at the most two,
it is actually a dog

and rules are made
regarding what it can or cannot do.
After that it becomes a dog-shaped person

and there's nothing it can't do,
nothing you wouldn't do or spend on it.
Love is now involved.

Nancy jumps up, because she did at Geoff's.
She follows me everywhere,
lets her daughter Eddi get away with things

and in this new life runs every day
through pink grass, bobbing up and down in it like
water,
this morning tried to catch a rat.

Wednesday 27 May

We continue in Lockdown, coming to the end of the 10th week, by my reckoning. I say that because I've heard it said that Lockdown began on 23 March, but in my diary, it was the week before. Such details seem to matter. With one exception the only place I have been to is the Field, at first once then now sometimes twice a day with the dogs. The exception was that we went to visit two friends, and stood at the gate at one's house, and at some distance in the garden with the other two.

Later, walking round the street with the dogs, I came across some Privet clippings.

Privet

Walking past those Privet clippings on the pavement, smelling of Privet

my dad could have just walked
down the path to get the brush,
in his gardening slacks and navy polo shirt,
saying *Eh up Eric* to the neighbour,
that it's a grand day,
thinking that after he's edged the lawn
he might re-paint the stones
that he individually placed, and painted,
that do for a rockery.

I might be about to walk in from school,
having come home the lane way today,
hawthorn blossom scent infusing the air,
the smell of warm green,
every inch of it grown up with me,

a place of secrets and revelations,
sometimes a horse, or a train,
finishing my *Caramac* before I got in,
running upstairs
and waving from the window.

Thursday 28 May

On my phone calls I learn how people who are well
are passing the time. iPad jigsaw puzzles feature, but
gardening comes out top, and baking quite high, the
daily walk being something most people do, and
skyping - or the equivalent - relatives and friends.

I think of our planet spinning away in the middle of
a vast nowhere, and imagine looking down on it, and
seeing all the blue and green, noticing the less-polluted
atmosphere, and zoom in, country by country, and see
those people who are out, masked, taking a daily walk
or going for essential shopping and medicines, for the
moment captured by a virus, something too small to
see, who's end aim, when it has replicated, infected,
struck down, killed, is what? To have the satisfaction
that it has ruled the world, driven wedges into
relationships, deprived people of comfort and love
when they were running out of time, driven people

out of their minds with money worries? If it killed everyone it would have nowhere to live itself, so mindless infecting would be counter- productive. And what do we people make of all this time, these new days, waking and sleeping? What meaning do we look for and find in it? There's a lot of talk about wine, and occupation. But throughout it all the religious go into chapel five times a day and pray for the world, the clergy and the people pray and pray. Yes, we pray for a swift end to this, for those who've been infected and those who died, for those who are separated, for those ill with other forgotten things, for those who've died of the usual things - all of that, but mostly to just sit with God, and for a while be in the bigger picture.

Saturday 6 June

Psalm for lockdown

From the Town Field I will praise you*
for all your marvellous works

while the enemy virus encamps around me*
I will praise you in voice and on drum

Many will say where is your God*
where is the God of your salvation

For our people have been slain*
and more will be slain, by the virus

A Glimpsed-at Reality

Our health workers will be snowed under*
our energy and resources will run dry

from where comes our hope*
from where comes the God of our longing

She comes in unknown places*
in strangers who do your works

He does not come in the strength of a horse*
or in the bottom of a glass, or on Zoom

She comes in friendship and companionship*
in sharing a laugh together

In a daily walk with a dog*
in the passing of time with a dog walker

He comes in a loving thought or a caring way*
in a smile or a wave on skype

She comes in a prayer*
like oil running down the beard

How great is your name O Lord*
How communicative and close in this lockdown

Many gods have aspired*
only to fail in being our God

Great is the Lord*
and worthy to be praised

Praise to Creator, God Incarnate, and Holy Spirit*
Blessed be God for ever.

Saturday 20 June

Geoff has fallen and broken his hip and femur. He was already in poor health, and now, after a spell in hospital, he is in a care home, the one where my dad was. It was a good care home then, and Geoff tells me it is now, which I am pleased about. I can't visit, because of the Coronavirus restrictions, but when I can I will take Nancy, Eddi's mum, whom he has given me. It is wonderful having her, and the two are really enjoying being together. From having a nice home and well cared for garden, he now has a bed, his phone, and whatever is in his head, some of it startling, as he is on hallucinogenic painkilling medicine.

The Centrepiece

You might say the weeping willow is the centrepiece,
mature, dripping its leaves,
a grotto among the twists of paths
and sculptural or natural surprises

but many plants catch the eye.
Geoff tells me about the decision to put this climbing
hydrangea here,
ever looking for the perfect match of colour or
timing

so that you could forget you are in a garden of
a council house that was a Thatcher's Right to Buy,
now extended and done up better than she would
ever have imagined.

A home, often full of people and dogs,
a trophy to outstanding breeding,
and even more to generosity and love,

that now, storing its many papers and bits and pieces,
drawers of clippers and scissors,
the starting point for many going home with an eight-
week-old puppy,

it stands empty,
the place where he fell and did the damage,
the wrist bracelet of no protection,

so that now, in the care home,
all he has been able to take is himself
and his phone.

A friend told me about a painting that had moved her,
depicting a man walking away, leaving his dog in the
place where they both were, to show that the dog had
died. After hearing that I wrote this poem.

Turn away

I wanted the pretty one, but Geoff had earmarked
her for someone else,
so I got the bolshy one. Who was stunning.

A climber - rocks at Pirnmill, little walls.
Not interested in the sea, or fetching balls, except for
a bribe.

You couldn't bear having your nails trimmed or your
feet combed.
Your paws smelled of sweet cut grass, any time of
year.

I was surprised to discover how much you liked
snow,
your legs with dangling ice balls, like four Christmas
trees.

Your smart fleece coat held no street cred for you
or the snow socks, or God forbid that scarf. Looks
and kill.

Many a time we danced to Comfortably Numb.
or you'd just walk out.

That image of you young and just groomed is one of
the most beautiful things I own,
as is your calendar pose in the garden.

A Glimpsed-at Reality

It never crossed your mind that you might not be
safe,
so recall was of no importance. Remember the
Hunmanby beach steps?

Sheringham was a better bet. It was a joy to see you
run, tinged with regret.
Candles on my cakes for you began to be less fun.

The ferry to Arran became not do-able.
Your way out of a room no longer sure-footed. Eddi
became your new guide.

I don't want to let anyone down, not that there's a
queue,
but you were a great love of my life.

On this day at the Pirnmill rocks I have to turn away
from you
and walk back alone to the cottage.

The wail you could not stop for twenty minutes
when I came for you after your eye op

is mine now. I asked you to let me know when you
were ready,
and you did.

The rocks are all yours now Phoebe
forever.

Tuesday 4 August

People are now making their own designer masks, to complement their outfits, or experimenting with visors, so that we might be eight year olds playing motorbike cops, except that we are attempting to protect others from the marching virus, which is not weary of us like we are weary of it, those of us who are currently surviving it.

Face coverings will be compulsory in the now open churches from next week. But no singing. Is the virus in its stomping advance obtaining any satisfaction from its effort to remove joy from our lives? In its rampant pursuit of life, what is it gaining? I would like to face it out and demand to know what is its purpose and meaning.

To The Virus

Spoilt, you sulk and skulk,
play with your food,
hang around doing nothing.

Bored, you hit on it,
get attention by annoying other people.
Make them cough.

Mindless, you move from one to another
not really caring,
but you decide the old and those of Asian origin may
as well go first.

A Glimpsed-at Reality

You start to get a bit fed up with it,
but you nod and smirk to yourself -
it is all about you now.

Most of the world is in lockdown,
you're making them die,
by the thousand

in South America coffins in gardens,
on the street,
the smell putting people off from taking them away.

You put those who love at a distance,
stop them singing,
grouping.

They can't be seen by a dentist or a clinician,
can't visit their ill or dying ones,
can't see them out of this world.

Still, back to you,
maybe a bit more out of hand than you'd imagined,
but still fun, and clearly a success.

You look blank when we ask you
'What's your game?'
As if there needs to be a reason.

I retired on 21st June. It feels very Benedictine going
nowhere, apart from in your head. But I did go to

church on Sunday, as a worshipper, for the first time in four months. It was like walking down your own street at the end of a long journey home.

Friday 14 August

My lovely friend Geoff, who gave me his beloved dog Nancy, has died. He was one of the most caring, generous, funny people I have ever known, and outstanding in everything he did - as a former head teacher, gardener, Kennel Club breeder, and as a person. He had many friends, and was a man of great faith.

Geoff

There should be a song for Geoff
who gets up every two hours
to take a dropper and feed
this pup who he believes will not survive,

but for days and nights he does this,
his knees killing him,
his constant dizziness made worse by the tiredness,

and she knows he will do this,
keep it warm in a shoe box,
love life into it.

Thursday 27 August

A rainy afternoon in the motorhome, after a walk

A pile of dogs in the crate,
a ploughman's lunch, then
sketching a stone arch for her,
learning the rests in *Cry Me A River* for me.

I wonder if Geoff's funeral has taken place yet?
Not that I could go, because of the restriction on
numbers.
I would have commended him to God along with the
priest
at that point in the ceremony.
But I've done that anyway.

The surround sound of tapping rain wraps us up.
The green outside is growing greener.
Earlier the dogs galloped full speed into the meadow,
disappearing in the long grass.
Nancy hadn't ever run like that.

There are 9.9 million dogs in UK households -
one quarter of homes.

Two of them are mine.
on the Field and the paths,
and soon All Saints' Day again.

A RED PATH HAIBUN

Tuesday 10 May 2022

This morning a friendly doberman/doberwoman bounded over, after rolling in a molehill, that after losing her footing near the stream and falling in. So an eventful walk for her.

My dogs, mother and daughter Miniature Schnauzers, Nancy the mum, Eddi the daughter, go charging about, happy to see every dog and person, Eddi puzzled today by a Border Collie being carried because of a pulled muscle, Eddi looking up again and again at the dog.

Having moved into a new house three months ago, one of the delights is the garden, now shooting up lots of perennials, many of which are unfamiliar. Someone told me about an app that identifies plants, so now, after some identifying, I discover that the garden has been designed for bees, alas not for dogs, and so many otherwise beautiful (but not yet out) Peruvian Lilies have to be dug up.

Having a coffee, Linda and I discuss this. She says, 'At the back two are laying down'. She is talking about plants she has dug up, but my mind is still on bees, so I think she is talking about two bees, unaccustomed to this cruise-liner style 24-hour buffet of a garden, exhausted after having eaten all they can eat, needing a deck bed and a nap.

Friday 13 May

I think about the liturgy of Baptism as I swim in the pool among wobbling, dancing shapes of light this morning, having been asked to pray for someone in need, who I don't know, who is very troubled. I swim reciting, 'God has delivered us from the dominion of darkness... You have received the light of Christ'.

I think of Baptism as a whole-life event, and wonder if the person concerned in this situation is baptised, and can derive some comfort and reassurance from that. I was born eight weeks early, and was given an emergency baptism. As I have said before, in my mind I think that's when I got attached to God, and God to me.

Saturday 14 May

Linda continues to dig up plants that are poisonous to dogs, if eaten or licked. The Dogs Trust has a comprehensive list. At this rate our very abundant new garden will soon be bald.

The dogs are already in the habit of scouring the soil for insect snacks. I don't remember them doing this before at the old house. There is more soil here.

Monday 16 May

Eddi is 4 today. On the walk I think back to when we were away this day four years ago and Geoff ringing, 'Do you want to hear the news? Nancy has had eight puppies' (I forget how many girls and how many boys), 'and one of them is yours'. I was thrilled. After a few weeks we went to see them, a beautiful picture of Nancy lying on her side feeding her litter, one of them Eddi. Little did I know then that Nancy would also become as much mine as her.

As I write this I am taken back to my Junior School and our wonderful Mrs Anderson, and English grammar, so I ask myself, should it be 'Little did I know then that Nancy would also become as much mine as she'??

We all loved Mrs Anderson, and she us, and her influence went deep. She read us poetry - a lot of Edward Lear - gave us a love of playing and listening to music, and singing, casting me once in the singing role of Angel Gabriel, and told us all about Scotland, whipping her glasses off one-handedly as she spoke, in the manner of someone else I love, Dan Cruickshank.

My friend Eon, (now departed this life) and I used to 'do' Dan Cruickshank when we went out - his mannerisms and delivery of words.

Dan Cruickshank, a few years ago, came to the minster to do a BBC programme about the design and architecture of the building. Although I was thrilled that he was coming, I felt too star-struck to dare speak to him. I confessed my shyness to the then Vicar, who said, 'Well ask Louise, she's got balls'. That did it. I said, 'I've got balls'...and so did speak to him, albeit in a cringingly star-struck hardly balls way.

On the evening walk an older man starts chatting to me and tells me to keep the dogs on the lead when I go to the Lake because earlier today someone's dog jumped in after a duck and despite calling the dog, it didn't come out for twenty minutes. Without the duck.

The nettles are prolific. I think of The Welsh Evening at the minster, a few years ago now, where I read *Tall Nettles* by Edward Thomas and *Nettles*, the response, by Gillian Clarke, saying, 'That's enough about nettles'.

Well, not quite enough:

Habitat

The Common Nettle has a preference
for damp, fertile and disturbed ground.

On this May evening unidentifiable birds, not beginners,
quickly and urgently singing,

the scent of Hawthorne putting me back in the damp Old Lane
as sure as a Cluedo piece being plucked from the Library and planted in the Conservatory.

This ground disturbed
when they built our new house,

people objecting (probably) to losing their fields,
places they had felt were theirs.

Along came the nettles with their toothed leaves
feeding, as Gillian Clarke notices, 'on what we leave
behind',

having waited for the right, fertile moment,
and armed to guard it.

Monday 30 May

A huge celebratory service today for a friend being
licensed to a team ministry. Lots of great singing and
piano playing. Several people talk to me - at length -
about toilets.

On my evening walk with Eddi and Nancy a tree's
leaves are shimmering and fluttering in the breeze.
They sound more like a rushing stream than leaves. I
look the tree up with my new app, and find it is a
White Poplar. The *Populus Alba* is described as magical,
its leaves as having irregular teeth round the edge.

All the better to eat you with, barked the tree.

Tuesday 31 May

I read the Church Times over lunch. Someone is
described as 'a lettering artist and influencer'. I read
the interview, all about his lettering work, but I
couldn't see that he was *especially* influential, so that he
would attract the title 'influencer'. I wondered, would
I ever describe myself as *A homeopath and an influencer*,

or *A poet and an influencer?* No. Would women in general refer to themselves as influencers? Do we just hold back on claiming influencing? Are men more ready to accept or recognise themselves as influencers?

I got on to stickier ground when I put to myself, *A priest and an influencer?* Well?? I hope so. But would I say that? *I'm Susan Bedford, a priest and an influencer?*

Haiku

Sitting with a friend
rain and hail drum down outside
thunder follows on.

Sunday 5 June

I heard from Peter, apologising, that I was not a winner in this year's Poetry Business International Poetry Competition, but that I had been shortlisted. *Shortlisted.* I couldn't be more thrilled!

Thursday 23 June

These last few days have been very hot. The grass on the field is straw. I took my dogs out at 7.30 this morning to avoid the too hot pavement.
In the house I choreograph the blinds for the time of day. Nancy works out which are the coolest places to lie. Eddi cosies up on the bean bag and pants. I move her.

Monday 27 June

On my walk this morning, just before the downpour, which worked out well for the dogs, as they don't like being out in the rain, I reflected on this weekend's ordinations at Sheffield Cathedral. I remembered my own ordinations, and the retreats leading up to them. All sorts of emotions ran high, but the emotion I remember most from my priesting was feeling overwhelmed.

Looking at the rain, in my mind's eye I'm back in the quadrangle corridor where Mrs Anderson took us to look at teeming rain, and to write rain words in new vocabulary books, *torrential* being a new word.
I am glad for our plants, who have to cope with very sandy soil, today their little roots smiling.

Thursday 30th June

Today is the fourth anniversary of my ordination to the priesthood, and I am staying with the sisters of the Order of the Holy Paraclete at Whitby. It's Ordination-day-hot.

The frequency of visits to the chapel means that the day is divided up into structured chunks of prayer, their regularity making it nearly impossible to get on with anything substantial, the point being made that they are the substance of the day, everything else is fitted around them.

What used to be the Priory, at the bottom end of the grounds, is now a wedding venue. The smart-suited and beautifully turned out are sitting around expertly dressed tables in the garden, laughing and occasionally shrieking. The nearest building to this is the chapel.

I read *A Child in the Night* by Elizabeth Jennings. In it she imagines how a child will feel when he, older, falls in love, that it will be like this time now when he gazes at stars, possessed. Elizabeth must have had a good experience of falling in love. I only remember the obsession, the aching longing, the skewed drag of time, and for all the desperation, the known impossibility of an anxiety-free manifestation of it, and I will be glad if I never feel as wretched again.

So, I have come here to have some dedicated time with God. I do like reflecting and contemplating, but I also like a task, so at first this feels like I am forcing myself to be more than I am. All the same, I accustom myself in chapel to the unfamiliar books, enjoy the mini homily about diversity, miss music, and wait to see why God has brought me here this time.

I think of Maitreyabandhu and his retreat to research Cezanne, thinking of his forthcoming month stretching ahead 'like an idling train, each day an empty carriage'. I feel similar.

A bee is flicked away by the Sister reading the New Testament reading, and then it rams against closed windows, again and again, ignoring every open one, the word buzz nowhere near describing its noise.

At the end of Vespers, as we are now in talking time, the species of bee is discussed.

Over dinner of egg and chips the two convent cats are much talked about, one of whom has wandered in to the refectory and been turfed out.

The View

A small wedge of high sea
looking like grey tissue paper
strung from trees to trees.

The Sisters in night silence,
the wedding revellers
raising a din over the de de de of the beat.

The night security man hoping the noise -
which will go on till one o'clock -
won't bother those Sisters who have their windows
open,
or me.

Friday 1 July

Psalm 148 at Lauds is recited with pleasure.
   I am given a lift from another guest after breakfast to Whitby harbour, so I am there early when there are only delivery drivers and harbour men.
Changing my shoes to slip-ons, so I can go for a paddle, I overhear a woman in a wet suit describing to her companion how a bird has just flown by her at eye level, much bigger than a seagull, black tipped wings. I chip in and ask her if it had a yellow head, and she

said yes, and I tell her it was a Gannet. She was thrilled, as anyone would be.

So I have the beach to myself for a bit, and then on with the dog walkers.

At lunch with the Sisters, we eat in silence to a thunderstorm that means business. One of the Sisters jumps at each lightning strike. All of us are dying to say something, but nobody does.

Psalm 148a

Praise the Lord from the heavens;
praise him in the cosmos all around!

Praise him all his angels
delivering daily unseen messages.

Praise him all planets, with and without moons
and all stars, light years away.

Praise him all navy brooding skies,
all thunder and lightning erupting.

Let them praise the name of the Lord,
for he creates them with love.

Praise the Lord what is under the sky,
all that that make the heavy grey North Sea their
home,

The Whitby Cod and low-flying Gannets,
torrential rain and beams beaming into the sea.

Praise the Lord West Cliff,
all those who live there,

And everything in their little or big gardens,
their dogs chasing balls on the beach,

The convent cat sitting by a corridor door
or laying on the reception desk.

You who are in charge of anything,
Sisters who lead worship, put the right flowers
together,

Attend thoughtfully to guests,
Let them praise the name of the Lord,

For She alone holds everything with love,
her splendour is all these, and that's just a start.

She gives strength, support and revelation to her
people
Who are close to her, knowing they need it.

Praise the Lord!

On the way back from the beach I bought a bottle of
water, that I put in an outside pocket of my rucksack,
which by the time I arrived back to my room I had lost.
Later, when I left my room, my water had been found
and left on the step for me.

It has taken two days to adjust to the rhythm here. Now I look forward to the repeated trips to the chapel, the rhythm of it.

In an article I read about retreat houses, one house has the rule of *No clergy shop talk*, so, it is explained, people can step back from the usual roles they inhabit.

Saturday 2 July

Today is the fifth anniversary of my ordination as a deacon. One of the Sisters today had the anniversary of her life vows, so a day for anniversaries.

I have just about got the hang of which book to use for what in chapel. At least I know what the actual contents of the Offices are, it's just a matter of working out where to find them. My confusion is nothing like it must be for people who have to turn up in church for the first time, such as at a Christening, which we insist on calling Baptism. It must be like, if you've never been in one, going to a betting shop for the first time.

This morning there was a huge downpour. A navy loaded sky over the sea turned in moments to a monochrome grey sea and sky. I was heading to a bench to read a bit more of *On Retreat with Henri Nouwen* when the rain was let out, like a massive bucket being poured over our heads. I just got into a shelter as couple walked past, soaked. The man said to us, 'Come on, what's the matter with you? English summer!'

Everybody in Whitby seems to have a dog, or two. Lots of Cocker-poos. This morning two Miniature Schnauzers, darker than mine, beautifully clipped.

Nouwen is asking us to ask ourselves the question Who am I? In another book of his, he talks about faith not being straight forward, saying, 'All authentic Christian lives know 'long tunnels' where you don't understand anything, where we go with Jesus to the tomb'. Of course, much of his writing is affirming and encouraging, but I think it is helpful for people to know that he had his struggles.

High evening sunshine is streaming in.

Sunday 3 July - Thomas Day

A bright baby-blue sky and white thin cloud, and cool. The beetle that walked in circles around the vase of flowers under the altar at yesterday's Vespers not there now. Not in it for the long haul. No anniversary for her.

I always feel sorry for St Thomas, his needing proof before he can take the next step with the resurrected Jesus being the main thing, we think about him. But he was not lightweight, as, even though it was dangerous for them all to go to Judea, Thomas was the one who said they should go, even if it meant possibly being stoned.

As I see Thomas, he was someone who wanted to clarify things, get things understood, and that mattered to him. I like that in a person. When he did actually see Jesus there was no longer any reason to touch his crucifixion wounds. But had it not been for his encounter with the resurrected Jesus, who wished to offer him proof, we would never have heard his dramatic, certain and beautiful confession of faith *My Lord and my God.*

And had it not been for Thomas needing to clarify things, we would also not have received the words from Jesus *I am the way and the truth and the life.*

So I would change 'Doubting Thomas' to 'Just Need To Get Things Straight Thomas', and thank God for him.

In the convent chapel congregation

A woman taking her glasses off
Holding them up
Bringing them down
Blowing on them,
Holding them up
Rustling in her handbag
Taking out a spray
Spraying her glasses
Taking out a cloth
Rubbing them
Holding them up
Then putting them on
During the excellent sermon

Same woman
Tapping out the hymn beat
With two hands

On the chair in front
Picking up her hymn book
And moving it up and down
As we sing

Saying to me as we leave
Are you enriched?

What day it is

The biggest choice in the day
Is when to take the walk to the sea

Finding the longest gap
Between services

Because they're not always at
The same times

Which helps you work out
What day it is.

When I want a change from Henri Nouwen I am
reading The Bloodaxe Book of Contemporary Women
Poets, and I read about Denise Levertov's childhood
perception that 'boys seemed, in fiction, to have more
adventures.'

To girls and women who refuse to be held back:

There was a woman from Sherburn in Elmet
Who liked to wear a knight's helmet
But it wasn't all armour
With nails and a hammer
She could knock up a kitchen pelmet

There was a woman from St. John the Divine
Who'd long had the priesthood in mind
Then in '94
Was allowed through that door
And now consecrates bread and wine

There were two electrical engineers
in volts up to their ears
One was paid a lot less
For wearing a dress
But she got equal pay - after years

There once was a woman who spoke
In a meeting as long as a bloke
That wasn't the norm
It caused quite a storm
But she's now CEO Pepsi Coke

Monday 4 July

I leave the Sisters, and Linda, Eddi, Nancy and I have a day in Whitby.

Walking by the harbour I am thrilled to spot a Shiba Inu, never having seen one live. I talk to the owners about it, and stroke it, feeling its dense neck hair. It's a beautiful dog, and similar colouring to me. A friend and I once wondered, if we were dogs, what we'd be. She thought that she would be a Saluki, and I would be a Shiba Inu.

Mrs Crimmonds School of Dancing, Whitby

Behind an ordinary window bay
Was the den of a brilliant spy
She had once hid in France
But now she taught dance
Or that's what it said outside.

Haiku

I must stop writing
Limericks. I am obsessed.
Get down to business.

Sunday 10 July

An exceptionally hot day. I think about the Sisters in their long-sleeved habits. Of course, the clergy have a lot of clothes to wear for services, but that's only for about an hour.

Later, when it's cooler, I take the dogs for a walk and get chatting to a man with a lovely young whippet, beautiful markings and eyes. He's only five months old, and even in this weather still wants a run. I say he's got the legs for it. The man says he's got two little ones at home, five and three, and I say, 'Are they whippets?' 'No, children', he replies.

Tuesday 12 July. St Benedict

The Number One of his Rule is Listen.

'Listen' is a translation of 'haiku'.

Haikus

Walking the Red Path
with two Miniature Schnauzers,
a runner phoning.

Heat we're not used to.
A woman in large headphones
talking by herself.

The midges bite on
There is nothing so itchy
from such tiny mouths.

Meet someone walking,
a woman new to the path,
loves it here, like me.

Listen to the air.
Put your ear to a tree trunk.
Open too your heart.

Wednesday 13 July

Happy birthday Nancy, who is six today. We had our first walk at seven this morning, 1) because I thought the day was going to be as hot as yesterday (which it hasn't turned out to be), and 2) because I am having two standard bay trees delivered, and the delivery notification said they'd be delivered *today*. *Today* is a lot of hours. Later I get a text to say they will be delivered between 14.2<u>4</u> and 16.2<u>4.</u> I think I might start using the 4. 'Yes, I'll be round at <u>4</u> past four, or I'll do Evening Prayer at 4.3<u>4</u>. If it's good enough for Marks and Spencer.

I wonder what treat to give Nancy. Eddi is easy - a ball on a rope always a winner, or a fabric toy with a loud squeak. Plastic toys, no.

Nancy shows little interest in toys, except now and again she'll play tug o' war with Eddi with the fabric squeaky banana or pheasant. Mostly, if they want to play together, they go in for tugging their bedding around the house, snarling and growling like sworn enemies, then drop the argument and roll on their backs together, eight legs waving in the air, at their own rave.

Cuddles and food are usually tops for Nancy, so it will be plenty of them.

I used to make a cake on Phoebe's birthday (for us), and take pictures of her sitting on my knee while I blew the candles out. But the fun went out of it when the candles were too many, and I've never done it for Edds or Nance.

I write a homily for this coming Sunday's Choral Evensong, mentioning that when we open a sermon with *In the name of the Father, and of the Son and of the Holy Spirit/Ghost*, we are then speaking in God's name. That focuses the mind. But as the Ordinal says, we cannot bear the weight of this calling in our own strength, *but only by the grace and power of God.* Thank God for that.

Thursday 14 July

A friend called round for a coffee, bringing with her some lovely Peruvian Lillies

The Peruvian Lily

The Incas might not be here,
but their Peruvian Lily insists on this home

its yellow and orange spots and stripes
in the garden; brought as a gift

symbolising friendship and devotion,
although neither of us knew,

and now I realise
is the pattern on my inherited wallpaper.

We were talking about friendship,
how some friends get lost

with the subtlest unexpected shift;
how ours will stay.

I have tried to dig up these *Alstroemeria aurea,*
their pollen reported to be toxic to dogs,

I have known friendship and devotion
with a toxic base note

not becoming apparent
until it's under the skin.

Sunday 17 July

Two lovely celebratory services today, one where the
Bishop of Sheffield officially opened our new servery
and toilet facilities, and one to mark the end of a very
lovely and enjoyable choir year.
Afterwards we discover that four cars in the Minster
car park have been bashed, one ours, causing a lot of
damage.

Sing to the rafters
Loud, joyful, and full of praise
while someone thumps cars.

Tuesday 19 July

Day 21. If I am writing after Maitryabandhu, this is the last day of this haibun. But it's not.

Yesterday and today are the hottest days on record in the UK, BBC Radio 4 saying Doncaster was the hottest place yesterday. A TV news team apparently gave a report from the grounds of Doncaster Minster.

Linda bought the dogs a cool mat. I put both of them on it to show them it. Eddi now has gone back to the bean bag...

Hottest Day

Even thinking feels like too much,
the thought of the sea and its breeze in my head

imagination not to be sniffed at,
the placebo effect, for example, being effective for years,

the mind assimilating a thought and the real thing
as the same,

so I take myself to Pirnmill,
a bit more seaweed now
than before

on the little rocks
where you can
barbeque sausages
and watch the baby waves lap in,
a place I don't want to have been for the last time.

Friday 22 July

Meeting with the Consultant

While the consultant is telling me very important
things

I can't help but notice how his shirt has been ironed,

that the yoke of the shirt has a crease in it,
where the ironer carried on after putting a crease in
the sleeve.

He says *Do you understand what I'm saying?*
I nod and say *Yes*, from behind a mask.

It's not important, his shirt, pale blue with white
stripe,
worn open at the neck; stone-coloured chinos,

conventionally smart-casual, meant to reassure me:
We're relaxed here but we know what we're doing.

He pulls forward an image, just given to him off the
computer,
and describes it to me, drawing on it to point things
out.

He suggests that in a moment I can ask questions,
and I'm guessing *Who irons your shirts?* is not the usual,

and it's not important, his shirt,
with the crease where it shouldn't be,

but if he ironed it, does that mean that he doesn't care
about getting it right,
and will he have that approach when I'm on the
operating table?

Tuesday 26 July

Depicted in the stained glass at Malmesbury Abbey, I
read in a booklet, the monk Eilmer, around 1010,
made himself some wings and leapt from the tower of
the Abbey, 'gliding for a furlong, before crash landing
and surviving with two broken legs'. Someone trying
to get above his station, one might say! These Middle
Ages monks and their fanciful life…

Malmesbury Abbey Stained Glass Window

The hours you'd spent observing birds,
picking up discarded feathers,
combing the dust out of them,

standing on the tower practising lifting your arms up
and down,
feeling them move the air,
imagining that air buoying you up;

trying out jumping on the spot,
feeling certain you'd be the exception
to shake off gravitational pull on a body,

and once airborne, soar like an eagle,
to where?
Is heaven up?
To join the angelic throng on some hillside,
singing and sparkling?

Yet angels always bear a message:
no mention of that.

The life of a monk must need a little diversion,
The Divine Office, and a silent walk with God
sometimes not holy enough,

but to fling yourself off your tower,
fall for a furlong,
break both legs,
then have to be looked after by the other monks??

You wouldn't catch a woman doing that -
but you did get yourself in a window.

Thursday/Friday 28 and 29 July

A friend and I spend two fabulous days in Durham
Cathedral, the shrine of St Cuthbert, St Oswald and
The Venerable Bede, where we are shown what

remains of St Cuthbert's coffin - which is a lot - his portable altar, and his pectoral cross, which was found in his coffin.

It was very moving to see his cross in real life, as opposed to in a book, something physical that you could see and (although we weren't permitted to) touch, as tangible as we are, bringing one significant Christian from the seventh century to the year 2022, making the apostolic succession feel real.

St Cuthbert's Cross

St Cuthbert's gold cross -
not like him the gold, the stones -
carried seven years.

St Cuthbert's gold cross
accompanying him dead,
showing us him then.

St Cuthbert's gold cross
six centuries along the
apostolic line.

Sunday 14 August

It is about thirteen days since a tick lodged in my back, which was removed by a friend because the doctors didn't have a tool to remove it, and the vets would not do it, and eleven days since I started antibiotics to prevent me getting Lyme Disease, which I may not have got, but because you don't want it, prophylactic antibiotics were given.

Well that's what the doctor at A&E told me, because my own GP Practice refused to give me antibiotics, preferring the option that I should get back in touch if I get Lyme Disease, so I had to take up valuable A&E time getting them.

On these antibiotics I am not allowed to go out in the sun, which means I am walking my dogs at dawn (5.30) and dusk. My nephew has started to call me Count Susan.

You do get lovely skies at these times of the day, and you do meet other dog walkers, who, as it is so hot during the day at the moment, are also finding these times to be the best for walks. Unless they've been bitten by ticks too and are on the same regime as me. Apparently, all this re-wilding of grassed areas is giving ticks the living and breeding conditions they could only have dreamed of.

Today is two years since Geoff died. May you rest in peace and rise in glory Geoff, with all your beloved dogs.

Creation

Turquoise glassy sea -
creation we are fond of -
pink, peach and blue sky

our dogs, birds, rabbits -
creation we are fond of -
butterflies, worms, frogs

polar bears, lions -
creation we are fond of -
ladybirds, ducklings.

Alligators, ticks -
creation we're not fond of -
ticks. Did I say ticks?

21 days not allowed out in the sun

In the house, looking out,
like a woman in a sweatshop
making cheap clothes for the West

like a patient on traction,
or who's had a stroke or broken a hip,
who is eight levels up

like a prisoner
having to keep face,
pretending she wants to go to chapel,

like a dog in kennels,
a rabbit in a rabbitry
a horse who can't quite reach the hay.

Monday 15 August

I collected today's windfall apples from our tree, and picked some new ones, for our neighbours, who give us plums and flowers.

Patience.

Eddi sits under the apple tree
waiting for a snack to drop,
as she would gaze at a Blackbird nest
in March.

I am half way through my vigil
of 42 Doxycycline's,
avoiding Lyme Disease.

Every ten years the Primates meet
and restate that some people's physical love is a sin
(not theirs), a turning from God (whose real name is
Love),

expecting continued patience
from those waiting to be affirmed,
accepted, treated the same as everyone else,

who, if they want to go to church at all,
have to seek out one of a handful of places
where they will not be given the hurtful gaze.

A midge has found the only part of me not covered up against the sun, my face, and bitten me on my temple. All around it is puffed up, including my eyelid.

Hive

I could be a bee-keeper here,
know all my bees by name -
if they're at all like cows.

Obsessed with Lavender,
the bee-centric flower beds
heave and hum.

The bug hotel has no vacancies,
pushy wasps the first to arrive,
the tick sneaking in on the insect cloud.

Wednesday 17 August

A nice plumber comes to service our new boiler, and tells us about his large pet tortoise, and its requirements, including a regular bath, in which it contentedly sits.

Thursday 18 August - Day 29 of the Haibun

Deep orange and apricot seep into the tumbled cloud over Barbara's house at 5.30 this morning, as if a pot of watercolour has been tipped over. By six o'clock it is as if it never was, and the sky is shades of pale grey. Maybe 50. No, I didn't read it.

We are walking on the streets, giving the path a miss for now, to avoid, if possible, insect life.

Friday 19 August

Christmas has crept in. It's August, so of course I've received my Dogs Trust catalogue. But this year the availability request for the clergy rota going up to next February arrived even before that. I might get my cards written this afternoon, my wrapping done, and I'm all ready...

The dogs see an enemy through the door and shriek and bounce at it. I let them out, and they go full pelt to the fence, one taking one side, the other the other side. The cat/squirrel/ bird has long gone, but they love the chase, and come in all pleased with themselves. In the UK Miniature Schnauzers are classed as Utility, but in America Terrier, which more fits their nature.

Eddi and Nancy like apple, and can hardly believe their luck when I am standing peeling apple after apple from our tree. But I can only give them so much, so it is with disbelief and sad resignation that they watch me put most of the peelings in the bin. If I had a compost heap or a wormery...

Eddi escaped into next door's garden, burrowing under the concrete fence bottom, not for ages able to find her way back, like a fly in the house, given a vast open window to fly out of, batting the closed window over and over again. Only it was Eddi, and until I heard her one bark, I was beside myself with worry.

Linda has now blocked up the escape hatch with rocks.

Tuesday 23 August

After several days of puffy and itchy insect bites, this morning I applied three lots of insect repellent to my arms and legs, and was bitten on my eyebrow.

We have some gardeners in clearing the flower beds that are to become lawns. The flowers will be replanted in the border or potted for the church Summer Fair plant stall. On considering where an Azalea is currently positioned, the gardener said, 'It isn't the plant's fault that it has been put there'.

The Plant's Fault

There are things I wouldn't have blamed on a plant,
but *if it's an option*
I could start with:
ATTRACTING TICKS AND MIDGES
(a current obsession),
Spiky stems and prickly leaves,
obviously,
Back spot (surely, they shouldn't just stand there?),
Seeds and bulbs that are toxic to dogs
toxic to dogs, come on,
High maintenance divas:
Ooo too much water / not enough water

Too much sun / not enough sun
Too near to that one / too much space
Compost too rich / compost not rich,

Being there as rain forests when people want to cut
them down,
Being there as woods when people want to make
fires,
Being under the ocean when people want to explode
nuclear bombs.

Maybe the plants are responsible too for
Cruelty, poverty, meanness,
over - industrialisation, self-centredness,
Or would that be just us?

Wednesday 31 August - St Aidan's day, Bishop of Lindisfarne in 635

Thirteen years ago, I decided it would be nice to memorise some poems, having committed myself to reciting from memory *The Green Eye of the Little Yellow God* by Milton Hayes, dressed in top hat and tails, for The Victorian Evening at Doncaster Minster.

I liked the idea that if I was somewhere without a poetry book, I could call to mind an entire poem. I think similarly now about the psalms. I managed to learn nine:

The Donkey by G K Chesterton, cheating really, as I already knew this by heart from schooldays.

You're by Sylvia Plath, being thrilled by the *travelled prawn*.

Not Waving But Drowning by Stevie Smith, remembering seeing the wonderful Glenda Jackson playing Stevie at the Vaudeville theatre in London.

Loss by Wendy Cope, because it's short and funny.

Self Portrait in the Dark by Colette Bryce, because of the emotion it so brilliantly conveys.

Pied Beauty by Gerard Manley Hopkins because of its excessive tongue-twisting descriptions and its exuberant joy.

The Triumph of Charis by Ben Johnson because it fell on a day in *Poem for the Day* that I was going out with friends, Anne among them who had bought me the book, who I thought would like it if I recited the poem for that day.

The Listeners by Walter De La Mare because it reminded me of Mr Akehurst and our delightful English lessons.

I have forgotten them by heart now, but I could resolve to relearn them.

Mostly psalm 27 is my favourite psalm, because of verse 4:

One thing have I asked of the Lord
and that alone I seek:
that I may dwell in the house of the Lord
all the days of my life

but psalms 148, 150 and 100 come close seconds.

Memories

I don't know how memories work,
some synaptical connection
embedding a chance transient moment

for a few minutes - as in a phone number being copied,
or a life time - as in *Watch that paint,*

residing in some cells,
banked up against other memories,
piling up like newspapers someone never throws away,

to be erased in dementia, or death,
to be taken to another consciousness,
a glimpsed-at reality
not requiring cells,

coming into its own
in some other place.

Thursday 1 September - St Giles's Day

I think of September as the beginning of Autumn. Dawn is getting later, this morning a golden glow, and then bright sun. In Morning Prayer I thanked God, as usual, for bringing us to this new day. Even though I have had many days every day does feel new at the beginning. I gather it is our Diocesan Bishop's practice to count how many days he has lived, to help him value each one. Today I have lived for 24,448 days.

St Giles is remembered for his compassion towards people with leprosy. He lived as a hermit, around year 710. It was understood at that time that an angel of the Lord might come in the guise of a demanding person to try you, and having put you to the test, would depart.

I suppose these days the only way of knowing if trying people are angels on a mission or not is to see if, having tried your patience, they depart.

Dogs

Two clipped and groomed dogs
scour the garden for insects
after their sardines.

Saturday 3rd September Doncaster Minster Summer Fair

The weather stayed dry, every group from the Minster community was involved, the new servery proved very popular, as did the hot dog stand, it was a good day for chatting to people, and we raised some money for church funds.

Sunday 4 September, dusk

Mussels-orange and prawn-pink seeps and is strewn across the grey-blue sky. Nancy, Eddi and I are out for a walk. When we get home, I stop to chat to my neighbour. She tells me that in Nairobi the elephants have no water and are collapsing. I cannot bear to hear it.

Where is God: A Lament Psalm.

Where is God when we need Him? Has He abandoned us for all our wicked ways, as the earlier psalmist wonders? Will He not listen out for us again?

Has our determination to kill off as much of Her nature, Her animals, Her people as we can get away with, finally driven Her away, tried Her patience a few thousand too many times?

A Glimpsed-at Reality

Has our refusal to love, our clinging on to selfishness,
position, control, proved too much for Them, that
They have taken their icons, their reredoses, their
incense away?

Is there another planet where it is all working out,
lambs lying with lions, weapons melted and sculpted
into objects of light and beauty?

But didn't once His love swallow all this up, accept it
and transform it? Aren't we redeemed, Kingdom
people, all who are, will be and have ever been?

Aren't we now, we who do church and those who
don't, all embraced by Her eternal love, including all
those we love who've died, in that reality now?

Don't They inhabit the universe and everything
created, including us, in us as much as out of us?

Is it our determination to see only what is outside us,
and our refusal to what is staring us in our heart, our
worst trait?

Was The Enlightenment so convincing that we really
believe that we only have what can be physically
demonstrated?

To which one-way pit have our souls gone? Are we
being crucified with Him, descending into hell with
Him today, having Holy Saturday again and again?

Or can we dare to believe that all those who
experienced your resurrection weren't mistaken,
All who were exhilarated by fire and language, not
hysterical

That You were there, that You meant it for then
and You mean it for now too.

Wednesday 7 September

An old friend, who's a farmer at heart, and in one way
as fit as a butcher's dog, is chopping logs ready for the
Autumn, and storing them in what used to be the coal
house, stacking them against blackened boards that
used to hold coal back.

I can see now our street, the separate tons of coal
deposited on the pavement by each gate, that our
miner dads would shovel on to wheel-barrows and
into our coal houses, building up the front boards as
the pile got higher, like you might a compost heap.
The overspill would be kept in another bunker
outside, and used first. It was important to keep it dry.
One of my jobs as an older child was to take a shovel
of burning coal from the kitchen/dining room (known
as The House) fire to the sitting room (known as The
Room) fireplace and start another fire there for the
evening, with newspaper up against the shovel to
'draw' the fire. That would never be allowed now.

I also did all the washing up, the ironing, and cleaned
the windows inside and out every two weeks. To

today's kids that would be equivalent of being sent up chimneys.

When I came home from college, older, the first smell I noticed was coal smoke.

Because of the open fires, and people smoking, my parents always seemed to be decorating. This poem *One House* was commended in The Ware Poets 14th Competition Anthology 2012

One House

I was born in a house of painters and decorators:
The paste table, the rolls of anaglypta, brick-effect, flock
slapped dry against plaster, one hand holding, the other
running down the side, the top flopping over,
a measured tear at the skirting board,
the unfurled roll hauled on to the table,
cut, pasted and slid up the wall,
 smoothed and eased into place,
air bubbles stroked out,
creases fingered flat,
and mind that paint,
watch that door.

A Tesco delivery man was at someone's door when I took the dogs out this evening. A Labrador came to the door, carrying its teddy. The delivery man gently pushed it back indoors. I said, 'That's part of your job!', and he replied, 'I do this more than I can count'.

Thursday 8 September

With great sadness we heard today that The Queen has died. May she rest in peace and rise in glory.

Sunday 11 September

On holiday. I went to St Andrews in Holt, Norfolk, this morning, where I sang for the first time 'God save the King'

At the end of the service The Vicar asked if it was anybody's birthday. So I thought *a few days doesn't matter*, stood up, blew out all the candles on the cake they gave me, and beamed as they sang me *Happy birthday to you.*

No I didn't.

We take an evening stroll on the cliff path at Weybourne, Nancy's first time here. We chat to two women, with a Shih Tzu (unfriendly) and a Border Terrier/Pug cross (wary), one of the women saying that her former Shih Tzu was like a Tasmanian Devil. So Tibet to Tasmania in one brief walk.

Monday Morning 12 September

Eddi, Nancy and me are the only ones about at 5.45, just light.

An hour later there is traffic.

I think about the pigeon in the *Peregrines of Norwich Cathedral* book, one photographed ascending live in the non-negotiable grip of the falcon, looking terrified. No moral agenda for the peregrine, no *we must treat it humanely, kill it speedily and without fear before we put it to our use.* No, it will get fed as it is to the young, becoming dead at some ghastly point.

I wonder what a non-killing Buddhist would think? I was at a lunch when I was a student teacher with some Buddhist monks, and found a caterpillar on my lettuce. After initially placing it on one side of my plate, after the meal I took it to the trolley for discarded food. One of the monks came after me, rescued it from the waste food, and took it outside.

I wonder what he would have done about the wasp nest we had recently, wasps coming into Linda's bedroom by the dozen, which we had a pest control man in to exterminate?

The sea is calm this morning. The little waves slowly lurching on to the pebbles, as if dragging themselves there after a bad night's sleep.
Standing on the edge of the cliff, on an edge of our island, I think of how of course we inhabitants of the British Isles are drawn to the sea.

I wonder what primitive tribal instinct makes us want to split ourselves up in the UK into separate countries? I remember, as kids, we identified as Elmsallites or Kirkbyites, a small distance allowing for a slight change of accent that could have been a chasm of miles.

Monday Afternoon 12 September

Happisburgh Owl Day, a birthday present to me from Linda. Before I go for my three-hour visit, Linda suggests I shouldn't wear my nice cardigan. She's thinking it might get pecked and pulled. I assured her it won't be Hitchcock.

I held around ten owls. All the owls are imprinted, which means that the birds have come to recognize the keepers as parents, whom they trust, so as long as a keeper is there, they're fine.

Happisburgh Owl Haiku

Learnt to trust, you could
forget she is a killer
could break your finger

or thumb with a grip.
But she allows this closeness
uninterested

in you and your gaze
but wouldn't come out if she
didn't want to, food

and being with the
keeper, her reward, the day
not exactly wild.

But they live longer
this way, are given all that
they need, and us too.

Owl

A job for every
feather and speckle and down
beyond sheer beauty

Tuesday September 13.

After Gerard Manley Hopkins

Speckled Beauty

Glory be to God for speckled things -
For birds of couple colour as a tawny owl;
For each speck on each feather forming a pattern;
Fresh evening's hoots and calls; scents smells;
Landscape netted in front of sky - panel, perch and
pot
And all things hiding, watching and poised.

All things that flutter, preen and fly
Whatever is transient, present (who knows how?)
With swivel, balance, leather and tether;
His name is written in every speckle; his delight
floods the universe at every new hatched egg:
Praise him.

Sheringham beach

Dogs are to beaches like Patsy is to Bolly,
these two going full pelt,
Eddi racing herself for her best time,
dropping deep after going for a gull,
Nance holding back. *It is water.*

A competition judge
said you shouldn't write poems about kittens and
babies,
and maybe she would have added dogs on beaches,
because joy and exuberance are harder to write about
than loss and heartbreak,
and wired though we are to dwell on sad,

to resonate with a friend after years,
despite many cell changes,
to prefer the tug and drag of a broken wave against
your feet
to that of a bad night,
to see your dog hurtle after a gull it could never catch
for just the thrill of it,

these things are worth a mention
even if impossible to convey.

Monday 19 September

The Queen's Funeral Haiku

Step step step step step
as the military march
The Queen to Windsor

faith, service, duty
kindness, care and love
people, dogs, horses.

The Queen's dogs are going to be re-homed by Prince Andrew, who bought her last dog for her. I wondered how they felt, sitting there as her hearse went by. Did they sense it was her, the one who fed them biscuits at the table out of a silver box, now being escorted out of smell's reach to her final resting place; did they know they would never again thrill at her voice, trot alongside her in the corridors, cut through all the human layers with a look?

Thursday 22 September

After ten days of reflecting on the qualities of, as Professor Linda Woodhead, quoted in the Church Times, put it, 'the give-your-life ethic' (as opposed to the current cultural norm of 'live your life ethic') of the late Queen, and the many other qualities of her, we are now back with an almighty thud into the world news: Putin threatening nuclear war, young people being gunned in Iraq, racist tension in Leicester, anxiety that people and businesses won't be able to pay their forthcoming energy bills, a desperate rise in people seeking the help of foodbanks, and less being offered to them, and so on.

We continue to pray.

Monday 26 September

I read Chrissy Banks' pamphlet *Frank*, Chrissy putting into words the surely universal feeling of love-loneliness, the universality, I feel, making the experience both better and worse.

A few weeks ago, I was also thinking about such things and put it this way:

The loneliness of grief, when the person is still very much alive but not to you

Tuesday 27 September

There's a noticeable nip in the morning air now, which the dogs prefer to the hot weather. The sun comes out when we're half way round the field, low and impossibly bright. I know a few people round here now and we stop to talk. We only talk dogs.

Eddi mercifully gets round the field without rolling in something. A few times this week she has had to suffer the indignity of being bathed outside after a walk.

A friend sent me a birthday card of a cartoon Miniature Schnauzer wearing a demonic expression, about to be bathed, saying, 'If I had wanted to smell like soap, I'd have rolled in it'. Quite.

On my second walk of today on the Red Path I say hello to an elderly woman with a walking frame, who says she wishes there were seats along the path. I think that would be nice.

On my third walk I consider that I have spent quite a lot of the day walking.

Wednesday 28 September

A fourteen-week-old liver Cocker Spaniel came speeding up to me and the girls on the field this morning, a right wriggler, full of exuberance and life.

Thursday 29 September

A green-soaked, green-scented walk through the wood at Chatsworth today, plugging me in to something essential.

Chatsworth Wood

There's no notice asking me not to touch
so I lay my hand on the bark of a thick high pine,
feeling its resolute roughness,
the years it has taken to get to this,
admiring its stance in its forever spot,
its acceptance of this September warm drizzle, and my
touch.

An ink picture of Chatsworth House is stamped on the
back of my hand
in case I want to come back

to have a last look,
stand for a bit.

Friday 30 September

Our Garden

Rods of rain framing the Celtic cross
Rain blurring the Canterbury Cross
St Cuthbert's cross drenched,
not for the first time.

Saturday 1 October

Attending a concert at the Minster I gaze at the rods of
light streaming through the clerestory windows, like
an ethereal bar code, as the brass band comes to a
crescendo in Wagner's *Procession to the Minster*,
generating an intense living-in-the-moment feeling,
which, having said that, is never possible as a moment
is in the past or the future the instant it arises.

Sunday 2 October

Harvest Festival this morning and I think of a friend who likes harvest hymns the best. I can see why. All that lovely flourishing of the countryside.

They remind me of school, and the hall, window ledges decorated with fruit and veg, the air heavy with the luscious smell of them. We would take boxes to the old people. I expect I'd qualify for one now, except that our church harvest produce is jars, packets and tins for the food bank. There were no such things when I was a child.

I remember reading Brian Keenan's *An Evil Cradling*, the account he wrote of his hostage experience, describing one day when, after months of horrid grey diarrhoea-producing swill he was given to eat, he was given an orange. The intensity of the colour, the smell, the texture were so wonderful he couldn't eat it.

Wednesday 5 October

I go to the Roman Catholic church to venerate the relic of St Bernadette of Lourdes, there for one day. Hundreds of Catholics queue up, the queue snaking up and around the aisles of the church, the faithful unselfconsciously devout. One woman in the queue remarks, as she inches towards the saint, 'We could be here all day'.

Saturday 8 October

Now the mornings are darker I am up before sunrise. Out of the kitchen window I see the cheery happy sunflowers pre-dawn, with nowhere to look.

On the path we crunch hundreds of acorns underfoot. The abundance of nature, that all those are dropped and maybe not even one tree will come of it.

Eddi and Nancy have a get together on the field with a Springer Spaniel, a Pug-cross, a very large tan woolly dog, and an unidentifiable dog who the whole time is on her back.

Tuesday 11 October

St Ethelburga's Day, Abbess of Barking in 625, the Venerable Bede saying that many miracles occurred around her.

How lovely to be in such a saintly presence that many miracles just occur. That makes up just a little bit for her name.

Walking along a woodland path by the red path, an oak leaf drifts down on to Nancy's head. Surprised that something should just touch her from above she looks up, sees nothing, and carries on.

Waiting for seed.

Unmanageable
those two deep high flower beds
now only soil, wait.

Wednesday 12 October

A day at the monastery at Mirfield, where I lead a group of lovely priests and a deacon on How to be a mindful Christian, and enjoy a Eucharist with the brethren. Good to be back.

Friday 14 October

The sky like an old English painting: light blue, irregular clouds of pink, beige, pale grey, white and dark grey, the greens of trees reaching up to it, the occasional bird in the air, the sun caught in a few clouds.

Saturday 15 October

A reflective, prayerful small service to mark the end of Baby Loss Awareness Week, with a compilation of prose and poems that I put together, a gathering of everyone around their lit candles on the altar, and nice cake afterwards. A good thing to do.

Sunday 16 October

I have an appointment at the hospital tomorrow, and with the appointment letter there arrived a questionnaire asking me if I was currently having, or intending to have, gender realignment. Well, to be honest, I've never thought of it, but if they think it will help?

Limp, tan oak leaves lie around the edge of the field, some sticking to my wet boots.

Soon it will be All Saints' Day.

Haiku

A poem can capture -
haiku in particular -
what nothing else can.

RED

Arrow

Setter

squirrel

button

light

rose

letter

robin

Rum

box

sky

onion

Sea

carpet

flag

planet

Riding Hood

cabbage

neck

brick

Kite

nose

Coat

pepper

head

line

corpuscles

herring

nose

Leicester

rash

hot

PATH

A PSALM OF THOSE WHO WALK DOGS IN THE PARK

With my whole heart I will give thanks for the dogs and the dog walkers and the paths of the park: the paths are long and straight. How can we count the paths?

In the midst of the park the dog walkers talk one to another: the dogs and the breeze are the words on their lips. Oh how much is the breeze on their lips. They say one to another Hello and Look at your dog.

For many years have the dogs and dog walkers walked the paths: though they may walk in the midst of trouble they are refreshed on the paths. I will slay my enemies who seek to destroy these paths.

How good and joyful are the dogs and their walkers on these paths. They are like precious ointment upon the head: this shall be their place for ever. Here will they walk and have delight therein.

Highly Commended in
Manchester Cathedral Poetry Competition 2013
Judged by Nicola Slee

Ways you can support Doncaster Minster

❖ Become a Volunteer Steward and help us to open longer for visitors;

❖ Attend events

❖ Support fundraising campaigns

❖ Visit shop for cards, souvenirs, books, preserves and much more

❖ Set up a Monthly Standing Order

❖ Donate cash, cheques or digitally at a donation station in the Minster

❖ Donate online at: www.doncasterminster.co.uk/donations and giving

❖ Donate as you shop online, at no extra cost to you: at Amazon Smile

AND GIVE AS YOU LIVE

Printed in Great Britain
by Amazon

19370991R00072

CW00392746

CITY BOYS
AT WAR

CITY BOYS AT WAR

The Lloyd's Battery 1938–1940

A gunner's perspective

Peter Ledger

UNIFORM

UNIFORM

Published by Uniform
An imprint of Unicorn Publishing Group
5 Newburgh Street
London W1F 7RG

www.unicornpublishing.org

All rights reserved. No part of this publication may be reproduced,
stored in a retrieval system or transmitted, in any form or by
any means, electronic, mechanical, photocopying, recording or
otherwise, without prior permission in writing from the publisher.

© Peter Ledger, 2018

The moral right of Peter Ledger to be identified as
the author and compiler of this work has been asserted.

A catalogue record for this book is available from
the British Library

5 4 3 2 1

ISBN 978-1-911604-83-9

Cover design Unicorn Publishing Group
Typeset by Vivian@Bookscribe

Printed and bound in the UK

CONTENTS

Dedicated to the Memory of Alfred and Marjorie

and

for Angela

*Those on both sides owe it to the dead to build on the experience
of war and to give Europe a new beginning.*

Richard von Weizsäcker, President of Germany,
speaking in the ruins of Coventry cathedral at the ceremony
commemorating the bombing of the city fifty years earlier.
14 November 1990

*I expect when all this is over and we are two dear old folks with
grandchildren dangling on our knees we will look back on these
days as a shady spot in our lives out of which we came into the
sunshine again, with our increased love, our memories and our
letters as mementos of them. Well, we hope so, anyway.*

Marjorie Ledger to Alfred Ledger
Boxing Day, 1939

FOREWORD

Throughout history, it is often only the story of the victor that remains echoing through the ages, a single narrative that obscures a multitude of alternative experiences and points of view. So when a book comes along that focuses, as *City Boys at War* does, on amplifying these untold stories, the experiences of ordinary people living extraordinary lives, it simultaneously refreshes the past and illuminates the present.

The true story in these pages is told from the perspective of an insurance broker in the Lloyd's market, Alfred Ledger, who joined the Lloyd's Battery in 1938 and was called up a year later.

It has been painstakingly put together from letters he wrote to his fiancée (later, wife) Marjorie Angel and her replies, diary entries and other first-hand accounts, creating great insight into the emotional reality of living in a country preparing to go to war – and then fighting one.

These were undoubtedly hard times and yet what shines through this book is the incredible resilience of Alfred and Marjorie, and everyone around them, as the world they knew and loved inexorably became a darker place. As the author notes at one point: 'Alfred's letters to Marjorie do not contain a single complaint about the harsh conditions the soldiers endured.' And yet they must have been unimaginably awful.

This life-affirming book is a salutary reminder to us all that the freedom we enjoy today was fought for by soldiers on the ground – including members of the Lloyd's market – and their loved ones back at home, living with the constant worry of bad news. Alfred and Marjorie, and others like them, are the true heroes of those times, regular citizens who sacrificed so much so subsequent generations could live in peace. It's time their part in our present was heard.

This book is a great achievement and adds another compelling chapter to the best story ever told: the triumph of the human spirit over adversity.

Bruce Carnegie Brown
Chairman, Lloyd's

PREFACE

Vast numbers of books have been written about World War II, most of them from the vantage point of the commanders and governments, describing and analysing great events and sweeps of strategy. This book considers a campaign of just eleven months, from September 1939 to July 1940, viewed at the micro level – the perspective of a gunner, his wife, his family and his comrades.

The period starts with the so-called Phoney War, the months up to the German attack in the west ending with Operation Dynamo and the escape of the British Army from Dunkirk. However, the events described here do not end on the beaches of Dunkirk but with a second, little known, rescue, Operation Ariel (also known as Aerial), the organised escape of allied troops and civilians from ports in Brittany and western France. Operation Dynamo succeeded in lifting 338,000 troops from Dunkirk. Ariel was just as successful in its objective, rescuing 190,000 troops.

Dunkirk has become part of British folklore. Ariel has been forgotten. As for Haddock Force, the units sent south to defend French military airfields in the event of RAF bombers using them as refuelling bases en route to bombing northern Italian cities, history moves into the realms of mystery. But it is these events that the narrative follows.

The genesis of this book was a conversation in the summer of 2014 between Angela Grant, the daughter of Alfred and Marjorie Ledger, and the author, their nephew. Angela reminded me that she had a large cache of letters exchanged between her parents throughout World War II. With the letters as the start point, I followed a trail which uncovered what follows.

Alfred was a marine insurance broker working for Gray Dawes in the London insurance market,[1] particularly Lloyd's of London. In 1938 he had joined the Lloyd's Battery of the 53rd (City of London) Heavy Anti-Aircraft Regiment, Royal Artillery, a Territorial Army unit based at White City. He was called up in August 1939.

The book sets out to capture the lives of Alfred and Marjorie through this correspondence – their hopes, expectations, fears and anxieties during a critical period in the recent history of the United Kingdom.

In one sense, Alfred and Marjorie were ordinary people, leading ordinary lives. In another sense, however, they were exemplars of that remarkable generation who, in their own way, anonymously stood up to one of the greatest tyrants in history, Adolf Hitler. As Colin Hall, an Arnhem veteran, put it,

> It was a grim time. We were just young men who would much rather be back at home, drinking, dating and living normal lives. We had been thrown into the defence of Europe, which although an honourable and worthy activity, was not our choice. Neither I nor any of my mates wanted to be there. I saw no cowardice, but I saw no heroics either.[2]

He spoke for Alfred and Marjorie and millions of others.

After the outbreak of war Alfred wrote to Marjorie as frequently as he could, generally every two or three days. Marjorie wrote virtually every day. Exchanging letters at this rate was exceptional, and a testament to their love for each other. Alfred had encouraged Marjorie to tell him what she was doing even if there was no news as such. On one occasion she opened by saying 'do you know I absolutely haven't got a scrap of news as I have done nothing since I wrote yesterday evening but knit'. She then went on to cover three pages describing her day.[3] For Alfred, her letters were a precious link with home, constantly boosting his morale. 'I marvel at the way in which you always have something of interest.'[4]

Alfred's brother Rupert and his friend Jack Davies, both of whom also joined the 53rd, were nothing like as assiduous. Marjorie wrote on 31 October 1939, nearly three weeks after the regiment had left for France, that neither of their wives had received letters, although Rupert's bank manager had heard from him. 'So evidently I am a woman favoured among women!'[5]

The letters remained in a closed black wooden box during their authors' lifetime. Alfred died in 1993, Marjorie in 1997. In 2014, Angela at last felt able to read the letters and agreed that they might give an interesting insight into a momentous time in the history of our family. Despite this, we opened the box with some trepidation. We should not have worried. It quickly became apparent that the cache of letters served not just as an extraordinary source of information on life during those difficult years but as a remarkable record of how a young couple, just married and very much in love, managed to survive the strains of separation while Alfred was on active service.

CONTEXT

Without context, however, the letters, which are the starting point for this book, lose much of their impact. I make no apologies, therefore, for devoting space to the circumstances leading up to the outbreak of hostilities in 1939 and the following events. War took Alfred to France in 1939 and forced his separation from Marjorie. Of necessity, news was managed by the Government and censorship applied. Today, we are privileged by our ability to access contemporary documents, even minutes of the War Cabinet. At the time, however, they were of necessity closely guarded state secrets. Censorship meant that for the participants the media were often compelled to be 'economical with the truth' and rumour thrived. By providing a minimum of context I have attempted to illustrate what Alfred and Marjorie's lives were really like.

THE SOURCES

There are two principal sources for this book. The first is the cache of letters, and a diary kept by Marjorie's father until his death from pneumonia in 1943. The second is the large number of documents, particularly military war diaries (battalion, regimental, battery as well as RAF records) held at the National Archives and the Imperial War Museum.

As sources, both are flawed. The letters are frustrating, as there are significant gaps. Marjorie's letters appear to be virtually complete, covering a period from mid-1939 to the end of the war in 1945. Alfred's letters, on the other hand, run from roughly the same start point but virtually cease on his return to England in July 1940. This is curious. Assuming that the letters were kept by both recipients, one would have thought it would be Alfred's letters that survived intact, not Marjorie's. Alfred was serving in the Army and moved fairly regularly. Marjorie, on the other hand, was by then living with her parents at Blackheath, Kent and later Claygate, near Esher in Surrey.

An interesting point about the letters is that they are virtually all numbered. The reason for this is that Alfred and Marjorie expected the mail delivery between England and France in wartime to be unreliable. By numbering each letter they would know if any had gone astray. From time to time this did happen, especially in the period when the 53rd HAA were on the move after the invasion of France.

Marjorie kept a list of her letters, and every time Alfred acknowledged receipt she crossed off the number. This was helpful when the exchange of correspondence slowed dramatically after the German invasion of the Low Countries and France in May 1940. Marjorie wrote: 'I'm glad you are getting my letters. You say 195 – 6 – 7 are missing. Well, since this trouble began I've ticked off the ones you say you have received, and according to my list the only one missing was 197.'[6] On occasion, the system could be the cause of some confusion: Alfred's letter of 1 December 1939 is marked 'p.s. numbering broken down'. But generally, it can be worked out when numbers and dates are compared.

The National Archives files are available in two forms. Some are online. Where these have been accessed it is indicated in the notes. The majority, however, are physical documents held at Kew. These bring different frustrations. The regimental war diaries, RAF and naval records are in poor condition. The daily entries in the war diaries were written in pencil and are often difficult to decipher. The same applies to appendices, embracing important documents such as special orders, patrol reports, gun station logs and Operation Orders.

Some of the war diaries and operational reports are typed, including that for Alfred's own battery, No. 159. It is almost certain that this was because the diaries concerned were damaged or lost in the confusion of the escape from France in June 1940. The war diary of 158 Battery, which is also typed, records that all the documents were burned on the quayside as the battery headquarters escaped from La Rochelle on 17 June 1940; it must have been recreated from memory after the Battery returned to England. The typed diaries are certainly much more cryptic, and thus less forthcoming, than the handwritten diaries.

The original documents all date from 1939 or 1940. These invariably give distances in miles. The present narrative uses kilometres as this will mean more to modern readers, but where distances are given in original documents miles have been retained.

The events recounted in the book are restricted to the period from Alfred's call-up in August 1939 through the arrival in France of the British Expeditionary Force in October 1939 to the withdrawal from France in mid-1940. I hope that this account will give the reader an insight into the contrasts faced by a group of ordinary City workers who were lifted out of their comfortable, perhaps rather mundane, lives and thrust into the hardship and deprivations of war. The narrative covers ten of the most critical months in the history of the United Kingdom, ending when the country, defeated in battle, withdrew behind the English Channel, leaving Continental Europe under the yoke of the Nazi regime. It is a sobering thought that between 1940 and 1945 it was only in these small islands that European civilisation, which we take for granted, remained intact.

ACKNOWLEDGEMENTS

In the course of writing this book I have incurred many debts. Angela Grant, my cousin, and her husband Mac, provided me with endless hospitality while I trawled through the correspondence exchanged between her parents, Alfred and Marjorie Ledger; their letters form the basis of this book. They may have wondered whether my visits would ever end, but they always made me welcome.

Ian Macalpine-Leny and Terry Pey, who heroically agreed to proof read the first draft, made corrections and suggestions which were unfailingly helpful and constructive.

The world of publishing is an intimidating place for a novice author. David Lermon provided me with invaluable encouragement, which helped me overcome many doubts.

The staff at the National Archives and Imperial War Museum Research Room patiently put up with my enquiries, on one memorable occasion resulting in an important discovery.

I owe a debt of gratitude I can never repay to Emily Lane, doyenne among editors, who, with generosity I did not deserve, offered to edit the book. With the eyes of a hawk and the patience of a saint she rigorously knocked the text into shape. Her critical vigilance, always wrapped in kindness, transformed my initial efforts.

My greatest debt, however, is to my cousin, Angela Grant. She it was who climbed into the loft of her home to recover a dusty black box, unopened for over seventy years, which contained the letters exchanged between her parents during World War II. Overcoming her understandable apprehension, she allowed me unfettered access to them. Without her generosity this book would not have been possible.

I am eternally grateful to all of them. It goes without saying, however, that any errors of fact or lapses in style or judgement are mine alone.

Peter Ledger, Midsummer Day, 2017

ENDNOTES

1   A shipping and insurance business founded in 1865 by the Scottish entrepreneur Archibald Gray and his partner Edwin Sandys Dawes. It was famous for arranging insurance for the P&O fleet, in the 1930s the largest in the world. Today it is a substantial travel agent (www.gdg.travel/history, visited 15.02.15).

2   Quoted in Buckley, *Monty's Men*, p. 18.

3   ML 03.11.1939.

4   AAL 25.11.1939.

5   ML 31.10.1939.

6   ML 31.05.1940.

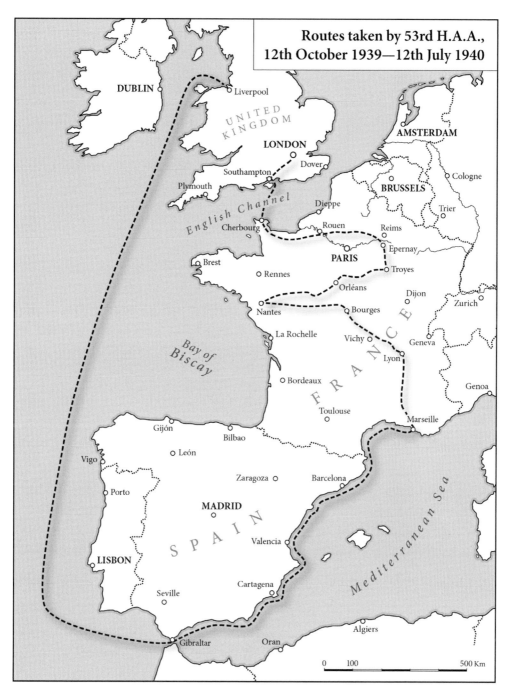

Routes taken by 53rd HAA 1939–1940

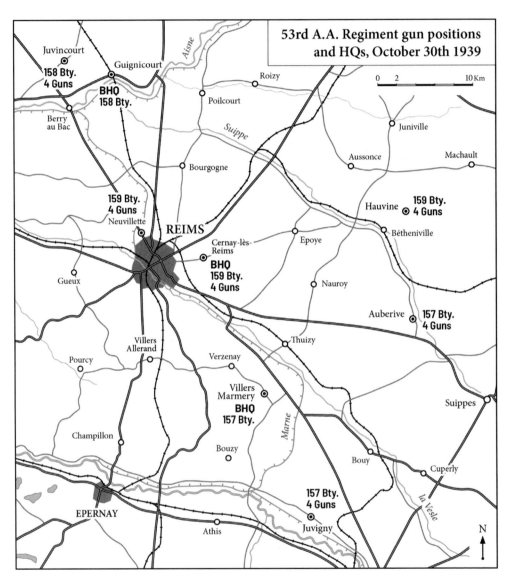

53rd A.A. Regiment gun positions and HQs, October 30th 1939

Juvincourt

158 Bty. 4 Guns

Guignicourt

BHQ 158 Bty.

Aisne

Roizy

0   2   10 Km

Berry au Bac

Poilcourt

Suippe

Juniville

Bourgogne

Aussonce

Machault

159 Bty. 4 Guns

Hauvine   **159 Bty. 4 Guns**

Neuvillette

REIMS

Cernay-lès-Reims

Epoye

Bétheniville

Gueux

BHQ 159 Bty. 4 Guns

Nauroy

Auberive   **157 Bty. 4 Guns**

Villers Allerand

Verzenay

Thuizy

Pourcy

Villers Marmery

BHQ 157 Bty.

Marne

Suippes

Champillon

Bouzy

Bouy

Cuperly

157 Bty. 4 Guns

la Vesle

N

EPERNAY

Athis

Juvigny

53rd gun positions and HQs, 30 October 1939

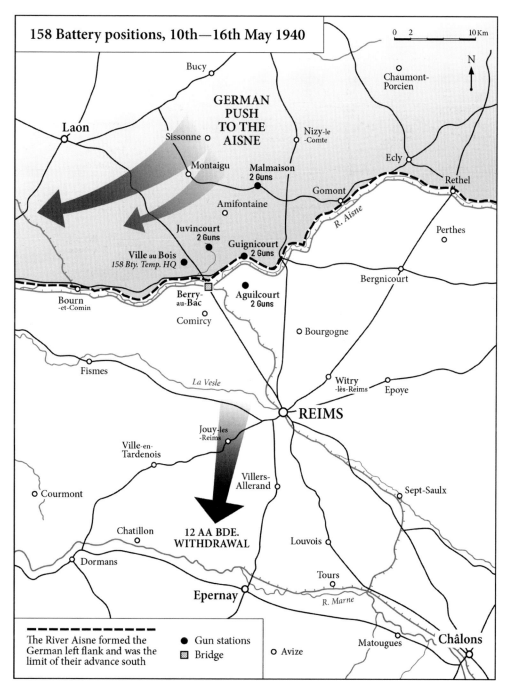

158 Battery positions, 10–16 May 1940

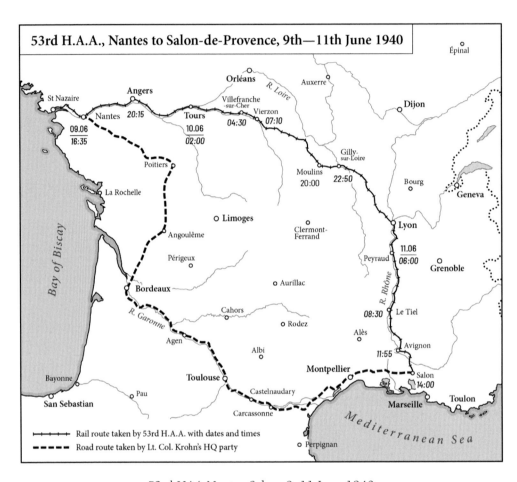

53rd HAA Nantes–Salon, 9–11 June 1940

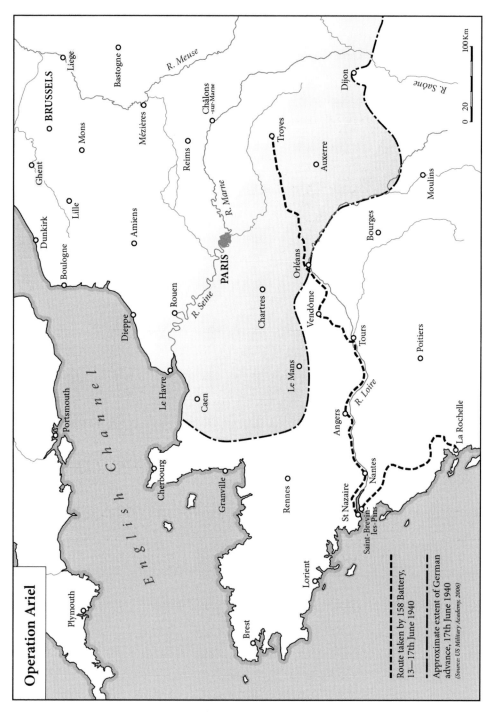

Operation Aerial

1
THE HUSH OF FEAR

Wednesday 20 July 1938 was hot and sunny. In apparent contradiction of the weather, Marjorie Angel went up to Brompton Road in Kensington and bought a grey lamb coat. She wrote to Alfred, commenting, 'what a ridiculous day to buy a fur coat! I think a bathing suit would have been easier!' It was her first letter addressed to 'Gnr Ledger, A.A. 883203'.

Her fiancé, Alfred Ledger, had volunteered for the Territorial Army on 21 March 1938. He was just twenty-five years old.

Marjorie and Alfred Ledger, 1938, after Alfred had volunteered for the TA.
© Angela Grant

Both families lived at Blackheath in Kent. Alfred and Marjorie met through the local tennis club. Her father Robert Angel was an architect with his own private practice. Much of his work came from local gas utilities. He was very artistic, an accomplished painter working in watercolours and engravings, even turning his hand to sculpture.[1]

Marjorie, aged 5/6 and her parents, Robert and Elenor 'Nellie' Angel. © Angela Grant

Marjorie inherited his artistic flair. On leaving school, with her father's encouragement, she attended an art college. She was a happy and accomplished student, studying life drawing and dress design.

Alfred had a fine voice and, until he was thirteen years old, had been a choirboy at Worcester cathedral. He moved to Caterham School in Surrey and from there went into the City, working for a Lloyds insurance broker, Gray Dawes. Starting as the office boy whose first job was to sweep the office floor each morning, including Saturdays. The firm was famous for placing the insurance on the P&O fleet, at the time the largest in the world. It was natural, therefore, that Alfred should progress to become a marine reinsurance broker, a specialism he retained throughout his career.

Marjorie was an only child. Alfred, on the other hand, came from a large family. He was the fourth child of Alfred and Dorothy Ledger. His father, Alfred senior, was a marine engineer who had spent most of his working life on cable laying ships owned by Cable & Wireless, eventually rising to be Chief Engineer.

Choirboy, eight years old, Worcester Cathedral, 1920. © Angela Grant

Alfred's siblings were his sister Eileen, married to a school friend, Charles Jarrett, and twin brothers, Rupert and Alan.

Rupert was a salesman for a building materials company. He and his wife rented the Elizabethan Cottage, a small café at Blindley Heath in Sussex. Alan had joined the Inchcape Group, at the time an overseas trader with operations in, among others, East Africa. Alan was company secretary and lived in Mombasa, Kenya.

Alfred's parents adopted a fifth child, Philip Bates, known in the family as 'Pip', the son of a friend of their mother, who had become pregnant after a liaison with her employer in Norfolk. In the unforgiving social environment of the time, Philip's mother found doors closed and turned to Dorothy Ledger for advice. Dorothy and Alfred senior said they would take in the baby, adopt him and treat him as their own son. They were good to their word.[2]

Alfred and his brothers were keen Rugby players. On leaving school they were instrumental in starting the Old Caterhamians Rugby club. At the same time Alfred kept up his singing. His voice had developed into a beautiful tenor and his sister Eileen would accompany him on the piano. Marjorie was also an accomplished pianist and, despite the socially restrictive customs of the time, was allowed by her parents to go to the flat Alfred shared with Eileen and Rupert, where she would also accompany his singing. It was a gentle, civilised time.

This was the world which Alfred, Rupert and a colleague of Alfred's, Jack Davies inhabited. It must have been with some apprehension, therefore, that they stepped into the unknown and volunteered for the Army. They signed on at White City Territorial Army Barracks, joining the 53rd (City of London) Heavy Anti-Aircraft Regiment, Royal Artillery. Alfred and Jack were given sequential service numbers and all three were assigned to 159th (Lloyd's) Battery.[3]

Why the 53rd (City of London) and the Lloyd's battery? During the Great War of 1914–18 the War Office had perceived benefits in recruiting men from the same locality. It meant that the men enlisting would be among friends and neighbours, with the expectation that this would produce greater cohesion in their units. They became known as the 'Pals battalions'. However, recruiting from a relatively small community brought risks. If heavy casualties hit one of these battalions then the community from which they were drawn would be devastated.

The majority of the Pals battalions were recruited from specific localities: the Leeds Pals, Accrington Pals, Sheffield Pals and so on. While perceived as synonymous with northern communities, they were in fact recruited from a wide variety of groups. The first Pals battalion to be raised was in fact the Royal Fusiliers 10th (Service) Battalion, formed in August 1914 when 1,600 members of the Stock Exchange volunteered.[4] It became known as the Stock Exchange Battalion.

The Pals Battalions and their communities suffered grievous losses in the First War. On the opening day of the battle of the Somme, in just twenty minutes the 11th Battalion, East Lancashire Regiment, the Accrington Pals, was shattered, losing seventy five percent of it strength, with 235 killed and a further 350 wounded.[5] Four hundred men of the Stock Exchange Battalion were killed on the western front.

The experiment was abandoned so the 53rd HAA was an exception, being recruited from the City financial community and 159 Battery, recruited from the Lloyds of London market, was a further exception. The other two batteries, 157 and 158 merely carried the sobriquet 'City of London'.

July 1938 found the Regiment at Weybourne Anti-Aircraft Practice Camp, near Holt, on the north Norfolk coast.[6] Alfred shared a tent with a soldier who had fallen ill. 'What

Jack Davies and Alfred (the two figures on the left) training with 53 HAA at Weybourne Anti-Aircraft Practice Camp, Norfolk, July 1938. © Angela Grant

has the chap in your tent got,' Marjorie asked, 'measles or leprosy? Don't come and give them to me!' With the weather so fine, she wrote that she was pleased he was not stuck in an office: 'scraping potatoes in the fresh air must be so much better!' He had got into trouble for having dull buttons on his uniform; Marjorie playfully chastised him in mock RSM tones: 'I'm ashamed of you having dull buttons. Mind you polish them up and get in training for next year.' For a young Lloyds insurance broker, however, it must have been a rude awakening.

The letter reflects Marjorie's characteristic sense of humour – but it also buzzes with a sense of excitement, which is hardly surprising. She and Alfred had just become engaged. Marjorie recounts that a number of family members had offered her their congratulations. (It seems her parents must have been spreading the news, as 'I haven't told anyone as yet'.) In a twist she added, 'I don't know whether to congratulate you would be to infer that in me you have acquired anything special! But – not taking it that way – may I tender *you* my congrats!'[7]

On another occasion, Alfred mentioned that he had been assigned to hut-cleaning duties. Marjorie teased him with the comment: 'That's right, you clean the hut & get into training – grand opportunity!!! I shall have a most useful husband by the time the army has finished with him – if they have anything of him left for me!'[8]

Marjorie's sense of humour must have lifted Alfred's morale on countless occasions – but why did a young man, only twenty-five years old, with a good steady job, who had just become engaged, decide to sign up and join the Territorial Army?

THE BACKGROUND

Twenty years before, the Great War, one of the most devastating in history, had ended, leaving 8.5 million dead and 21 million men maimed and wounded. Britain alone had suffered 2.43 million casualties, including 730,000 dead. With the benefit of hindsight, and from the perspective of the twenty-first century, it would be natural to deduce from these appalling statistics that the nations of Europe would vow that such trauma and suffering must never again be allowed to happen.

Britain was exhausted, economically and psychologically. The result was political consensus, with both the Conservative and Labour parties pursuing a policy of disarmament.[9] Understandably, however, there was strong support for the view that Germany must pay for its aggression. French public opinion was even more hawkish, demanding harsh reparations, as France had suffered even heavier casualties.

These demands were reflected in the terms of the Treaty of Versailles, despite the misgivings of the Prime Minister, David Lloyd George. As an elected politician he had to retain the support of the voters, but privately he was concerned about the rise of Communism in Russia. He saw Germany as a bastion against Russia, and while believing that Germany should be punished, he did not want her left destitute and her disaffected people espousing

Communism.[10] He regarded the Treaty as little more than a temporary measure 'to satisfy public opinion in the belligerent countries'.[11]

His economic adviser, John Maynard Keynes, was open in his disagreement. He resigned in disgust, writing, 'The policy of reducing Germany to servitude for a generation, of degrading the lives of millions of human beings, and of depriving a whole nation of happiness, should be abhorrent and detestable.'[12] Harold Nicholson, a member of the British delegation at Versailles, considered the Treaty 'neither just nor wise'.[13]

Germany had financed her war effort by loans, and the reparations imposed at Versailles exacerbated her economic plight. Within a few months the currency had collapsed. In January 1914 there had been 4.2 marks to the US dollar. By July 1921 the rate was 76.7; the decline then plummeted to 17,972 in January 1923, and by November it was 4,200,000,000,000 marks to the dollar, a number beyond comprehension. As Gordon Craig observed: 'For millions of Germans these figures created a lunatic world.'[14]

The result was the rise of the National Socialist Party, formed in 1920, initially to counter the threat of Communism in Germany. Founded on opposition to the Treaty of Versailles, German nationalistic expansion and anti-Semitism were central to the party's ideology. An early member was Adolf Hitler, who rapidly came to dominate the party, so much so that by July 1921 he had been elected chairman with absolute power and the title *Führer*, leader.

The National Socialists' rhetoric, articulated by Hitler's mesmerising oratory, appealed especially to unemployed young men. Their membership exploded to around 20,000 when, in January 1923, France occupied the Ruhr following Germany's failure to make its reparation payments.

During the mid- to late 1920s Germany had made an astonishing recovery,[15] but membership of the Nazi Party, as the National Socialists had become known, continued to expand. Surviving the failure of their Beer Hall Putsch in 1923[16], the party adopted a lower profile and bided its time. Hitler's opportunity came with the Great Depression, which struck in 1930, leading to mass unemployment and widespread business failures. The democratic parties were unable to form a united front and became discredited. Following the July 1932 election, by which time membership had risen to 200,000, the Nazi Party emerged as the largest in the Reichstag, the German Parliament.

Neither the Nazis nor the Communists would join or support a ministry, so government by decree ensued. A second election was called, producing a similar impasse. Hitler made his move and in January 1933, supported by a number of press barons, President Hindenburg appointed Hitler Reich Chancellor. The Reichstag Fire, when the Parliament building was destroyed by arson, gave Hitler the *raison d'état* to eliminate his political opponents. He persuaded Hindenburg to suspend civil liberties, and by March 1933, after the necessary legislation had been enacted, Hitler had secured dictatorial powers.[17]

Hitler immediately set about reducing unemployment, and by a combination of measures, including sleight-of-hand in bookkeeping, Nazi propaganda was able to proclaim 'an economic miracle'. In contravention of the terms imposed at Versailles, conscription was introduced in 1935; by 1939 the Army was 1.4 million strong. Equipping these men required rearmament, which was delivered by rebuilding German industry.

Voices of concern began to be raised in Britain. One was that of Major Desmond Morton, head of the Government Intelligence Unit responsible for monitoring the import of materials used for armaments. He had met Winston Churchill – then a backbencher – on the Western Front in 1916 and, by chance, was a near neighbour of Churchill's in Kent. With the tacit approval of the Prime Minister, Ramsey MacDonald (who, paradoxically, was pursuing a policy of disarmament), Morton fed secret government information to Churchill. Armed with this, on 16 November 1934 he broadcast about Germany: the Nazis, he said, were seeking 'the submission of races by terrorising and torturing their civil population'.[18]

By 1936 Germany had become, in the words of Norman Gelb, 'an armed, swaggering colossus. More than that, it had become a bully and a menace, a threat to other nations in Europe'; Hitler proclaimed his determination to use this rebuilt military power 'if necessary to get what he wanted'.[19] In March 1936 Hitler sent troops into the German Rhineland, which had been demilitarised under the terms of the Treaty of Versailles. He also renounced the Locarno Pact, by which the signatories were required to come to the aid of France if the Rhineland was remilitarised.

The occupation of the Rhineland demonstrated the extent to which Hitler was a risk-taker. His instinct that the French would do nothing proved ominously accurate. The British and French governments, fearful of another major conflict, backed down.[20] Harold Nicolson, then an MP for the centrist National Labour Organisation, recorded in his diary on 9 March 1936: 'Great excitement about Hitler's coup. House crowded. Eden [Foreign Secretary] makes his statement ... Promises to help if France attacked, otherwise negotiation. General mood of the House is one of fear. Anything to keep out of war.'[21] Two days later, he wrote:

'If we do nothing, then finally the League of Nations and collective security will cease to have any meaning. All this is indisputable, but what is also indisputable is that the country will not allow us to take drastic action in what they regard as a purely French interest.'[22]

Hugh Dalton, a Labour MP who usually advocated stiff resistance to Germany, endorsed Nicolson's view, stating that neither the British people nor the Labour Party would support military or economic sanctions.[23] Public opinion, which in 1919 demanded revenge on Germany, had swung full circle and was firmly against a return to war. Appeasement prevailed.

Hitler took note but bided his time, continuing to rearm. Then on 12 March 1938 he struck, annexing Austria, in the *Anschluss*. Once again, the signatories to the Versailles Treaty were challenged to act, as the treaty explicitly forbade the union of Germany with Austria. Later the same day Neville Chamberlain, Prime Minister since May 1937, told the House of Commons that 'nothing could have arrested this action by Germany unless we and others had been prepared to use force to prevent it.' Once again, Hitler's gamble paid off.

By now Nicolson was convinced that Chamberlain's policy was disastrous. He spoke openly against him, and was forced to resign his Vice Chairmanship of the Foreign Affairs Committee.[24]

Alfred, Rupert and Jack shared Nicolson's view. However, it must have taken courage and determination to go against the prevailing anti-war mood but, for the three of them, the invasion of Austria was the final straw. They believed that Hitler would not stop there and that war in Europe was inevitable.[25] On 21 March, nine days after the invasion of Austria, they enlisted as reservists.[26]

There was an advantage in doing so: the volunteer retained some control – at least over timing, and, with luck, his unit. When conscription was introduced, the conscript was told where and when to report. Alfred acknowledged this when writing to Marjorie in May 1940: 'I think I have been fortunate really in the fact that I joined up when I did and where I did because, had I not joined 159 … I would be called up any moment now with little or no choice of what I joined.'[27]

ANTI-AIRCRAFT DEFENCE

The government was under severe pressure from influential commentators in the press and Parliament to increase Britain's air defences. Churchill, speaking from the back benches on 28 November 1934, counselled the government that 'to urge preparation of defence is not to assert the imminence of war. On the contrary, if war was imminent preparations for defence would be too late. [Germany is re-arming] though little is said about it in public'. He believed that over a week or ten days of intensive bombing of London '30,000 or 40,000 people would be killed or maimed … Birmingham and Sheffield and the great manufacturing towns will likewise be targets of bombing in the event of war.'[28]

William Deedes, a correspondent on the *Morning Post* (later the *Daily Telegraph*), wrote in 1938 that 'London had recruited less than one-fifth of the air-raid precautions volunteers it needed … the same state of affairs prevailed in most of our big cities – Liverpool, Manchester, Sheffield and so on.'[29] In May the Air Minister, Lord Swinton, was sacked, when it became clear that such an important minister had to be a member of the House of Commons. Swinton confided to a friend of Deedes' that Chamberlain 'gave me no reason: but the row over air strength was going on in parliament. He wanted a quiet life and didn't believe war was coming.'[30]

Despite being far from the seat of power and without access to government intelligence, Alfred, his older brother Rupert and friend Jack Davies, saw things very differently.

TENSION INCREASES

The situation in Europe had further deteriorated in March 1938 when three million ethnic Germans in the Sudetenland demanded autonomy in the newly created state of Czechoslovakia. Hitler used this as a cover for his expansionist plans. Chamberlain sympathised with the Sudeten Germans but mistakenly believed Hitler's demands were limited. The situation deteriorated throughout the summer, with the Czech government ordering a partial mobilisation in response to a possible German invasion.

Britain was gripped by apprehension. Marjorie was acutely aware of the looming crisis. She confided to Alfred in August that 'although I don't like the look of things in the very least I'm still trying to be hopeful! Maybe we will be repaid for our optimism!'[31]

In a desperate attempt to defuse the crisis, Chamberlain travelled to Germany three times in September 1938 to negotiate with Hitler. Their last meeting was on 29 September in Munich. The Italian dictator, Mussolini, and French Prime Minister, Daladier, were also present.[32] It was a desperately anxious time. Marjorie wrote to Alfred on the 29th: 'Chamberlain and others are deciding our fate … I'm afraid on Monday and Tuesday (until the evening), I had just about given up hope but since Wednesday morning I have been becoming more cheerful. [33] Marjorie's emotional roller coaster reflected the swings in Hitler's demands, first belligerent then apparently conciliatory. [34]

Finally, on 30 September, desperate to avoid war, Britain, France and Italy signed the Munich Agreement, giving the Sudetenland to Germany. Czechoslovakia was not involved in the negotiations and was presented with an ultimatum – face Germany alone or accept the agreement. History has judged the terms hammered out in Munich to be a cynical act of appeasement. It is easy to forget, however, that in signing the agreement Chamberlain merely reflected prevailing public opinion. Most of the national press supported Chamberlain. Under the banner headline 'PEACE!' the *Daily Express* trumpeted:

> Be glad in your hearts. Give thanks to your God. People of Britain, your children are safe. Your husbands and your sons will not march to war. Peace is a victory for all mankind. [35]

To post-war readers the tone and sentiment are surprising but it does reveal the relief felt at the time. But there was criticism. The *Manchester Guardian's* editorial the following day observed:

> The pacificators of Munich returned home yesterday to receive greater gratitude than has ever been given to any conquering hero… But at the same time we must not delude ourselves that we have not paid a high price… Politically Czecho-Slovakia (*sic*) is rendered helpless with all that that means for the balance of forces in Eastern Europe, and Hitler will be able to advance again, when he chooses, with greatly increased power. [36]

Marjorie for one couldn't believe that the crisis had been resolved. 'For some unearthly reason I can't realise that all the trouble should by now be over! I feel I must be told again in case it isn't true and that the papers and news this morning might have been mistaken!' This is hardly surprising. At the same time as Chamberlain was negotiating with Hitler, the country was making preparations for defence. The evidence was all around. Marjorie mentioned that trenches were being dug in the open spaces of Blackheath – the heath and the park.

The family's neighbours were so nervous that many were making plans to leave. 'Mrs

Page insists on going tomorrow afternoon [30 September 1938] whether necessary or not. Mrs Brown would go too. Mrs Usher – next door to us would, & Miss Clark, Miss Simes & June… Mother and I tried to persuade Daddy to say he would go, but he said nothing. However, I think if the worst came to the worst he would decide to shift.'

Perhaps most unsettling of all, air raid practices were being held in anticipation of bombing. Travelling home by train on 26 September Marjorie had fallen into conversation with a young railway electrician who had been summoned to Waterloo Station at short notice, as he was a volunteer air-raid warden. 'He had been told he might be kept at this work for 8 hours or 48, so he was in a fit about his wife (yes, he had one!) whom he had left all alone with no warning and no company for the night.'[37]

Chamberlain's catastrophic misjudgement was exposed when on the morning of 15 March 1939 German troops crossed from the annexed Sudetenland into Czechoslovakia. Equally disastrous was the misplaced sense of confidence within the government that, if it came to war, Britain would win.[38] It is hardly surprising that the population at large suffered from the same delusion. Marjorie wrote that she felt 'very sorry for the German people as they must realise that if there is war Hitler is more or less forcing them to commit suicide.'[39] Her prediction of the German people's fate was prescient, but neither she nor the British people realised what it would entail.

Six days later, Churchill received a visit from Forbes Leith Fraser, Chief Intelligence Officer of the Air Raid Precautions Department, and was briefed on the deficiencies in his department. Churchill wrote at once to Chamberlain urging an immediate state of 'full preparedness' for Britain's anti-aircraft defences: 'The temptation to make a surprise attack on London or on the aircraft factories, about which I am even more anxious, would be removed if it was known that all was ready.'[40]

The situation continued to deteriorate rapidly. On 8 August Churchill had made one final effort to rouse 'the Great Republic', his term of endearment for the United States: 'There is a hush over all Europe … What kind of a hush is it? Alas! It is the hush of suspense, and in many lands it is the hush of fear.'[41]

CALL UP

Despite these warnings, the 53rd HAA was not activated until late summer. Alfred and the other reservists were called up, and on 5 August they reported to their base at White City.[42]

The first entry in the regimental war diary noted:

> White City, 5th August
> Following stations (gun positions) occupied by the Regt (53 HAA) this day at
>   14.00 hours:
> 157 Bty (HQ Southwark Park) – Brockley Park
> 158 Bty (HQ Fairlop) Hyde Park – Wormwood Scrubs
> 159 Bty (HQ Finsbury Park) Friern Barnet – Burnt Farm
> Very wet most of the day.[43]

Alfred and Marjorie had been married just five weeks earlier, on 1 July 1939. They must have dreaded the moment when his call-up papers arrived, but Marjorie put a brave face on it. There were people who were worse off than they were, she wrote. She had met a young woman who had just married a doctor. While on honeymoon he was called up and immediately sent overseas. They had not even had time to return to their new home, and now 'she feels she can't go near it.'[44] She immediately swung into action, sending Alfred a cake to supplement his Army rations. She was to keep him supplied with cakes, made from her precious rations, throughout the war.

But worry crept in as well. 'I'm also glad you've come off the guns. I'd rather you peeled onions. If you ponk [sic] of them I'll have to call you Alfonso,' presumably the closest reference she could contrive to a French onion-man.[45]

Training became more intense and in August 1939 the Regiment was away for a month in the north of England. This proved a strain: 'Nearly 7 days gone! 23 more to go – no 22 – my mistake! … I'm glad you've come off the guns'; but she confessed that 'it's quite impossible to concentrate in the midst of all this'. As training came to an end, they agreed to meet at the first possible opportunity, when Alfred disembarked from the train at King's Cross station, rather than wait for him to arrive at their home at Blackheath.[46] Little did they know that far longer absences and even greater worries lay in store.

WAR DECLARED

In the east, Russia was especially fearful of the rise and expansion of Nazi Germany, so much so that the Soviet government made overtures to Britain and France, proposing an anti-Nazi pact. However, the Western allies shared a deep suspicion of Bolshevik Russia; and knowing that the Soviet Army officer corps had been emasculated by political purges, Britain and France were sceptical that the USSR would add anything militarily to the alliance. The Soviet government's approaches therefore fell on deaf ears, and it concluded that the Western allies intended to drive the Nazi threat east. The unpalatable alternative was to neuter the threat from the West by signing a pact with Germany. Feeling that there was no other option, the Soviets threw in their lot with the devil and signed a non-aggression pact with Nazi Germany on 23 August 1939.

Seven days later, Hitler, now assured of no threat from Russia, invaded Poland. Britain and France each issued an ultimatum to Germany. Again, these were ignored. War with Germany was declared on 3 September.[47]

ENDNOTES

1   Angela Grant, email 26.11.16.
2   Richard Ledger conversation with the author, 21.11.16.
3   T.A. Attestation form.
4   http://www.iwm.org.uk/ (visited 10.11.2016).
5   *Accrington Observer*, 30.06.06.
6   Address on the envelope of Marjorie's letter.
7   ML 20.07.1938.
8   ML 03.10.1938.
9   nationalarchives.gov.uk/cabinetpapers (visited 04.05.2016).
10 historylearningsite.co.uk (visited 15.02.15).
11 Nigel Nicolson, ed., *Harold Nicolson Diaries & Letters 1930–39*, p. 79.
12 Keynes, *The Economic Consequences of the Peace*.
13 Harold Nicolson, *Peacemaking 1919, Being Reminiscences of the Paris Peace Conference*, p. 187.
14 Craig, *Germany 1866–1946*, p. 450.
15 Bullock, *Hitler, a Study in Tyranny*, p. 151.
16 The Nazi Party was proscribed and Hitler imprisoned for twelve months, during which time he wrote *Mein Kampf* ('My Struggle').
17 ibid., Chs. 3–5.
18 Gilbert, *Churchill, a Life*, pp. 515–16.

19 Gelb, *Dunkirk, The Incredible Escape*.

20 ibid., pp. 7–8.

21 Nigel Nicolson, p. 242.

22 ibid.

23 Taylor, *English History, 1914–1945* (1965).

24 Nigel Nicolson, p. 322.

25 AAL conversation with the author

26 AAL attestation form.

27 AAL 05.05.1940.

28 Gilbert, p. 536.

29 Deedes, p. 56.

30 ibid., p. 60.

31 ML 24.08.1939.

32 Gilbert and Gott, p. 178.

33 ML 29.09.1938.

34 Gilbert, pp.591-99.

35 ukpressonline.co.uk (visited 30.11.2016).

36 static.guim.uk/Guardian (visited 30.11.2016).

37 ML 29.09.1938.

38 Bell, *The Origins of the Second World War in Europe*.

39 ML 29.09.1938.

40 Gilbert, p. 611.

41 Broadcast to the USA, quoted in Gilbert, p. 618.

42 NA – WO 167/617, letter 09.12.1939, Lt. Col. V.R. Krohn to C.O. 12th AA Brigade.

43 NA – WO 167/617.

44 ML 09.09.1939.

45 ML 11.08.1939.

46 ibid.

47 Gelb, pp. 8–17.

2
THE 53RD MOVE TO FRANCE

The misjudgements of appeasement now became apparent. The bulk of the German Army and almost its entire air force were committed to the invasion of Poland. French forces, although not fully prepared, far outnumbered the German forces manning the Siegfried Line. In some places, German defences didn't exist at all. Despite this, the French made no move against Germany.

Britain was similarly inactive. RAF Bomber Command was restricted to dropping propaganda leaflets on the German population. The allies' indecision was a monumental blunder.[1]

FIRST STIRRINGS OF ACTIVITY

A start was made by dispatching the British Expeditionary Force to France. In early September two divisions were moved, building up to ten divisions during the autumn and early winter.[2] Marjorie realised that the 53rd would probably be involved, but remained as phlegmatic as ever. 'The thought of you having to go abroad is too awful for words but as it has to be faced. There is no use fibbing about it.'

Alfred had heard a rumour that the Regiment might be sent to one of the many British colonies, news that Marjorie greeted with mixed feelings. The possibility of U-boat attack made sea crossings hazardous, but 'it might not be so bad as somewhere on the firing line'; however, she asked, 'What is the point of having anti-aircraft men in the colonies?' She concluded, 'The only thing we [women] can do is to accept the decisions when they're made.' She did allow herself to ask: 'I wonder if and where we can see each other again? Aren't I greedy?'[3]

Greedy? In five weeks since his call-up Marjorie had seen her new husband for just twenty hours. Her stoicism was typical and would stand her in good stead throughout five years of war.

The 53rd had spent August establishing their batteries in North London and being inspected by the CO, Lt. Col. V.R. Krohn. On 1 September their war started, the Regimental diary noting dryly: 'general mobilisation ordered'.

The sense of impending disaster can be felt when, the next day, the Regimental Headquarters moved from the building it occupied in the White City barracks to the Royal Army Service Corps Drill Hall, 'and prepared buildings against air attack'. Life for the gunners became rigorous. It was not unusual for Alfred to be on overnight guard duty and then expected to man the guns all day. Marjorie felt helpless. 'What wouldn't I give to be able to help you and give you more rest!' [4]

Life in the army was a rude shock for many recruits. Alfred complained about some of the treatment he received, but by the end of September 'the City boy' was clearly adjusting to military life: Marjorie wrote that she was pleased to hear he was 'in a more cheerful frame of mind. Goodness knows how you manage to keep so bobbish considering all you are having to put up with.'[5]

And then the event everyone dreaded happened. A short, factual entry in the Regimental war diary states:

Sept 3rd AM
Declaration of WAR against GERMANY announced by PRIME MINISTER. AIR RAIDS WARNING sounded at 11.15 hrs – FALSE ALARM.'[6]

EVACUATION

Several days followed with air-raid warnings sounded, only to be declared false alarms. As things calmed down, the war diary reverted to a series of daily reports, just single-line entries: 'nothing to report'. The truth was that the Luftwaffe was completely occupied by the invasion of Poland.

Chamberlain and his government have received a bad press as 'appeasers' but, given the catastrophic events in Flanders and elsewhere little over twenty years before, it is understandable that they were deeply reluctant to confront what was happening in Germany. Behind the scenes, however, the government was pragmatic, and, despite opposition from the Labour party, began to rearm. By 1939 defence expenditure consumed well over half the government's revenues. The RAF was the main beneficiary, at the cost of the Army;

between 1934 and 1939 it enjoyed a huge expansion, with new aircraft, bases, and trained personnel.[7] Home frontline squadrons were increased from fifty-two to seventy-five.[8]

The government also understood the risks to the population of aerial bombing of urban centres. With considerable foresight, planning had begun in the summer of 1938. The initial evacuation from the big cities and centres of production took place at the beginning of September 1939. Over three days, an astonishing 1.5 million people were moved.[9]

Civilian evacuation September 1939. Wikimedia Commons – IWM HU 36238

Twelve months before, in September 1938, when many of the Angel's neighbours at Blackheath were leaving for the country Marjorie's father, Robert Angel, had decided to stay put. This time he didn't hesitate. Even before the formal declaration of war he decided that it was unwise to continue living in Blackheath, which was near the naval dockyard at Chatham, an obvious target for enemy bombers. The family had an invitation to move in with friends, Mr and Mrs Hunt, who lived at Godalming in Surrey. He wrote in his diary on 1 September:

> We heard on the wireless that war had commenced between Germany and Poland, that G had bombed Warsaw and other towns, so as things looked grave, we packed our things on the car with the intention of getting away as soon as possible and going to Godalming … at 3.30 pm, Friday September 1st we started off for Godalming. We went through Croydon and going our way were many cars similarly loaded up like ourselves, getting away from London. On the same day motor buses and trains were taking mothers and children out from London to the country. We met long streams of buses returning to London having taken the mothers and children to their destinations.[10]

Marjorie and her parents found moving out of their home in London an unhappy experience. She described Godalming as 'a rotten sort of a village away at the bottom of a steep hill … I can't imagine anyone coming to live here.'[11] Their hosts were friends, and they had proffered the invitation to stay. However, despite paying rent, sharing the house proved difficult. Robert Angel looked for an alternative. By chance, the house next door to Alfred's parents in Claygate, near Esher, Surrey, was vacant, and they took it 'for the duration'. The rent was £2 per week.[12]

Dalmore Avenue, Claygate. Alfred's parents lived in the left hand semi, from which the Union Jack is flying. Alfred's father flew the Union flag every day throughout the war. Marjorie's parents rented the other half.
© Angela Grant

When the family announced that they were leaving, the owner's wife said it was probably the best thing, prompting the comment from Marjorie: 'so evidently we are not wanted here. Poor old refugees!'[13] Being treated 'as a glorified skivvy in what is supposed to be a friend's house is rather apt to get on one's nerves!'[14] The relief is palpable when they finally moved to Claygate on 1 September, especially as Alfred was able to get forty-eight hours' leave. 'The happiest & most precious 48 hours I have ever lived', wrote Marjorie.[15]

Most of the evacuees did not know the people with whom they were billeted, so it is hardly surprising that things didn't always work well. An acquaintance of the Angel family, Mrs Harvey, moved down to Gillingham in Dorset to stay with friends. It was an arrangement that didn't work, and she was summarily asked to find somewhere else. They 'bundled her into their car & took her all round the country trying to find her lodgings … Eventually they got her into a farm where she was half starved & treated like dirt!'[16]

In the end, after their move to Claygate, Marjorie's family took in Mrs Harvey, and happily for all concerned the arrangement did work well. Mrs Harvey was quite a character. 'It is always "duckie" when she wants some help! She is great company here, we love having her.'[17]

CIVILIAN LIFE

Immediately on arrival in Claygate the family registered at a local butcher's shop in anticipation of the introduction of rationing. On 23 September billeting officers called to check on occupancy. 'I informed them that there were my mother and father, myself & my husband when he was here! (I didn't tell them how often he was here, poor dear!) and a friend, yes a permanent one, and two dogs! So they were fully satisfied!'[18]

Even here life wasn't all plain sailing. Marjorie might have been living next to her in-laws, a comforting reminder of Alfred, but she missed the family home in Blackheath. She wrote in December 1939 that she would 'give anything to go home again. I've been so homesick since we left in September' but she understood the reason for the move to Claygate.[19] For the modern reader, however, it is curious to find her referring to Claygate as being in the country; today it is almost part of Greater London.

Anyone with an extra room might find someone billeted on them. Alfred's uncle and aunt, 'Egg' and Cis Eggelton, took in a nursing sister. 'She appears to be very nice & doesn't mind helping them. She is attached to an ambulance train at Walton &, so far, is having a cushy time.'[20]

Despite the mass evacuation of London and the anticipated introduction of rationing, an air of unreality prevailed. 'Isn't this a tedious war? Nobody seems to be getting anywhere. I wish to goodness it was over.'[21]

Very soon, however, the reality of life in wartime Britain was becoming more evident. On 4 September, Marjorie's father wrote in his diary:

> I went to London by train to see if all was right at our house and collect papers etc.
>
> The barrage balloons, which formerly were only about a few hundred feet up now were up at their full height – some so high up that they could scarcely be seen. There were hundreds of balloons in the sky over London and the neighbourhood. Another striking feature was that nearly everyone in town carried their gas mask boxes; merchants, clerks, girls and children.

In late September he observed:

> It was very noticeable that very few private motor cars were in the streets. Place seemed empty of traffic, quite easy to cross the road. A very large number of shops and other buildings were sandbagged. Some of the bagging projected out onto the footway. Windows were covered with strips of gummed paper to prevent glass splinters flying everywhere. I saw several temporary tanks built in the roadways, made of either iron or waterproof sheets and sandbagged all around, full of water for washing poisoned gas off roadway. They were about twenty feet across.[22]

There was no disguising the extent of the crisis facing the country. The evidence was everywhere. Marjorie commented that the small town of Esher, less than 3 km from the new family home at Claygate, was full of soldiers who were camped there. Over at Blackheath, trenches were being dug, and 'we got our gas masks on Tuesday morning – beastly things!'

Fear of gas attack was understandable. A young friend, Kitty, was especially worried 'what she would do with the baby in the event of a gas attack. She refuses to put him in a baby's gas mask & I don't blame her. Next door to her home a friend has a bomb-proof, gas-proof shelter & says Kitty and the baby … can go in it.'[23]

Rationing began to bite. Petrol was the first commodity to be controlled, restrictions introduced in late September. Robert Angel received his petrol coupons – '2 books, one for each month, allowing me 6 gallons per month, i.e. 144 miles of travel. The petrol is called "pool" and will cost 1/6 per gallon, not 1/7 as at present for National Benzol and Shell – I wonder what it will be like. Some people say it is paraffin oil.' Just before Christmas 1939 Robert noted: 'for some days we have been in straits with butter. We have each got our pots of butter, containing ¼ lb to last for a week. We cut the bread thick or use Velveeta cheese instead, which spreads like butter.'[24]

The most obvious impact of the war was the 'blackout'. Street lights were switched off and windows covered so no light was emitted. Driving became especially difficult, and road accidents increased markedly despite the severe reduction in traffic. In September 1939 '1,130 people were killed compared with 617 in August and 554 in Sept. last year, of these 633 were pedestrians. Among the motor accidents most were head on collisions.'[25] On 4 February 1940 Robert observed that 'it seemed strange to be going along Cheapside in the blackout. Could not see one's way, only the dim lights of cars, shops quite blacked out.'[26]

Refugees also began to appear and, with them, the evidence of Nazi prejudice. Marjorie met a 'very romantic couple. [She] is a very beautiful German girl who was brought up from childhood by her German aunt and Scotch uncle in Scotland. Because she won't say "Heil Hitler" her family [in Germany] have cut her off!' Matters were made worse when she married a Czech Jew, 'a very handsome English-looking young fellow'. They were a wealthy young couple living in a '£3,000 house' in Hampstead and had given a Christmas party for Czech refugees. The latter had been wealthy members of society but were now 'poor as church mice & some [of the women] are maids in houses & some of the men are butlers'. One young man couldn't find employment, so planned to join the Czech Army in France. Another was a brain specialist. Their one remaining asset was the 'dazzling' jewellery worn by the women – 'the only remains of their fortunes'.[27] Unlike the desperate refugees that Alfred was to encounter later, these people were well connected and had managed to escape to England and safety. Nonetheless their lives had been devastated. Marjorie's heart went out to them: 'Isn't it terrible for them?'[28]

THE 53RD ORDERED TO FRANCE

The scepticism felt by the British towards the Nazi government's announcements can be detected when the adjutant allowed himself to express an opinion in the 53rd's war diary entry for 6 October: 'Hitler made his Reichstag "Peace" Speech today – His so-called "last offer".'

The following day the Regiment received orders of such importance that the entry is underlined:

> 7th October, 12.01 hrs
>
> <u>Instructions for move of unit Overseas received</u>. 53rd HAA to prepare to move overseas, date unknown.

The change of atmosphere is stark. There is a feeling of apprehension in the urgent series of entries in the war diary. Where the late September activity reports are restricted to single-line entries, the entry for 7 October describes a flurry of activity. Operational Orders were received throughout the day instructing batteries to be moved, detailing locations and deadlines.[29] The momentum was maintained, and on 8 October the Regiment was ordered to prepare its three batteries to vacate their positions in London and move to 'the assembly point at Arborfield[30] on 10.10.39'.[31]

Alfred was home on twenty-four-hour leave on 8 October.[32] Presumably he did not explain why the Regiment had moved to a location south of Reading (in fact a staging camp). Once again, Marjorie's life was filled with uncertainty. She quizzed him by letter: 'why send guns and men to a place so far out of London? Or have you only gone there to pick up your kit? Have you heard any more of your future plans?'[33]

When she did find out, it was the news she had dreaded. Alfred must have written on 12 October, as she replied the next day: 'I've got your letter this morning, love, and now know the worst. I didn't expect you to go so soon, and it was a bit of a blow to know that probably by this time you have left.'[34]

The strain of separation was already considerable. In late September Marjorie had confessed that 'there is one thing above all others that a soldier's wife must learn to do and that is to keep her chin up the same as her husband has to & the sooner I learn to do that the better it will be! Maybe in time I will! But I'm ashamed to say it, I always was an awful cry-baby.'[35] By mid-December, she confided that when she was cold in bed she hugged her hot water bottle and imagined that she was with Alfred. 'It takes some imagination, I can assure you, to convert a hot water bottle into you!'[36]

Her worst fears were now realised, and Marjorie had to steel herself to the news that

Alfred was on his way to France. She immediately replied to his last letter from England, her letter a mix of emotion, impotency and uncertainty.

> Darling … I can't begin to tell you all I feel for you, and how every atom of me goes out to you at this time. I can imagine what your feelings must be like, being bundled off to goodness knows where without seeing your loved ones just once more … I'm afraid that God will have to bear with an incessant prayer from me for your safety, health & happiness & speedy return home, &, as you say, our permanent reunion.

It is a moving letter, Marjorie reassuring Alfred that she will do her best not to worry 'more than I can help' and urging him not to 'worry your dear head about me. You know I'm safe, & so long as all goes well with you, that is all I ask.'[37]

The move to France affected all the troops. Alfred later recalled, 'when we left England originally, we ourselves were plunging into the dark unknown without the slightest idea of what we should have to tackle and naturally felt full of forebodings, optimistic though we tried to be.'[38] The shock affected the entire family. Marjorie wrote that 'Naturally your Mother & Father were not too happy to hear the news.' In their case, the Regiment's move to France meant that two of their sons, Alfred and Rupert, were going to war. This was compounded a week later when their adopted son, Pip signed up to join the forces. 'There goes another one from family Ledger', commented Marjorie.[39]

On 27 October Alfred's brother-in-law, Charles Jarrett, who had joined the RAF, was also called up.[40] In two weeks, four men in the immediate family were either in the forces or about to join their units. It is hard to imagine what Alfred's parents felt.

Alfred was sympathetic. Pip didn't receive orders to report until 11 December when he was instructed to report to Richmond, North Yorkshire on the 15th. 'Poor old Pip. So he's going at last – & just in time to miss Christmas. I do think that's jolly hard lines. How I wish he could be spared so that the folk could have just one of us nearby.'[41] Military bureaucracy was never sensitive to such feelings, but in the event Pip got seven days' home leave, one of only a handful of recruits at his training camp who did so. According to Marjorie he managed this by telling the best tale: 'He said he had 2 (or 3) brothers in the army and his mother was all alone! Trust Pip to swing a good one!'

Marjorie, for her part, was full of regret at Alfred's sudden, unannounced departure for France. She had not been able to say goodbye. 'If only I had known what was going to happen so soon I would have done [things] differently.' Ever practical, she bemoans the fact that she couldn't send a food parcel she had prepared, together with some warm clothes.[42] Looking back at the end of the year, she wrote that she would never forget 'as long as I live, that black Friday when I got your letter to say that you were going without another chance to say goodbye'.[43]

Despite the very real concerns that she must have felt, Marjorie had no resentment towards the German people. She firmly blamed Hitler for the war. 'I don't suppose [the Germans] wanted war any more than the British. Anyway, they are somebody's sons and husbands.'[44]

MOVING TO FRANCE

The logistics of moving 800 men and their equipment were formidable. The batteries and their gun stations were widely dispersed. 158 and 159 batteries were located in London between White City and Dalston, with gun stations at Hyde Park and Wormwood Scrubs. 157 Battery had been moved to Bramley, Hampshire, close to Basingstoke. The first requirement, therefore, was to assemble the three batteries and then move them, together with the Regimental Headquarters, to Arborfield. This was completed as scheduled by 10 October 1939, most of the officers and men being moved 'by charabanc'.

A further three days were required to transfer the Regiment to Southampton: '12th Oct, 07.00 – Advance party of 7 officers and 140 [other ranks] and all vehicular transport … start for Southampton'.

The Regiment required a fleet of 96 vehicles, made up of the following:

30 × 3-ton lorries
23 × 30-cwt lorries
18 × motor cycles
20 × medium and light cars
 5 × towing vehicles

They moved in convoys at intervals spread out over two hours, and included 20 'semi-mobile 3-inch guns'.

The last four guns moved the next day and on 15 October the remaining troops moved from Arborfield on two trains direct to Southampton Docks. Moving so many soldiers and equipment to France at short notice was a logistical nightmare. Around 10,000 troops were moved in October 1939. The 53rd was just one regiment, but it required three ships, all requisitioned civilian vessels: the *Princess Maud* and *Manxman*, both passenger ferries; *Achilles*, a cargo vessel.[45]

The men and officers boarded the *Princess Maud* at 14.00 on 15 October. The advance road party travelled separately on the *Manxman*, with the guns and transport loaded on to the *Achilles*. The convoy of three vessels moved into the Solent off Bembridge in the Isle of Wight and sailed for Cherbourg at 2.30 the next morning, 'weather cold and very wet'.[46]

The requisitioned passenger ferry Princess Maud. *Normally sailing the Stranraer-Larne crossing, it was one of three vessels needed to move the 53rd HAA to France in October 1939.*
© Ian Boyle/Simplon Postcards

The succinct, economic notes of the war diary do not convey the reality. The men were roused at 4.00 am, given breakfast, and then kept on parade in the rain for about an hour. 'We fortunately went to the station in coaches which at any rate kept us dry for a while.' However, on arrival at the station the Regiment had to stand in the rain for another hour until the train arrived.

Alfred was already learning how to look after himself: he found a shop where he stayed in the dry on the pretext of buying some cakes and fruit.

Alfred must have been part of the main body of the Regiment on the *Princess Maud*.[47] Once aboard, not all the troops could be accommodated under cover. Alfred resorted to 'a little judicious wandering about in the breeze on deck and leaning up against the funnel stack', and so managed to dry out. Sleeping arrangements involved 'the so called cabin with about 50 other blokes'. Alfred wasn't having this, and with a friend 'found a nice quiet & warm spot along the corridor outside the dining saloon', where he managed to sleep from 10.30 pm until 6.15 the next morning.[48] His first letter home is evocatively headed '16th October 1939, 10.00 am, Somewhere off France', and opens: 'Well here we are lying off our port of disembarkation awaiting our turn to draw alongside the quay.'

ORGANISATION

The British Expeditionary Force, or BEF as it was known, was hamstrung by professional jealousies among its senior generals. Lord Gort, entrusted with its command, was a brave soldier, but General Allan Brooke, one of three BEF corps commanders, said he had 'no confidence in his leadership'.[49] Allan Brooke must have had his reasons, but the observation is curious. Gort had won the VC, DSO and Bar and MC, the citation for his Victoria Cross stating: 'For most conspicuous bravery, skilful leading and devotion to duty'.

This unhappy state of affairs was compounded by an inefficient command structure. Air cover was provided by the British Air Forces in France (BAFF), which commanded nine reconnaissance and four fighter squadrons; the latter were increased to thirteen after the German invasion of France, although six remained based in England, flying sorties on a daily basis.[50] The Advanced Air Striking Force (AASF) consisted of ten Fairey Battle light bomber squadrons based around Reims; initially it reported direct to the Air Ministry, but the flaws in that arrangement were rapidly exposed and in January 1940 command was transferred to the BAFF.

The truth was that the Army and RAF units rushed to France in late 1939 were commanded by men who distrusted each other, operating within a structure which was neither efficient nor effective. Events were to expose these weaknesses. Happily, the units doing the fighting were blissfully unaware of this.

12 ANTI-AIRCRAFT BRIGADE

The 53rd, together with a second heavy anti-aircraft regiment, the 73rd HAA, and three batteries from other regiments, made up the 12th Anti-Aircraft Brigade. Their role was to provide protection for the AASF airfields.

The first deployment of the BEF was completed by 11 October, five days before the arrival of the 53rd. Over a period of five weeks 158,000 men were transported to France. By 19 October the BEF had received 25,000 vehicles, and by mid-March 1940 Britain had 316,000 men in France. The transport infrastructure was essentially late nineteenth/early twentieth century; no roll-on roll-off ferries, no motorways or high speed trains. Moving so many troops and their equipment was an astonishing logistical achievement. However, moving troops in large numbers was one thing; housing, feeding and keeping them supplied was another matter.

On arrival in France, the 53rd was billeted in an area 10 km south of Cherbourg, at Sideville. The arrangements were unsatisfactory: the men were housed in farms and villages spread across a wide area and feeding them was a particular problem. With no adequate equipment the cooks were forced to prepare food over wood fires in the fields.[51]

Alfred, on the other hand, considered that the barns in which they were billeted were 'really quite comfortable. They are very clean & only used for storing hay & straw, which is also scattered about quite liberally for our bedding. They are strongly built of local stone & we sleep about 20 in one 30 feet square. I have slept like a log each night & have been perfectly warm.'[52] He also felt that the cooking arrangements, 'although somewhat primitive and 'impromptu', had worked excellently. As far as he was concerned, having spent the previous 48 hours on iron rations, it was a relief to get some proper cooked food.

Much to Marjorie's amusement, he tried his hand at some laundry, 'French style – by the side of a fast running brook'. His comrades did the same, 'and we have a long line of washing hanging out in our backyard'. The washing place was '*publique*' (*sic*), with a 'proper cement kneeling place ... & we bagged this after one [of the women] had finished'.[53] Marjorie replied that she would keep him busy 'when we get home again, but not in a stream, though!'[54]

TO ÉPERNAY

The Fairey Battles had been moved to air stations in the Reims area in September 1939.[55] 12 and 142 Squadrons were at Berry-au-Bac, about 20 km north west of the city. The

AASF headquarters and 226 Squadron were at the French Reims Air Base, also north of the town. Greatly expanded and modernised in the 1930s as the showcase of the French Air Force,[56] it boasted a concrete parking apron, hangars and a support area, and a grass field for takeoffs and landings. A large concentration of French squadrons was already there.

Rearming and refuelling between sorties – a Hawker Hurricane of 73 Squadron RAF at Reims-Champagne Air Base. Wikimedia Commons – IWM C 1551

Seven of the ten squadrons assigned to the AASF were clustered in a small area around Reims: 88 Squadron at Mourmelon-le-Grand, 105 at Villeneuve-lès-Vertus, 103 at Plivot, 150 at Ecury-sur-Coole and 218 at Suippes. Later 103 squadron moved to Challerange and were replaced at Plivot by 142 Squadron. It was this concentration of aircraft that the 53rd HAA were to defend.

The Regimental HQ of the 53rd was quickly established at the Hotel Royal on the Boulevard de la République in Reims. Its three batteries were to defend the airfields to the north, south and east of the city, and the town of Épernay in the Champagne region, not far to the south, was selected as the base for 159 Battery (it was initially based at Cernay-lès-Reims, to the east).[57]

The move from Cherbourg took place over three days, 20–23 October, and required four personnel and transport trains. Each train took between twenty-four and thirty hours to complete the journey,[58] and worse still, the rolling stock used to move the men were cattle trucks.[59] Gunner Roy Harvey later described:

> A long journey to the NE of France, Épernay in packed cattle trucks each labelled '20 hommes et 5 Chevaux'. We ploughed on through the night. Somewhere en route, at a stopping point, a German plane machine gunned the train killing 3 soldiers. Because of overcrowding I found space on top of the loaded ammunition truck enabling me to stretch out. Thankfully Jerry did not hit this – hells bells! We eventually reached our destination at a little farming village called Vaudesencourt.[60]

The 53rd was in position at gun sites protecting the RAF airfields around Reims by 24 October – but the haste of its dispatch to France and lack of planning were now revealed. Although they were no longer in transit, there were no cooking facilities, as the Regiment had been ordered to leave all its stores at White City. Food was again cooked over wood fires in the fields.[61] Sometimes there were no supplies, and the men had to buy food at their own expense.

Neither had any thought been given to providing shelter. Alfred's section was allocated 'a huge wine warehouse', the only gesture of comfort being six inches of straw on the floor. Marjorie observed, 'I imagine the wine store is empty otherwise it would be rather rash to put a Regiment in it'.[62] Eventually they were provided with *paillasses* (straw mattresses); but Alfred, Rupert and their friends elected to move to a 'sort of store room on the ground floor [where we] piled all our straw together because we find it much more comfortable'.[63] A few days later they were moved again, the Regimental war diary reporting that 26 October was spent constructing temporary shelters using straw bales roofed over by tarpaulins. Once again the weather was against them – 'cold and wet'.[64] The 12th Brigade war diary noted that 'the rain [turned] the gun positions into seas of mud. Approach roads, being nearly all country tracks, rapidly broke up and became almost impassible for [motor transport] except by the use of tracks.'[65]

Incredibly, it was not until late December that proper sleeping quarters were available at the gun parks. They were slowly built by the gunners themselves and were in reality 'glorified dug-outs'. However, they were fitted out with bunks and spring mattresses. 'They look extremely comfortable and I am sampling one tonight and am quite looking forward to the occasion – it will be the first bed I have slept in since leaving England. So we do progress, even if slowly.'[66]

Alfred's stoicism is staggering. Far from resenting the fact that the Army had failed to provide him and his comrades with adequate shelter, the sense of excitement at sleeping in a comfortable bed is palpable. It was 23 December, over two and a half months since their arrival in France. The huts were far from ideal. Each had a corrugated iron roof, camouflaged by a covering of earth a foot deep, and warmth from the fire created condensation 'in great drops which keep on splashing down'. Despite this, Alfred reported that he enjoyed 'a glorious night's sleep – lovely and warm and beautifully comfortable'.[67]

ENDNOTES

1   Gelb, p.11.
2   ibid., p. 12.
3   ML 09.09.1939.
4   ML 12.09.1939.
5   ML 25.09.1939.
6   NA – WO 167/617.
7   Philpott, pp. 255–56.
8   raf.mod.uk/history (visited 19.05.2016).
9   spartacus-educational.com/2WW evacuation (visited 19.05.2016).
10 RJA diary, August 1939-May 1943.
11 ML 04.09.1939.
12 RJA 16.09.1939.
13 ML 13.09.1939.

14   ML 15.09.1939.

15   ML 19.09.1939.

16   ML 21.09.1939.

17   ML 25.09.1939.

18   ML 21 and 23.09.1939.

19   ML 22.12.1939.

20   ML 18.10.1939; At the outbreak of war the rail companies were put under government control and special ambulance trains built. The train was probably parked at sidings at Walton station. Rail. co.uk (24.08.15).

21   ML 05.10.1939.

22   RJA diary, 04.09.39, 19.09.1939.

23   ML 26.09.1939.

24   RJA 20.12.1939.

25   RJA 19.10.1939.

26   RJA 04.02.1940.

27   ML 27 & 28.12.1939.

28   ML 27.12.1939.

29   NA – WO 167/617.

30   Arborfield Garrison, Berkshire, 8 miles south of Reading.

31   NA – WO 167/617.

32   RJA 08.10.1939.

33   ML 11.10.1939.

34   ML 13.10.1939.

35   ML 20.09.1939.

36   ML 18,12,1939.

37   ML 13.10.1939.

38   AAL 05.05.1940.

39   ML 22.10.1939.

40   ML 27.10.1939.

41   AAL 15.12.1939.

42   ML 14.10.1939.

43   ML 31.12.1939.

44   ML 06.11.1939.

45   The *Princess Maud*, 2,917 tons, owned by the London Midland Scottish Railway and used on the Stranraer–Larne crossing; the *Manxman*, 2,000 tons, built in 1904, owned by the Isle of Man Steam Packet Co., sailed between Douglas, I.o.M. and Liverpool; the *Achilles* was owned by the Blue Funnel Line.

46 NA – WO 167/617.

47 He arrived at 10 am; the war diary notes that the *Manxman* was disembarked at 8, the *Princess Maud* at 10.30.

48 AAL 16.10.1939.

49 Gelb, p. 12.

50 Richards, p. 125.

51 NA – WO 167/617.

52 AAL 18.10.1939.

53 AAL 22.10.1939.

54 ML 21.10.1939.

55 Richards, p. 125.

56 *History of Base Aérienne 112.*

57 NA – WO 167/617, 24.10.1939.

58 NA – WO 167/617; AAL 6/22.10.1939.

59 AAL 22.10.1939.

60 deardad blog (visited 12.02.16).

61 AAL 18.10.1939.

62 ML 27.10.1939.

63 AAL 14.10.1939.

64 NA – WO 167/617, 26.10.1939.

65 NA – WO 167/370, 26.10.1939.

66 AAL 23.12.1939.

67 ibid.

3
PHONEY WAR AT ÉPERNAY

It was not until 1 November that the Regiment saw any action, when 159 Battery had moved and set up gun stations at La Neuvillette, just to the north of Reims and Hauviné, 30 km east of the city.[1] A lull followed and they did not see action again until seven weeks later, when twelve rounds were fired at enemy aircraft on 21 December.[2] The gunners of the 53rd didn't realise it but the Phoney War had started, so-called because, despite the French and British rushing troops to the German border, virtually no significant action took place for eight months.

For much of November and December the war diary consists of single-line entries: 'nothing to report'. Time was taken up on training and routine tasks, such as the RAF using the Regiment's gun positions to practise low-flying attacks, and 159 Battery working with French anti-aircraft gunners to set up a barrage system.

The population back home sensed the unreality of the situation. The BEF had hurried over to France, but then nothing happened. All they wanted was for the inconveniences to stop and for their menfolk to return. As early as November 1939, after the 53rd had been in France only three weeks, Marjorie wrote: 'Isn't this a queer sort of war? I wonder when it will start? I don't want it to for your sake, but if it has got to start in order to stop I almost wish it would get on with it so that you can come back home.'[3]

The batteries were allocated the code names Pip, Squeak and Wilfred (assigned to 159 Battery), names of cartoon characters taken from the *Daily Mirror*.[4] In a curious contradiction, the war diary Anti-Aircraft Logs are regularly headed with the relevant battery number and its code name. No doubt the enemy would have been completely confused.[5]

From time to time German aircraft dropped leaflets. On 9 November the diary reported that leaflets had been dropped overnight 'presumably by hostile aircraft'. (Who else would have dropped them?) More leaflets were dropped six days later.[6] As the French Army made up the greatest proportion of the forces in northern France (2.24 million men as against the BEF of around 500,000) the leaflets were aimed at ordinary French soldiers. A typical example was headed:

Soldats français
Pourquoi vous battez-vous?

German propaganda leaflet dropped over the 53rd's positions in November 1939. 'Why do you fight? … England wants you to fight to the last to maintain the world hegemony of Great Britain and to perpetuate the injustices of Versailles.'
© Peter Ledger

It then set out to persuade the reader that the French government was only following the urging of the British cabinet, '*qui veulent rester des milords*' (who want to remain the boss).

When enemy aircraft were occasionally sighted, they were invariably out of range. This was because the 53rd was equipped with 3-inch anti-aircraft guns, firing 12.5lb shells. These were old, World War I guns. While they were effective against zeppelins and slow-moving early aircraft, they were not very effective against the modern fighters and bombers deployed by the Luftwaffe.[7]

One of the 159 gunsites, Wilfred II, spotted a Dornier twin-engined bomber on 23 November but at 6,000m it was well beyond their reach. It was another four weeks before the battery saw action again – a Heinkel III bomber sighted 'very high' on 21 December. Twelve rounds were fired, but the Heinkel flew on.[8]

RUMOURS

Invariably rumours thrived, often emanating from official sources. On 15 November a message from Regimental HQ sought information on 'suspicious characters' who had been sighted: 'two girls dressed in leopard skin coats and Wellington boots carrying attaché cases selling postcards and envelopes'. It hardly seems a convincing front for spies. The report alleged that the women were asking about particulars of British units, but nothing more is mentioned in the diary.[9]

Such rumours could spread far and wide. The BBC's Charles Gardner picked up gossip that two women had been arrested near Mourmelon where 88 Squadron were based. They were selling picture postcards to the airmen and 'at the same time asking them questions about their unit … [they] were said to have been dressed in trousers and thick boots' – adding 'I don't know how true it was.' In a footnote, he says that 'some weeks afterwards … it was said that the French decided not to shoot the women as they had been very brave and no damage was done.'[10]

Rumours weren't always about the enemy. A problem encountered by the pilots of the AASF was trigger-happy anti-aircraft gunners. Aircraft recognition was purely by sight, and even with the slowest planes it proved problematical for the gunners and high risk for aircrew. Gardner recounted an incident near Speke in Lancashire when a Wellington bomber was fired on. 'Crack went a gun and off went a bit of the Wellington's tail.' The pilot landed in a field, and, borrowing a car, drove back to the gun site. Approached by an officer, he asked him whether he was in charge. When told he was, the pilot punched him on the nose, got back in the car, and drove away. Gardner commented dryly that he'd heard the same story told 'of a Wellington at Speke, a Whitley at Manchester and a Hampden at Worcester. Soon it'll be a Gypsy Moth at Inverness.'[11]

One rumour, however, did prove to be true. The war diary noted on 10 November that there were reports of an attempt 'made yesterday on the life of Herr Hitler after his speech in Munich'. This was the assassination attempt at the Bürgerbräukeller where Hitler was due to make a speech celebrating the 1923 Beer Hall Putsch. The incident took place on 8 November and was reported in the British press on the 9th. Marjorie commented, 'isn't it a thousand pities that whoever timed the beer house bomb didn't set it a bit earlier? … But one great comfort is that if it has been done once it shows that it is not impossible to do it again.'[12]

LIVING CONDITIONS

Two overwhelming problems faced the troops living under canvas in northern France in early winter – the weather and a lack of washing facilities. Alfred managed to have one shower and one bath between early October and mid-November. He only removed his 'jacket and trews' to sleep in case there was a call-out.

There were no laundry facilities. On 1 December Alfred reported to Marjorie that he had changed his underpants for the first time in three weeks. He took things into his own hands, and eventually, in late November, he found a French housewife who agreed to wash and darn his clothing.[13]

To compound their discomfort, the troops had to put up with intense cold. The winter of 1939–40 was one of the coldest on record.[14] Alfred wet-shaved throughout his life using a cut-throat razor: the advantage of this was that, whatever the conditions, he was always able to sharpen the razor.[15] At Épernay the troops had to shave in the open. From late November through to mid-December it was so cold that on several occasions Alfred's shaving brush froze to the lid of the dustbin he was using as a table. Marjorie was furious. 'It makes me feel mad when I think of all you must be putting up with for one little squit of a man.'[16] Later, on 14 February 1940, he wrote to Marjorie that the cold was so intense that his 'flannel, toothbrush, shaving brush, scrubbing brush and toothpaste all froze together in my wash bag'.

Eventually, the troops moved from the temporary straw-bale shelters into agricultural

Airmen of No. 226 Squadron RAF pushing a Fairey Battle out of its hanger at Reims-Champagne Air Base during the winter of 1939–40, one of the coldest on record.
Wikimedia Commons – IWM, C 783

buildings. These, again, were a temporary measure while permanent structures were erected. While they were an improvement on the initial straw shelters they brought their own problems. Alfred was woken one night by a mouse nibbling his ear. Marjorie hoped his ear had recovered 'after the mouse sampled it', and suggested he should put mustard on his ears in future to deter the little rodents.[17]

Gunner Hewitt-Taylor described the ingenuity of all ranks when living in the open as amazing. 'During the Phoney War, slit trenches were lined with beaten tin containers (fuel came in 10 gallon tins) and made very comfortable, earthed on top.'[18]

CENSORSHIP

Alfred's letters to Marjorie do not contain a single complaint about the harsh conditions the soldiers endured. Rather, he seems to treat them as a sign of his ruggedness, of defiance in the face of the enemy.

There was one thing he resented, however: censorship of his letters home. He understood the need for censorship, explaining not long after arriving in France that 'you will appreciate that it is impossible for me to say much about my movements'. But he was aggrieved that the Army intruded on his privacy, and constantly railed against it. 'I dislike the idea of anyone who is directly in charge of me reading my letters to you. That, briefly, explains why some – in fact most – have probably appeared a little bit cold.'[19]

Marjorie sympathised. 'It must be horrible to write knowing that someone else is going to read it all before I get it'; but then she reassured Alfred: 'I don't really suppose that they read it properly so long as they don't see anything censorable in it.'[20]

Censorship came in three forms: (1) Letters, to which censorship was strictly applied. (2) 'Green Envelopes', issued on trust and read on a random basis at Regimental HQ. (3) Pre-printed open postcards.

Letters were read by one of the battery officers, and without exception signed by the officer at the end. To Alfred's consternation, an early letter from Cherbourg was mutilated by the censor, most of the first page cut out and a number of words scored out. He only discovered this from Marjorie's reply:

> Well, your letter No. 5 arrived this am. Unfortunately I was quite unable to read the first page as it hardly existed at all! In other words the censor had cut away all of it from the end of the first paragraph to almost the bottom of the page, leaving a thin margin on the right hand side to hold it together. Besides that there were whole lines and half lines blocked out so that I was none the wiser over what was left! Of course the back page was missing too so I had to begin on page 3. Mr Belson[21] must have been very busy, and I don't know what Ru and Jack did! Anyway thank you for what was left![22]

Needless to say Alfred was taken aback: 'How on earth my first letter from France came to be so mutilated I don't know because I had been extremely careful not to mention anything

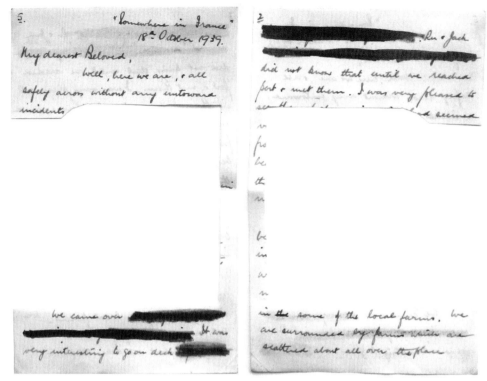

Alfred's first letter from France (No.5, 18 October 1939) heavily censored.
© Angela Grant

that I thought I shouldn't so I will have to make enquiries.'[23] From then on he was more cautious, and only the occasional word is deleted by the censor.

And then comes the first complaint about censorship: 'You apparently are not bothered with censorship so you at least have the comfort of knowing that your letters have not been scrutinised by a third party. I find it very difficult to fall into the way of writing under such conditions but maybe I shall soon get over that.' However, Alfred's comment was not quite accurate. Marjorie's letters were censored. In late October 1939 she wrote, 'there is much more I would like to say to you but as our letters are no longer for our eyes only they are not quite the same now, so I will leave you to imagine it.'[24]

By November Alfred was able to joke to Marjorie: 'Well my love, I must get cracking or the censor will be on my track for making him read such a lot of twaddle.'[25] It was a heartless censor if he failed to have a smile. Marjorie in return asked whether Alfred had been in action 'when the Germans paid France a visit? But I suppose you won't be able to tell me because of Mr Belson!'[26]

With 'Green Envelopes' the writer was required to sign a statement printed on the envelope: 'I certify on my honour that the contents of this envelope refer to nothing but private and family matters.' Alfred didn't find these so objectionable as, even if they were opened, the officer reading the letter was not someone he knew. They were supposed to be issued once a week, but it seems they were infrequent, and whenever they were handed out Alfred's delight is obvious: 'Hooray! A Green Envelope!' Marjorie was indignant when she discovered that one of Alfred's prized Green Envelopes had been opened – possibly, she suggested, as it was 'a fat one!' nine pages long. She felt the contents were 'for my eyes only'.[27]

Open postcards were a quick method of communicating with home. They were pre-printed, and set out a number of statements which the sender deleted as appropriate:

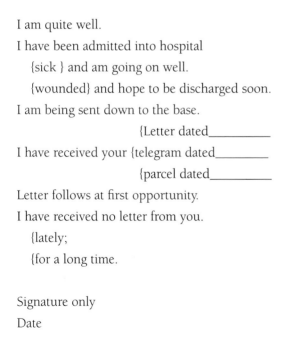

I am quite well.

I have been admitted into hospital

    {sick } and am going on well.

    {wounded} and hope to be discharged soon.

I am being sent down to the base.

                {Letter dated_____

I have received your {telegram dated_____

                {parcel dated_____

Letter follows at first opportunity.

I have received no letter from you.

    {lately;

    {for a long time.

Signature only

Date

The postcards were prefaced by an instruction that the only writing permitted was the date and signature of the sender. If anything else was added the postcard would be destroyed.

Alfred referred to these as 'whizz bangs', explaining that they were really meant for troops in trenches who didn't have time to write home. However, if the recipient wasn't aware of the context they could cause alarm. When the first one reached Marjorie in December 1939, she wrote, 'my heart sank into my shoes'.[28]

NOTHING is to be written on this side except the date and signature of the sender. Sentences not required may be erased. If anything else is added the post card will be destroyed.

[Postage must be prepaid on any letter or post card addressed to the sender of this card.]

I am quite well.

I have been admitted into hospital

{ sick } and am going on well.

{ wounded } and hope to be discharged soon.

I am being sent down to the base.

I have received your { letter dated _____

{ telegram ,, _____

{ parcel ,, _____

Letter follows at first opportunity.

I have received no letter from you

{ lately

{ for a long time.

Signature only

Date *1st Feb. 1940.*

Forms/A2042/7. 51-4997.

Field postcard, dubbed by Alfred and Marjorie 'whizz bangs'.
© Angela Grant

While understanding the need for censorship, most people found it exasperating at best, and at worst shared Alfred's view that it was an intrusion into their privacy. Some censors were so pernickety that their deletions bordered on nit-picking. Alexander Clifford, the Reuters correspondent assigned to the AASF, fell foul of an Army censor checking one of his dispatches. The censor insisted that he delete a reference to the moon shining. Clifford commented that he 'expected hourly to hear that the sequence of night and day was "information likely to be of help to the enemy".'[29]

Amazingly, Alfred and Marjorie devised an ingenious method to circumvent the system. Before Alfred's departure to France they agreed a simple code so that Marjorie would always know where he was. Whenever Alfred arrived in a new location the first letter of the second and succeeding paragraphs would make up the name of the town or village.[30] That their ingenious cipher worked beautifully is confirmed by checking letters against the war diary. Thus, on arriving in France, Alfred's letter of 16 October 1939 revealed that he was at Cherbourg:

Chance would have it …

How irony combines with fate …

Early yesterday morning …

Rain – even the continuous drizzle …

But some of the poor militia boys …

On arrival at the station …

Unlike some of the other batteries …

Rather than sleep in the so-called cabin …

Going back a bit …

Six days later, Marjorie knew he had moved to Épernay:

Each section …

Please don't start bothering your head …

Eventually we should get …

Regarding the correct method …

No, my love, there is no need …

Are you still banging away …

You will appreciate …[31]

Robert Angel noted in his diary: 'by a code we heard that he was at Reims'.[32] In late November, Marjorie suggested a second code:

> I suppose you are manning now till tomorrow morning. I'll think of you tonight in the cold keeping watch. If your battery shoots a plane down do you think you could make a blot on the page of your letter, or something? I would love to know if you do. I hope that won't entail your rewriting a page if one comes by accident. In that case just apologise for it, and don't if it is intended, see?[33]

Alfred replied cryptically three days later: 'I will certainly take up your suggestion of the blot.' However, he is careful to reassure Marjorie that 'I don't think you'll see any – not at the present rate anyhow. Actually it seems to me that we are safer here than in good old England!'[34] This was a 'Green Envelope' letter, so it escaped the critical eye of the battery censor. It would have been a neat irony if it had slipped past Mr Belson.

As time went by, Alfred's understanding of what he could and could not say improved. There are relatively few deletions, and one of these was not terribly effective. The area around Reims was hit by hurricane force winds on 14 March 1940, the war diary observing: 'Signal communications suffered much interference and damage.'[35] Alfred wrote that two days later he was still unable to deliver messages to either of 159 Battery's gun stations as 'the ~~telephone lines~~ had come down in a ~~gale~~… but what a ~~gale~~ we had!'[36]

SANDES HOUSE

Despite these early disruptions the Regiment settled into life at their gun stations around Reims. After the initial hiccoughs with catering, the troops were well fed, so much so that they were better off than their families back at home. Gunner Hewitt-Taylor described how meals were delivered to the gun positions by truck. 'Breakfast, brought up in hay-boxes, was always fried bread, baked beans, fried meat loaf and tea. I often had two helpings.'[37] Alfred asked Marjorie not to send precious rations but to keep them as 'we get plenty'. Food in France was plentiful and cheap.[38]

Living in accommodation that ranged from temporary straw-bale structures in the open, then agricultural buildings and eventually, when winter bit, in rough corrugated structures, meant life for the troops was harsh. However, the lack of basic facilities, particularly washing, was alleviated by Sandes House in the village. This was one of the many soldiers' homes established in the late nineteenth century by a remarkable Irish woman, Elise Sandes, an evangelical Christian and philanthropist. Her original intention was to draw young soldiers away from public houses and offer them an alternative centre for friendship, entertainment and self-improvement. The ethic was based on homes run by women with an emphasis on creating a welcoming atmosphere. While the women were clearly missionaries, prayers and religious services were always voluntary for the soldiers.[39]

Elise Sandes died in 1934 but the principles she established continued into the Second World War. Sandes House in Épernay was supervised by two elderly English ladies. It had rooms for reading, writing and games – chess, draughts, and table tennis and, most importantly, bathrooms. Best of all, the two ladies served 'real English tea – impossible to obtain in France'.[40] From time to time Alfred had a meal at Sandes, followed by reading magazines. 'What a luxury it is to sit in something soft.'[41]

DAILY ROUTINE

Life in France was physically tough for recruits who had been used to comfortable lives. As the title of the Regiment indicated, the 53rd was drawn from there City of London, with 159 Battery recruited from Lloyd's of London and the London insurance market. The troops would have spent their working day in the buzz of commercial offices, returning each evening to the comfort of their homes. .

By contrast, life in rural France must have seemed dull for much of the time. Efforts were made to alleviate this, and provision of entertainment for off-duty soldiers gathered pace. Local cinemas put on English films such as *Souls at Sea*, *The Wedding Night* with Gary Cooper and Anna Stein, *She Married her Boss*, *The Return of the Flag*, and Alfred Hitchcock's *The 39 Steps* (Alfred commented, 'I understand it's a very good film'[42]). Eventually the local Paramount Cinema put on 'buckshee [free] shows for British troops every Tuesday and Wednesday'.[43]

On occasion the troops could prove a sceptical audience. In late December *The Silver Butterfly*, starring Katherine Hepburn and Billy Burke, was shown in one of the local cinemas. Alfred observed that while the acting was splendid 'the plot was absolute drivel – in fact I have never seen so much "bear-hugging and slob stuff" on the screen before', and the audience shared his disdain: 'We just roared with laughter at parts which were presumably meant to bring tears to our eyes. I couldn't help thinking how shocked an English audience would have been.'[44]

ENSA concerts began to be organised, with the emphasis firmly on variety.[45] In November alone big names such as Gracie Fields and Josephine Baker appeared, followed by less illustrious but no less appreciated acts such as Harry Blam and the RAF Band. Blam, now long since forgotten, produced a burlesque act that included a tap dancer, a conjuror, and an acrobat who amazed the troops by continuing to play a trumpet while doing the splits. 'It was grand to see real English people on the stage, speaking and singing in a language we could understand … to say nothing of some decent looking English girls', Alfred adding 'now don't be jealous!'. In February 1940 the troops were entertained by a xylophone player who was 'an absolute genius … simultaneously playing the big instrument with his feet and a smaller one on his lap with his hands'.[46] Memories of entertainers such as Harry Blam have passed into the mists of time, but clearly the ENSA concerts were a huge boost to morale.

ENSA concert with Gracie Fields entertaining airmen at their Christmas party, 1939.
Wikimedia Commons © IWM, C 212

In addition, the troops were adept at creating their own entertainment. Alfred and his brother Rupert were keen rugby players and spent much time trying to organise a game. This was a frustrating process; several letters comment that they had not succeeded; but eventually two teams were formed from the three batteries in the Regiment, the objective being to select a XV to represent the Regiment against the AASF headquarters. Alfred's hopes of selection were put back when he sprained a shoulder, but the game was a great entertainment as 'it got us out of uniform'.

But there were no bathing facilities, despite assurances that they would be available. The players had to put on their uniforms over the mud and try to beg a bath from the hotels in Épernay, but the hotels were unable to oblige: the intensely cold weather had prevented deliveries of coal for hot water. Was this just a diplomatic way of getting rid of thirty muddy soldiers? They eventually persuaded the good ladies running Sandes House to allow them a bath.[47]

'MILITIA BOYS'

Despite the Chamberlain government's pursuit of appeasement, prudent preparations for war were slowly put in place. In May 1939 the Military Training Act was passed, requiring all men aged twenty and twenty-one to register for military service. They were referred to as 'militiamen', to distinguish them from the regular army. It was the first peacetime conscription in the UK, and it was immediately superseded on the outbreak of war by the National Service (Armed Forces) Act, that extended conscription to all males aged between eighteen and forty-one.[48]

The 53rd was brought up to strength with 'militia boys' from the East End of London. 'They turned out to be very good lads'[49] and there were several in Alfred's battery. However, most had never left home before and were homesick. Their unhappy state was compounded, as their families did not understand that they needed support from home. Marjorie felt sorry for them. 'It probably comes very hard on them at first if they are not used to roughing it. Not like our "he" men who are used to camping & playing that gentle game of rugger, to say nothing of all they have gone through before they start on the "real thing".'[50]

Alfred was able to write to Marjorie and request additional items such as clothing for himself. In addition, he received constant support from a variety of sources – family, friends and even colleagues at his company, Gray Dawes. Marjorie's letters constantly mention items of clothing which she, family and friends were making for him (knitting was a favourite occupation), and he regularly received parcels of clothing, food and cigarettes. His father-in-law, Robert Angel, seems to have gone a bit far: Marjorie reported, 'Daddy has bought a hand weaving machine! So now he is going to weave ties and scarves & goodness knows what! Any orders?'[51]

The militia boys, on the other hand, did not have this level of home support. With the onset of winter, they suffered from lack of clothing to augment the inadequate uniforms hastily distributed by the Army on their departure for France. A number of them never received a parcel from home, and some never even received a letter.

Throughout his life Alfred was marked out as an extraordinarily generous and compassionate man. He discovered that two militia boys, Gunners R. Fothergill and T. Jackson, had not received a single letter or parcel. They were typical cockney lads, only nineteen or twenty, 'always cracking jokes … and keep us in fits of laughter'.[52] Fothergill was an orphan, a fact disclosed when he gave Alfred his Green Envelope. Alfred wrote to Marjorie, 'I can't sit here & receive things myself when I know they won't' and asked her to send them each a parcel of 'choc, cigs, biscuits & anything that might make something interesting for [them] … but you'll know – that's a woman's instinct!' He urged her not to spare the cost. 'Nothing will please me more than to know that some of [my bank balance] will be used for something useful.'

Marjorie was the same. She thanked Alfred for telling her about Fothergill and Jackson. 'It came in most useful to know of them as I had that 10/- from May and Edie. So I spent it on them, love, instead of you as I think I can provide your few wants myself … Poor souls, I feel very sorry for them … Which one was it that gave you the green envelope? Bless him!'

May and Edie were Marjorie's cousins and the money was their birthday present to her. Perhaps to protect Alfred's identity she enclosed a note in each parcel telling the two gunners that the money to pay for the food came from her cousins, suggesting that they write to thank them for the gift. 'I know they would be delighted to hear from them.'[53] More like surprised, as the two cousins had no idea what Marjorie had done. Alfred was able to report to her that the parcels had arrived and they 'seemed bucked with them'.[54]

Happily, most of the militia boys were able to adjust to army life. Many thrived. The senior clerk at Gray Dawes, Alfred's employer, commented to Marjorie that it was an eye opener seeing some of the 'little fellows' in the office set off as apprehensive militia boys only to return on leave 'big strong looking lads & one of them is a sergeant!' As Alfred was still a gunner, Marjorie teased him: 'So there! You had better not meet him or you will have to salute and say "Sir"!'[55]

'AGONY AUNT'

At the grand age of twenty-seven, Alfred was older than most of the conscripts. As a result they appear to have respected his greater experience of the world, and, on occasion, confided in him. While delivering rations to one of the gun stations in April 1940 he was taken aside by Gunner Basted, 'who seemed very bucked to see me … Poor lad – he had a long tale of woe to confide to me.' It transpired that while on leave Basted had become engaged and his fiancée's family had thrown a party to celebrate. During the party, Basted's sister offended his fiancée, who was reduced to tears and fled from the room. She wouldn't be pacified and forced Basted to take back her engagement ring. Basted wanted to speak to Alfred as he had received a letter from her saying she wanted nothing to do with his family and, because she hadn't 'smothered the letter in Xs and said she loved him', he assumed she didn't want him. Alfred was confident he could 'read between the lines and told him he hadn't much to worry about and suggested what he should write in reply – so by the time I left he was once more full of beans and his hopes raised. Now I only hope what I told him comes true!'[56]

On another occasion, while 'quietly installed in the café' Alfred was irritated when a gunner nicknamed 'Scruffy' joined him 'and would insist on talking despite my efforts to stop him without causing offence'. This was twenty-two-year-old Crombie, who Alfred knew from Lloyd's. Alfred couldn't understand why Scruffy had latched on to him, until it transpired that, 'all confidential like', he was seeking advice. The young gunner was in love with more than one girl and didn't know which one to marry. Alfred had to sit through an account of Scruffy's love life, including how he had met the girls. Eventually he counselled that it would be foolish to marry without being sure he had chosen the right partner. Only Scruffy could judge that. Scruffy was impressed by this advice but asked how he could be certain. Alfred replied Delphically that the answer would come to him naturally. Apparently, this left Scruffy 'completely mystified'.[57]

The incident brought some light relief back home: 'Your Mother and Father were highly amused over the tale of Scruffy and his love affairs.' Marjorie offered the advice, though, that rather than asking Scruffy 'can you live with the girl in question?', Alfred should ask: 'can you live without her?'[58]

Within two weeks, Scruffy was a POW, captured trying to recover the guns abandoned by the 53rd after they received the order to withdraw.[59]

CHRISTMAS 1939

The arrival of November reminded the troops that Christmas loomed and that most of them were unlikely to be with their families.[60] There was a determination throughout the Brigade to ensure that, as far as possible, and despite their circumstances, traditional festivities would be celebrated.

At home, however, reminders that the country was at war were ever present. The blackout dominated daily life, with most people scurrying home before dark. On 30 November 1939 Russia had attacked Finland, on the spurious excuse of recovering territory. Finland was expected to capitulate rapidly – but Stalin's purge of the Russian officer corps, and the high morale of the Finnish forces, enabled them to hold out for several months. Marjorie's letters are full of admiration for their resistance. She wrote just before Christmas: 'Isn't it amazing the way the Finns are keeping the Russians on hot bricks so to speak.'[61]

Alfred conceded that things were a muddle, summed up by a colleague of his: 'the Germans love the Italians but want the Balkans which are wanted by the Russians and the Italians. The Germans love the Russians but the Italians hate [them]. The Russians don't like anybody but they've got the Baltic and now the Germans want it'. It reminded Alfred of the old ditty:

The other day upon the stair
I met a man who wasn't there.
He wasn't there again today.
I wish to hell he'd go away[62]

Inevitably, the prospect of Christmas brought home to the troops and their families their separation from each other. Alfred wrote that 'somehow I am afraid I shall miss Christmas tremendously – especially the preparations beforehand. I might be childish but I loved such simple things as decorations, wrapping parcels in fantastic wrappings & sending stacks of cards.' If Alfred felt childish then he never grew out of it. He always loved the paraphernalia and traditions of Christmas.[63]

Ever the optimist, he told Marjorie that he and his comrades would make the most of things 'and a committee has been formed to organise things'. His section would be manning the gun stations on Christmas Day, so planned a 'beano' on Boxing Day – a running buffet in the gun-park. They planned to drink the health of 'our loved ones' at 8 pm on Christmas Day and suggested that Marjorie and the family 'complete the circle' by doing the same at the same time.[64]

Christmas proved to be an opportunity to introduce some form of home familiarity to their lives. By 22 December plans had advanced, and the section intended to have a 'proper feed of traditional fare cooked by the staff of a local hotel & served by the sergeants', the latter a long-standing Army tradition. His one concern was that the turkey might be like the chicken that some of his comrades had eaten in one of the cafés the previous evening. 'It was so tough (like rubber they said) that they couldn't carve it themselves & had to call "monsieur" to their assistance. He had to take it to the kitchen & use a chopper on it!'[65]

Efforts were made to maintain 'good old English traditions as far as possible', and one hut was decorated with paper chains and mistletoe, which the soldiers had gathered from trees around the gun stations.

It was appreciated that the servicemen were far from home. Every man in the Regiment received a gift from the 53rd's Honorary Colonel of a pair of socks and mittens and a scarf, 'plus either half a cake or Xmas pudding, all of very good quality'. The Committee of Lloyd's sent each man in the Lloyd's Battery either a cigarette case or a pipe, and Alfred's colleagues at Gray Dawes sent a parcel of 'Players cigs' as well as a number of Christmas cards.[66] Rupert also received parcels, one friend sending a thousand cigarettes. Alfred was so inundated by gifts of cigarettes and 'baccy' that he wrote to Marjorie: 'Methinks I will have to open a shop.'[67]

Committee of Lloyd's Christmas card sent to members of the Lloyd's Battery, 1939. © Angela Grant

Best of all, the King and Queen sent Christmas cards. Alfred described his at some length and sent it to Marjorie for safekeeping.[68] Reminders such as these that the men had not been forgotten were clearly a boost to their morale.

Alfred welcomed Christmas morning at 1 am, wishing the guard he was relieving a happy Christmas. All was quiet, the only sound the ringing of church bells some distance away. 'It was a unique and even enjoyable way of "hailing the happy morn".' It was also a white Christmas and bitterly cold, the gun station 'like a fairyland, with every twig and branch of bushes and trees, even telephone poles and the guns covered with a coating of about half an inch of frost'.[69]

Despite the weather and the absence from home Alfred clearly enjoyed the festivities. 'We had a pretty good time – at any rate as far as grub is concerned!' The Regiment made an effort to ensure that things were as relaxed as possible. Parade at 9 o'clock was held as usual but followed by the announcement that 'no work would be done today. A great concession!' On Christmas Day and Boxing Day 'we mooched about doing nothing in particular until lunch time'.

Despite the war it seems there was no shortage of food for the BEF: the two days were largely spent consuming festive picnics and dinners, interspersed with visits to the café

'Our café', the café adopted by the Battery, a postcard sent by Alfred, marked by him.
© Angela Grant

adopted by the Battery. The proprietors must have realised that the presence of so many men a long way from home offered an opportunity to make some money, and it remained open for business throughout the two days of Christmas. The men clearly liked the owners. They announced their arrival on Christmas Day by 'singing *Noel* outside, much to the amusement of m'sieur and m'dme', and on leaving they 'dragged m'sieur into a ring while we sang *Auld Lang Syne*.'

The informal 'picnics' consisted of the random ingredients of food parcels, with some curious results. Although the soldiers' usual diet was fairly basic, 'tinned roast duck, two smallish Christmas puddings plus all sorts of choc. biscuits' can't have been everyone's preferred choice.

The traditional Christmas lunch, with the sergeants acting as waiters, was of a different order. Alfred was pleasantly surprised when he found what was involved. 'I must admit that the meal was excellent and it seemed strange to see tables laid with table cloths, paper serviettes, plates and the usual Xmas nuts and fruit – even crackers!' The lunch menu was the traditional turkey and sprouts with baked potatoes. 'This disposed of, the lights were turned out and the puddings brought in all alight … The party then began to liven up' with impromptu entertaining 'chiefly supplied by the militia boys and we just howled with laughter at the various antics they got up to'. The party ended with the men all dancing. 'Just imagine about a dozen pairs of soldiers with paper hats on (chiefly fezzes) all toddling around in hob-nailed boots dancing waltzes and fox trots to the accompaniment of a badly tuned piano.'

The following morning the section marched down to the gun park 'all dressed in our paper hats, much to the amusement of the few French bodies that we passed!' So the men were able to let their hair down despite the threat of hostilities. Little wonder that these months were dubbed 'the Phoney War'.[70]

CHANGE OF DUTIES

Recruiting from a relatively small community brought risks, and it is surprising that the government had learned nothing from the experience of the Pals Battalions in the First War. The attraction for the men enlisting from the same area was that they would be with friends and neighbours rather than being arbitrarily allocated to different regiments. However, if heavy casualties hit one of these battalions then the community from which they were drawn would be devastated. For example, the 11th Battalion, East Lancashire Regiment, nicknamed the Accrington Pals, suffered severe losses on the opening day of the battle of the Somme: of roughly 800 men, 235 were killed and 350 wounded in just twenty minutes.[71]

At the same time, the benefits originally driving the recruitment policy held good. Many of the men in the Lloyd's Battery knew each other, so even when they were training in 1938 their families were able to support one another. In September that year Mrs Jacobs, the wife of one of Alfred's Lloyd's acquaintances, phoned Marjorie and 'gave me the message that you were alright and you can imagine how thankful I was to hear that'.[72]

Alfred had wangled a place for Rupert in the Regiment and they were both assigned to 159 Battery. Alfred describes Rupert, along with Jack Davies, as 'my only genuine friend' in the Regiment.[73] Jack Davies worked in the Lloyd's market with Alfred and was one of his closest friends.[74] It was a blow, therefore, when he was assigned to the transport section and became the driver for one of the senior officers in the Regiment. His friends regarded this as the ultimate 'cushy number', away from the rigours of life as a gunner on one of the gun stations.

Worse was to follow in late December. The Regiment needed more drivers. Rupert had good engineering knowledge and probably caught the attention of those responsible. His transfer to the HQ Motor Transport Section was logical, but it clearly left Alfred bereft. 'I am afraid I have suffered rather a nasty blow as Rupert has been

Rupert Ledger, in the uniform of a captain, 1944.
© Margot Westmacott

taken away for good as a lorry driver at HQ so with both he and Jack gone I am sort of on my own … It is a good job it happened after Christmas and not before because we did manage to have as enjoyable a time as possible.' Alfred would dearly have liked to have been transferred with him 'but I expect my hopes are a little forlorn'.[75]

Happily, he did not remain on the gun park for long. Jack Davies had promised to try to put in a good word. He 'keeps nagging away … swearing I am a good driver'.[76] This paid off, as Alfred joined him a few days later, designated as an HQ driver.[77] His relief leaps off the page of his letter to Marjorie. He admitted to leaving the gun park with mixed feelings,[78] but he soon got over that, and his expectations of an improved life were realised: 'It's a welcome change from pick and shovel'.[79]

Jack Davies, Alfred's closest friend in the Lloyd's Battery. © Angela Grant

Alfred's surprise at the improvement in living conditions shines through his letters. 'We are living in luxury compared with the gun stations … We even get wakened with a cup of tea at 6.30! … Breakfast is HOT!'; and the men did not have to wash up after meals. Ten days after his transfer Alfred exclaimed: 'Fancy being waited on in the army! … I wouldn't go back to the gun station for anything – this is a life of luxury by comparison.' It seems that every soldier's impression that life at headquarters was easy had been proved correct.[80] It was a welcome change to get away from the hard, physical work in the gun park, and he had the bonus of rejoining Rupert and Jack. He confided that 'I'm a bad soldier as I never had much liking for killing; I used to think how unpleasant it was for the other chap.'[81]

Alfred's transfer to the Motor Transport Section meant he had to learn to drive a 3-ton truck, something he had never done before, and in unfamiliar conditions – on the right-hand side, complicated by the French road signs and the mysterious system of *priorité à droite*. Initially it must have been a daunting task, even after the Regiment helpfully issued guidance on an A4 typed sheet with illustrations of signs, quaintly drawn and coloured by hand. (Just how daunting is illustrated by an accident which occurred just before Alfred's

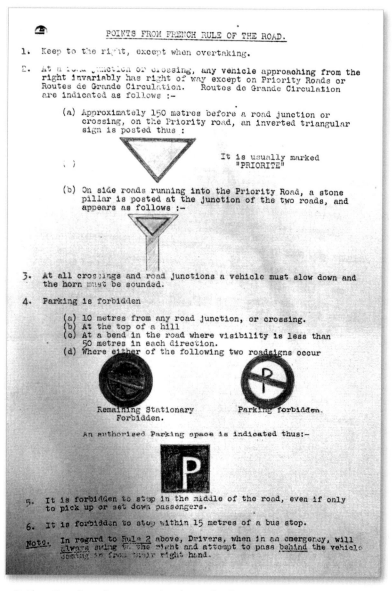

POINTS FROM FRENCH RULE OF THE ROAD.

1. Keep to the right, except when overtaking.

2. At a road junction or crossing, any vehicle approaching from the right invariably has right of way except on Priority Roads or Routes de Grande Circulation. Routes de Grande Circulation are indicated as follows :-

    (a) Approximately 150 metres before a road junction or crossing, on the Priority road, an inverted triangular sign is posted thus :

        It is usually marked "PRIORITE"

    (b) On side roads running into the Priority Road, a stone pillar is posted at the junction of the two roads, and appears as follows :-

3. At all crossings and road junctions a vehicle must slow down and the horn must be sounded.

4. Parking is forbidden
    (a) 10 metres from any road junction, or crossing.
    (b) At the top of a hill
    (c) At a bend in the road where visibility is less than 50 metres in each direction.
    (d) Where either of the following two roadsigns occur

    Remaining Stationary   Parking forbidden.
    Forbidden.

An authorised Parking space is indicated thus:-

5. It is forbidden to stop in the middle of the road, even if only to pick up or set down passengers.

6. It is forbidden to stop within 15 metres of a bus stop.

Note. In regard to Rule 2 above, Drivers, when in an emergency, will always swing to the right and attempt to pass behind the vehicle coming in from their right hand.

Guide to French road signs issued to drivers by the 53rd HAA. © Peter Ledger transfer to the MT Section. On 8 December a British Army truck collided with a French train on a level crossing close to Le Mesnil-sur-Oger, 15 km south-east of Épernay. The train was carrying British troops, and thirteen men from the 2nd Air Formation Signals were killed or injured.)

In addition to driving, Alfred was expected to maintain and service his vehicle. Before volunteering for the Army he had been an insurance broker. Unlike Rupert, therefore, he had little knowledge of vehicle mechanics. The wartime Army, however, was a great place to learn a trade. Early January was spent learning about motor engines.[82]

The cold weather made driving conditions difficult, especially at night. Fog was a particular hazard. On one occasion in January Alfred's spectacles misted up so badly that he was forced to take them off while driving through the dark for 30 km.[83]

Driving was interesting and living conditions were better than those with the Lloyd's Battery, but the work involved was often just as heavy. Bedford 3-tonners were the workhorses of the Army. The Regiment's vehicles were constantly required to collect and deliver a wide variety of loads – coal, sand, ballast, concrete pipes, often consignments of 20 tons.[84] No sooner had Alfred arrived at the transport department in early January 1940 than he was dispatched to collect and load 4 tons of sand. As no equipment was available, he had to shift it by hand. On one occasion he delivered 10 tons of gravel, while the gunners worked 'in a lake of mud and slime'.

However, the street awareness that Alfred was acquiring in the Army increasingly stood him in good stead. English cigarettes were popular with the locals as they were far better quality than French cigarettes, and he regularly used them to 'sweeten' French labourers to help with the heavy work. On one occasion in January a few cigarettes facilitated the use of a mechanical grab to load 4 tons of sand rather than the loading party doing it by hand.[85]

The unreliability of vehicle engines in 1940 gave endless opportunities for skiving. Early morning parades and square bashing are a bane of life in any army. Rupert, in particular, considered parade-ground marching to be an exercise in futility, and devised a ruse to avoid it whenever possible.

The Regiment was short of mechanics and Rupert had gained a reputation as someone who could fix engines. A favourite trick, but one he could only use sparingly, was to check the vehicle dispatch roster. If the morning parade was at 8.00 am he would identify a vehicle scheduled to leave a few minutes beforehand. He would wander into the parking area, find the vehicle, and switch the leads to the spark plugs. With the vehicle immobilised he would close the bonnet and amble out. Without fail, just after the morning parade had assembled, a driver would appear from the lorry park and speak to the parade sergeant. 'Ledger! You're needed in the lorry park. Look sharp!' Rupert would respond: 'I'll need my brother to help, Sarge', and the two of them would disappear from the parade ground. By judicious use of the prank they were never rumbled.[86]

HOME LEAVE

The Regiment had been called up in August and left for France on 15 October. Understandably Marjorie's letters are full of longing for Alfred's first home leave.

For his part, Alfred seems to have been a paragon of stoicism. Perhaps this was deliberate, as they both had to endure several disappointments when leave was cancelled.

By December 1939 the Regiment had 'served continuously at Home and in France since being called up' and no one had received more than forty-eight hours leave. This so concerned the 53rd's commanding officer, Lt. Col. V.R. Krohn, that on 9 December he wrote to Brig. W.T.O. Crewdson, commanding 12th AA Brigade, formally requesting that leave be granted. Krohn was a compassionate officer, concerned for the welfare of the men under his command. However, even though Britain had been at war with Germany for three months, formalities had to be preserved: 'I have the honour to request that this, my Considered Opinion [sic] in regard to the granting of Home leave to the Officers and Other Ranks of this Regiment, may be submitted with all possible speed to higher authority.' Three tightly typed pages follow setting out his concerns.[87]

Although the letter was marked 'Confidential' in red capitals, just two days later Alfred had picked up a rumour that home leave might be looming and wrote accordingly to Marjorie.

The possibility of leave, however, was the cause of enormous disappointment. The rumour was confirmed on the 19th, but it transpired that only three men from a unit would be allowed home at any one time. On the 23rd the Regiment was told that the first men would depart 'in ten days time' but, before that happened, all leave was delayed for two weeks. Leave was then suspended. The excitement of anticipation turned to anguish, Alfred writing that his 'dreams of heaven have been dashed'. Alfred then learned from the BBC 7 o'clock news that 'BEF leave has been reinstated'. Through all of this he maintained great stoicism, cautioning Marjorie 'don't raise your hopes, wait for the knock on the door'.[88]

His circumspection was wise. 'The army works on strange lines at times and arrangements are always being altered or cancelled or sprung on us without warning.' He cited as an example a soldier who had been waiting for months to be transferred to a different corps. Without notice, he was told to pack his kit for home leave and be ready to move off within an hour. 'His mother will have a pleasant surprise when he knocks on the door tomorrow!'[89]

Despite Alfred urging Marjorie not to pin her hopes on his early arrival she could not help but get excited at the prospect of a visit from him. 'If you really do come in the second week of January we have only got another week to wait!!! I can't believe it is really true, it seems far too good. Oh, if anything happened now I would just pass out!' Her patience would be tested. Her father wrote tersely in his diary for 9 January: 'Alfred was expected home on leave today but did not arrive'.

Then, eleven days later, the moment they had both waited for: 'Alfred came home on leave last night (Sunday) quite unexpectedly.'[90] The Army certainly liked to keep its men, and their families, guessing. After five months continuous service in France, Alfred was granted ten days leave on 22 January 1940. As this included travel he would have had only seven days at home, rejoining his regiment on 2 February.[91]

Enforced separation needed some source of comfort to mitigate the strain. Marjorie worked out 'by the aid of atlas and compass that you are situated somewhere behind a very big tree that I can see to the S.E. from my bedroom window. It is a great comfort to have a spot I can look towards & think that if I could see far enough I would be able to see you.'[92]

While this might have mitigated the strain of being apart, especially as they had been married such a short time, it only served to dull the pain. At the end of November 1939 Marjorie's thoughts turned to Christmas, which brought back all the emotion. 'How I would give anything to be with you for a while. It's queer how, although one is surrounded by folks one loves, one can feel lonely just because the most loved one isn't there.'[93]

However, the moon also became a secret source of comfort, often featuring in their correspondence. On Christmas Eve 1939 Marjorie wrote: 'Good old moon! That is something we have in common, isn't it? I often wonder when I look at it if you are doing likewise and thinking thoughts like me?'[94]

TRAGEDY

Unquestionably, life in France during the winter of 1939–40 for the ordinary soldier, or 'other ranks' in military parlance, was tough but boredom must have been a problem too. So, was it a lapse in discipline that resulted in two fatalities before the Regiment's war had really started?

A short, almost brutally factual report in the war diary noted on 31 December: '20.35 hrs message received from BHQ 158 that No 1490670 Gnr. Burns A. had been shot by a member of the guard at Squeak II … He is dead.' It transpired that the incident occurred when sentries were changing over. Gunner Hancock was about to go on guard duty and 'picked up a rifle from the table'. On the way to the sentry post he called in at his hut. Burns was sitting by the stove. Hancock said he was going on guard duty and 'had one up the spout'. What followed is not clear. Hancock may have playfully pointed the gun at Burns or have sat down. Either way, the gun discharged accidentally and Burns was hit in the head, dying instantly.

A second incident followed on 7 February 1940. Gunners Dixon and Ridger were on guard duty at the Brigade ammunition dump. The officer in charge of the dump, Lt. G.L. Owen, left the guard room 'for toilet purposes', and before leaving removed his revolver and left it on the table in its holster. Dixon was in the guard room at the time. Ridger entered and, as he described the incident, 'went to look at the revolver … And as I was lifting it out of the case it went off.' According to his account he did not think the revolver was loaded. The bullet struck Dixon in the shoulder, and he died of his wound two weeks later.

Both Hancock and Ridger faced field general courts martial. The charge against Hancock was that 'in the field he so negligently handled his rifle as to cause it to discharge, thereby causing the death of 1490670 Gnr. Burns A'. He was found not guilty. Two charges were brought against Ridger under the Army Act: manslaughter, and 'neglect to the prejudice of good order and military discipline'. At a court martial on 4 April he was found not guilty of the first charge but guilty on the second count. The war diary does not comment on the sentence.[95]

Both incidents reflected a lapse in discipline. The 53rd was a Territorial Army Regiment, consisting of volunteers who had made considerable sacrifices to serve their country and endured considerable discomfort. It had been ordered to France to defend the AASF in the event of an anticipated attack by Germany. But instead of action the men had spent months engaged in tedious tasks, many, it seems, devised merely to keep them busy. The Phoney War was just that. Was this lapse in discipline the result of boredom?

If so, it wasn't confined to the 53rd. The BBC correspondent Charles Gardner was told by a number of Army correspondents in February 1940 that British troops in Lille had been getting restive at the non-activity. To relieve the monotony they had strung up their sergeant major on a lamppost. He was found dead early the next morning.[96] It seems that in some units boredom morphed into mutiny.

ENDNOTES

1   NA, WO 167/617, 01 & 02.11 1939.
2   NA, WO 167/617, 21.12.1939.
3   ML 01.11.1939.
4   The strip cartoon featured an orphaned family of animals. It continued to appear in the *Mirror* until 1956: screever.org/2012/03/18/pip-squeak-and-wilfred-1938 (visited August 2015).
5   NA, WO 167/617, 03–20.12.1939.
6   NA, WO 167/617.
7   They were replaced by the 3.7-inch AA gun. This was so effective that it continued in service after the war, until replaced by missiles in the late 1950s. (N. W. Routledge, *History of the Royal Regiment of Artillery – Anti-Aircraft Artillery 1914–55*, Brasseys, 1994).
8   NA, WO 167/617, 23.11 and 21.12.1940.
9   NA, WO 167/617, Appendix D.
10 Gardner, pp. 49–50.
11 ibid., p. 33.
12 ML 11.09.1939.
13 AAL 11.11, 17.11 and 27.11.1939.
14 ww2today.com/a-cold-winter-arrives-in-europe (visited 21.05.2016).
15 Conversation with the author.
16 ML 29.11.1939.
17 AAL 17.12.1939 and ML 27.12.1939.
18 Hewitt-Taylor papers.
19 AAL 27.11.1939.
20 ML 16.12.1939.
21 2nd Lt. P. C. E. Belson, 159th Battery; NA, WO 167/617, Nominal Roll of Officers, 26.11.1939.
22 ML 21.10.1939.
23 AL 26.101939.
24 ML 22.10.1939.
25 AAL 11.11.1939.

26 ML 12.11.1939.

27 ML 18.12.1939.

28 ML 03.12.1939.

29 Gardner, p. 19. Clifford was a distinguished war correspondent, who reported on the Spanish Civil War and World War II. (wikipedia.org/wiki/Alexander Clifford visited May 2015).

30 AAL, in conversation with Angela Grant.

31 AAL 16.10.1939 and 6/22.10.1939.

32 RJA diary 30.10.1939.

33 ML 23.11.1939.

34 AAL 27.11.1939.

35 NA, WO 167/617 14.03.1940.

36 AAL 16.03.1940.

37 Hewitt-Taylor papers.

38 AAL 12.02.1940; 17.11.1939; 27.11.1939.

39 Elise Sandes' organisation survives today as Sandes Soldiers' and Airmen's Centres. Bryan MacMahon, *History Ireland*, vol. 13, 2005. historyireland.com (visited 22.04.16).

40 AAL 5/10.02.1940.

41 AAL 8/16.02.1940.

42 AAL 15.12.1939.

43 AAL Nov.1939 letters.

44 AAL 23.12.1939.

45 The Entertainments National Service Association was set up in 1939 to provide entertainment for British armed forces during World War II.

46 AAL 31.12.1939; 16.02.1940; 22.02.1940.

47 AAL 11.02.1940.

48 Wikipedia.org/wiki/lary_Training_Act_1939 (visited July 2015).

49 Hewitt-Taylor papers.

50 ML 18.10.1939.

51 ML 25.11.1939.

52 AAL 23.12.1939.

53 ML 18.12.1939.

54 AAL 02.01.1940.

55 ML 28.11.1939.

56 AAL 14.04.1940.

57 AAL 30.04.1940.

58 ML 07.05.1940.

59 Gardner, p.144, AAL margin note.

60 Some men had the good fortune to be on leave. The first leave contingent arrived in the UK some

      time on 23 December 1939. AAL 23.12.1939.

61   ML 22.12.1939.

62   AAL 09.12.1939.

63   AAL 09.12.1939.

64   AAL 09.12.1939.

65   AAL 15.12.1939.

66   AAL 27.12.1939.

67   AAL 02.01.1940.

68   AAL 23.12.1939. Disappointingly, the card is missing.

69   AAL 25.12.1939.

70   AAL 27.12.1939.

71   *Accrington Observer*, 30.06.06.

72   ML 29.09.1938.

73   AAL 8/31.10.1939; 22/01.12.1939.

74   He remained a life-long friend.

75   AAL 29.12.1939.

76   AAL 16.01.1940.

77   AAL 31.12.1939.

78   AAL 31.12.1939.

79   AAL 02.01.1940.

80   AAL 40–43 01.1940.

81   AAL 16.01.1940.

82   AAL 05.01.1940.

83   AAL 40/09.01.1940.

84   AAL 09.01.1940; 01.01.1940.

85   AAL 09.01.1940.

86   Conversations with the author.

87   NA, WO 167/617, letter 09.12.1939, Lt. Col. V. R. Krohn to C.O. 12 AA Brigade.

88   AAL 30–32/38/44.

89   AAL 23.12.1939.

90   RJA diary.

91   Army Form B199A – AAL service record.

92   ML 12.11.1939.

93   ML 26.11.1939.

94   ML 24.12.1939.

95   NA, WO 167/617.

96   Gardner, p. 85.

4
RABBITS IN THE HEADLIGHTS?

FRENCH FOREIGN AND DEFENCE POLICY

Between 1919 and 1935 France had spent a far higher proportion of its GDP on its forces than the other great powers. However, it had a severe manpower shortage relative to its population, which was half that of Germany. To compensate, France had mobilised about one-third of the male population between the ages of twenty and forty-five, bringing the strength of its armed forces to a staggering 5,000,000.[1]

Poland was a cornerstone of interwar French foreign policy. A number of agreements of mutual support were concluded, culminating in the so-called Franco-Polish Alliance. Under the terms of the agreement either army would come to the aid of the other in the event of invasion by Nazi Germany. In reality this was merely a military convention between the French and Polish armies, not a signed treaty.

On 7 September France triggered the alliance with Poland and launched the Saar offensive. However, the reality was that the French government was caught like a rabbit in the headlights. Their policy was founded on static defence – hence the massive investment in the Maginot Line, a series of concrete fortifications and obstacles 20–25 km deep and stretching 720 km from Switzerland along the Luxembourg and German borders. Fatally, it did not extend to the North Sea, as France did not wish to compromise Belgian neutrality.

France enjoyed an enormous numerical advantage along its German border when it declared war against Germany on 7 September. The Wehrmacht was still occupied in the east with the invasion of Poland. Despite this, the French government dithered and so missed the opportunity to launch a decisive attack in the West. Outdated World War I tactics, dependent on dominance by static artillery, combined with a woefully inefficient mobilisation system, meant that only eleven divisions out of a possible ninety-eight were available for the attack.

Underground tunnel and narrow-gauge railway at Ouvrage Hackenberg, part of the 450 km Maginot Line, the fortification built by the French along the Franco-German border. © Peter Ledger

French forces advanced 8 km along a 32-km front but were under orders to halt 'not closer than 1 kilometre' from the Siegfried Line. Their half-hearted push through territory deliberately abandoned by the German Army never reached the thinly manned German defensive positions and the opportunity was lost. Between 16 and 17 October, at the very moment that the 53rd HAA were landing at Cherbourg, the German Army launched a counter-offensive. Reinforced with troops returning from the Polish campaign, they retook all the territory gained by the French forces in the Saar Offensive. As planned, the French Army withdrew to the Maginot Line and, along with the much smaller British Army, settled into an eerie wait.[2]

BRITISH FOREIGN POLICY – APPEASEMENT

A similar reluctance to move decisively gripped the Chamberlain government. Churchill had been invited to join the Cabinet in early September as First Lord of the Admiralty. Significantly, Chamberlain also appointed him to the War Cabinet Committee. From the outset he sought every opportunity for action but was frustrated. The Air Ministry objected to his plan to drop several thousand mines in the Rhine. Concerned about the 320 km gap between the Maginot Line and the North Sea, he proposed that British troops be allowed to move forward to fill it, but was thwarted when the Belgian King objected. Similarly, the War Cabinet rejected his recommendation that Norwegian waters should be mined to interrupt Germany's access to Swedish iron ore. It was not until early February 1940 that it was decided to take control of the Swedish iron ore fields, but once again Churchill was forced to postpone the mining of Norwegian waters by opposition from Chamberlain.[3]

Harold Nicolson's diaries confirm the failure of the government to grasp the gravity of the situation. On 25 October he wrote, 'There is in fact a general feeling in ministerial circles that the war will peter out before the spring. I cannot get anyone to give me any serious grounds for such optimism.'[4]

But it wasn't just the appeasers in the government who had unrealistic expectations: the ordinary people fervently hoped the war would be over quickly. Unlike Chamberlain's government, however, they quickly realised their mistake. In November 1939 Marjorie reminded Alfred that he had been in the Army 'for 15 weeks. Just fancy 15 weeks! And to think of the fuss we made when we thought you would be away 4 weeks! Silly little things!'[5] Although unintended, her comment aptly described the government.

Gradually, however, the government managed expectations, so much so that by late November Marjorie was writing to Alfred telling him of warnings that the war could last between three and six years. 'By that time we will have white hair and false teeth!'[6]

In early December Nicolson joined a group of MPs on a visit to the Maginot Line. They were hugely impressed with a demonstration of the Line's defensive capabilities.[7] On their return to Paris the MPs were 'driven off at once, without being allowed to wash, to the Ministry of Finance. Paul Reynaud[8] is there to meet us. He is very anxious to hear what we think of the Maginot Line and is frankly delighted by our enthusiasm … He keeps repeating, "We've got them already, and they know it!"'[9]

Never was hubris more misplaced. The fixed defences of the Maginot Line were already hopelessly outdated. Leading military authorities, and the young French *commandant* Charles de Gaulle, who in 1934 had published *Vers l'armée de métier* (translated as *The Army of the Future*), were highly critical of the plan for a massive static defensive line. De Gaulle advocated a professional army based on mobile armoured divisions. The book sold only 700 copies in France, but 7,000 copies in Germany, where it was studied by Hitler.[10]

The advocates of the Maginot Line within the French military establishment not only ignored the prescient advice available to them within their own ranks but also misjudged the effect of air power.[11]

Despite the odds stacked against Britain, Churchill's defiant eloquence continued to rouse the morale of the nation. On 12 November, after his appointment as First Lord of the Admiralty, he broadcast a speech which commented on progress in the first ten weeks of the war. Pathé News observed that it was 'a speech laden with sarcasm [attacking] Göring and Hitler in particular'.[12] Marjorie was ecstatic. 'I can't think I have heard anything more funny and caustic in my life. What he didn't call Hitler and the Nazis wasn't worth mentioning.'[13]

But life was an emotional roller coaster. Russia's pact with Germany and subsequent invasion of Finland in late November 1939 caused consternation. Marjorie wrote that 'things seem to be getting in such a hopeless tangle that I can't imagine what the end of it all will be. Certainly not what we imagined – a short war with Germany. [With Germany] taking Norway and Sweden things are turning out very different to what we expected.'[14]

GERMAN WAR PLANS IN THE WEST

Unbeknown to the allies of the Entente Cordiale, Hitler was in a bellicose mood. The diplomat Ernst von Weizsäcker heard him say that a campaign in the West 'would cost me a million men, but it would cost the enemy too – and the enemy cannot stand it'.[15] Intoxicated by his triumph in the East, he moved men and equipment to the West to prepare for an offensive there. His generals were in despair, considering that an attack in the autumn would be a disaster. Hitler overruled them and ordered an offensive for November. Bad weather led to a postponement and a new date set for 17 January 1940.

However, a fortuitous accident led to a further deferment. On 10 January, an officer carrying the German war plans was arrested in Belgium when his aircraft made a forced landing. He was unable to destroy the documents, which quickly fell into the hands of the Belgian intelligence services. British and French commanders received full details from the Belgians and put their forces on alert.[16]

Curiously, this alert does not seem to have reached the 53rd. The war diary entries from 10 to 17 January 1940 are mostly single lines, largely concerned with the weather: 'cold, visibility poor … snowing. Nothing further to report.' Amazingly, considering the intelligence received from the Belgians, a group of twenty-two men returned to the UK to undergo officer training at Ascot. Clearly local commanders had no idea of the impending threat facing the BEF.[17] Was this due to a policy of caution, or just plain incompetence?

BRITISH INDECISION

Unsurprisingly, the planned attack did not materialise, and life returned to its torpid normality. Churchill visited the headquarters of the AASF near Reims on 7 January 1940 and inspected gun positions and airfields, then moved on to Arras and visited a number of military units. Afterwards he released a press statement which confirmed the impression received from the 53rd's war diary that, despite the hardships, the morale was surprisingly high: 'Anyone at home who feels a bit gloomy or fretful would benefit very much by spending a few days with the British and French Armies. They would find it at once a tonic and a sedative.'[18]

At the same time, Churchill was under no illusions as to what lay in store. Exasperated by Chamberlain's prevarication over a landing at Narvik in northern Norway,[19] on 12 March 1940 he wrote to Lord Halifax, the Foreign Secretary: 'Britain has sustained a major disaster by not acting in the North … Whether [the Germans] have some positive plan of their own which will open upon us, I cannot tell. It would seem astonishing to me if they do not … Surely they have a plan. We have none.'[20]

In fairness to Chamberlain, the leaders of the Labour Party, Clement Attlee and Arthur Greenwood, had declared their opposition to the landings, and there was concern that the

United States might also object.[21] Marjorie had no such qualms. 'Isn't it too bad that the Socialists are making such a bother in Parliament … I do think that the [they] are humbugs, when it was their fault we disarmed some years ago, to blame everyone for our shortage of striking power.'[22]

THE WEATHER!

Throughout all of this, life at the 53rd HAA carried on unchanged. Single-line entries describing the foul weather proliferate in the war diary: '12th January 1940 – Little to report. Weather cold and clear.' The reports for the next two days contained no words, just dittos along the lines.

Alfred's transfer to the transport section coincided with bitterly cold weather. The unit soon learned that large lorry engines seized up in sub-zero temperatures, so night pickets were mounted between 7 pm and 7 am. Working in pairs, the drivers moved round the vehicle park turning over the engines of lorries and cars by hand every thirty minutes. It was backbreaking work, made worse by the blackout, and a job that Alfred did not relish.[23] In a letter of 11 January Alfred describes how the Regiment had suffered what he judged to be the coldest night so far:

> One lorry was frozen in the mud & had to be towed out. This morning was no better and water spilled out of the radiators was soon hanging down in icicles. Even a tin of water that wasn't far short of boiling cooled down and had a film of ice over it within half an hour. My poor old lorry has anti-freeze mixture in so that the rad. was alright but the pipe from the petrol tank to the carburettor got blocked through the petrol freezing and although I started trying to get her going at around 8.00 I eventually got underway at 11.15![24]

The weather was so harsh that on 8 January Col. Krohn had instructed that all personnel should receive a half rum ration.[25]

Occasionally there were reports of high-flying enemy aircraft being sited. These were reconnaissance flights. One was a Dornier 17P from Reconnaissance Squadron 4/F/122, shot down on 23 November 1939 by Hurricanes from No. 1 Squadron near Ste-Ménéhould, east of Reims.[26] Three airmen parachuted to safety but one died before landing. He was found to be carrying his 'order of mission', even though it was marked, in German, 'NOT TO BE TAKEN DURING FLIGHT OVER ENEMY TERRITORY'. The crew must have become lost, as their orders were to fly a loop to the north-east of Reims, south of the Belgian border, reconnoitring railway lines and roads, looking especially for 'enemy A.A. Defence (fighters and A.A.)', French and British fighters, any important locations of unloading operations, and 'to be on the lookout for the most minor details', with important features to be photographed. 'Under no circumstances are the Belgian and Dutch territories to be violated.'[27] There was no risk of that happening. The plane was shot down 200 km off course, well south of the Belgian border.

EARTHWORKS

The war diaries show that from January to April 1940 the 12th AA Brigade was preoccupied either in training or in building works to establish the gun stations and living quarters for the troops. The 159th's diary reads more like the daily record of a building contractor: 'Outdoor work continued and site levelled for new Nissen Hut … Battery position moved due to increasing bad state of dugouts … Much progress with field works … Lewis Gun pits and dugouts prepared …

Alfred Ledger digging out a drain. In between training, troops spent much of their time excavating pits for gun positions and accommodation huts.
© Angela Grant

Nissen Hut flooring completed … wattle collected for revetting of gun walls', and so on. Over Christmas 1939 Marjorie asked whether the troops had had to do any digging. 'You must be sick to death of it. Won't you feel funny when you get back to the office? Will you prefer it to a navvy's job? I'm sure Daddy will put in a word for you in the Bermondsey Council!'

The weather continued to be a concern. In January a number of daily entries are limited to noting that frosts made cementing difficult.

It would be difficult to guess that these were the diaries of an artillery brigade at war.

MEDIA REPORTS

Charles Gardner had contacted the Brigade and arranged to record a broadcast for the BBC. This was set up at Alfred's gun station, Wilfred II, and a fake attack organised using a Fairey Battle flown by Flt Lt. R.G. Hurst from 226 Squadron. Gardner wrote that he was 'glad to get something over about the "jolly gunners," because they had had a dull time through the spring and a backbreaking time in the winter, when they were digging the pits for their guns in iron-hard ground.'[28]

It was probably not the first media report describing the 53rd. Marjorie read 'an account in the *Telegraph* by their war correspondent, Peter Lawless. It seemed to fit your crowd very well' – a battery recruited from City men who had been in the Army since 5 August, now with the RAF. 'It described how they were dug into trenches & covered in mud & had a severe attack from mosquitoes! But I've no doubt that all the AA batteries are more or less the same.'[29]

Life for the people of France also carried on with a considerable air of normality. Thursday 2 May 1940 was Ascension Day, a public holiday. Schools were closed, and the villagers processed through the village to church. Alfred was intrigued when around a dozen young children aged from seven to twelve or thirteen 'went round the houses of the village singing something corresponding to our carols and then knocked on the doors for alms – who for I don't know, but I imagine for the poor as today there are a couple of nuns round collecting for the same purpose.'[30]

Home leave continued to preoccupy the troops. Alfred wrote on 5 May that he hoped to get home either at the end of the month or in early June. He and Rupert would be on leave with some of the Battalion HQ staff, but, with past disappointments in mind, he cautioned Marjorie that 'we must be prepared for "muck-ups" so don't get over-confident!'[31] As he wrote this, French aerial reconnaissance was sighting a 100 km column of German armour moving towards the Luxembourg border.[32] Little did he realise the scale of the 'muck-up' looming.

On 9 May the Brigade war diary wearily noted: 'A generally quiet day with little activity.' However, it did go on to observe that the international situation was tense and all leave was cancelled. On the same day Marjorie observed: 'I am scared to death that if [the Germans] begin to speed things up they will do it in France, and that – above all places – I want to stay quiet (no need to say why!).'[33]

In the early hours of the next morning the Luftwaffe attacked.[34]

ENDNOTES

1   Dear and Foot, p. 318.
2   Kaufmann, p. 97.
3   Gilbert, pp. 623–635.
4   Nicolson, p. 35.
5   ML 17.11.1939.
6   ML 28.11.1939.
7   Nicolson, pp. 36–9.
8   French Minister of Finance, appointed Prime Minister in March 1940.
9   Nicolson, p.39.
10   wikipedia.org/wiki/Charles_de_Gaulle#Between_the_wars (visited 25.08.15).
11   Gelb, p. 8.
12   ww2news.com (visited 25.08.15).
13   ML 13.11.1939.
14   ML 06.12.1939.
15   Bullock, p. 570.
16   Gelb, p. 17.
17   NA, WO 167/617.
18   Gilbert, p. 631.
19   Landings in Norway to prevent German access to the Swedish iron-ore fields.
20   Gilbert, p. 635.

21 Gilbert, p. 634.

22 ML 08.05.1940 and 09.05.1940.

23 AAL 05.01.1940.

24 AAL 11.01.1940.

25 NA, WO/167/639.

26 Luftwaffe data: www.luftwaffedata.co.uk/wiki/index (visited 14.05.15).

27 NA, WO 167/617, Appendix E.

28 Gardner, pp. 143–4 and AAL margin note.

29 ML 17.11.1939. Peter Lawless MC was with the RAF in France until May 1940. A war correspondent with the *Daily Telegraph*, he was released to report the invasion of Normandy. He was killed by shellfire in March 1945, while covering an action to cross the Rhine during the Battle of Remagen, aged fifty-three. (wikipedia.org, visited 25.08.2015).

30 AAL 02.05.1940.

31 AAL 05.05.1940.

32 Bond, pp. 36–46.

33 ML 09.05.1940.

34 NA, WO/167/443/182.

5

'THINGS GOT A BIT HOT'

INVASION!

'REIMS, 10.5.40 – Germany invaded Holland and Belgium in the early hours of the morning.' The opening line in the 53rd's war diary's entry was a masterful understatement. No hint of panic, even though the adjutant went on to record that before dawn the military aerodromes being defended by the Regiment were attacked and that 'all gun stations in this unit were in action'.[1]

Alfred had spent the previous day collecting sand. In the evening, as the Germans were about to launch their attack only 140 km to the north-west, he went into Épernay for the evening with Rupert 'and had a most enjoyable time – nothing out of the ordinary, just a bath, tea, a visit to the flicks and a wander around'.[2]

Nothing out of the ordinary? Neither he, nor for that matter anyone in the Allied High Command, had any inkling that Hitler was planning something very much out of the ordinary that night.

ALFRED'S AND MARJORIE'S CONCERNS

His letter to Marjorie written later in the day on the 10th attempted to convey studied nonchalance. He had 'a welcome surprise when I received two letters from you, Nos. 192/3'. The French farmers in the fields around the gun stations were bringing in hay and he comments on the woods being full of arum lilies and 'one or two fields of a glorious golden colour from masses of buttercups [which] made a very pleasing sight – although I don't suppose the farmers think so!' His principal concern was not that the Phoney War had definitely ended and the action was about to start but that one of the brake drums on his lorry had oiled up again and he had spent the previous afternoon removing it – 'most annoying'.

The catastrophic failure of Allied intelligence is vividly illustrated by the fact that home leave for the BEF had only just recommenced. Alfred suppresses any disappointment at this news. The scale of the Allies' complacency and the troops' misplaced trust in their commanders is illustrated by his reassurance to Marjorie: 'We mustn't give up hope [that leave will be reinstated] & once we have given Jerry a pretty good pasting of his own making & things have settled down a bit again I expect that "the powers that be" will turn up trumps once more … Who knows? I might be home for my birthday.' As that fell on 14 June his optimism was sadly misplaced.

Rather than any sense of apprehension, Alfred expresses relief that 'things have livened up a bit because it ends that seemingly endless period of suspense & now we can get cracking'. He felt that as the allies had not 'made the initial move & can't have that blamed on us … it gives us a free hand to pay Mr. Adolph back … I am afraid after recent events a major engagement was unavoidable, so now we have started in earnest we won't call a halt until we have again smashed the misled and foolish Germans. It's a pity it has got to be done because no one really profits in the end.'

Marjorie shared his sentiments. Quite independently, as neither had seen the other's letter, they both seem to have been resigned to the inevitability that hostilities would break out. 'So at last the war has really started and reached you, and although we hoped it wouldn't, we knew perfectly well it would have to, and [if it] means it will be over all the quicker then it is just as well it has.' By now, she had become accustomed to disappointment and continued: 'I guess this is goodbye to your leave.'

At the same time, Marjorie in turn tried her best to reassure Alfred that she wasn't worrying. On 10 May, the day the nation woke up to discover that Germany had attacked Holland, Belgium and Luxembourg she wrote to Alfred. Over the first page and a half she urges Alfred to take care of himself, 'if only for my sake', and telling him she was praying for his safety, then discusses the possible outcome of the war and urging him to take care of himself.

She then deliberately changes the subject: 'Well, to talk of something more cheerful … so you have become a fully qualified coal man' followed by three pages of mundane home news.[3]

But these developments were a huge worry for her: 'Your Pops bets you are wearing your tin hat today, and I hope you are.' In an emotional paragraph she pours out her concerns for

Alfred's safety, writing: 'you are absolutely the very soul of my life and centre of my whole world'.[4] It must have weighed heavily on both of them that there was a real risk their world could cease to exist after only ten months of marriage.

Simultaneously, Alfred's principal concern was that Marjorie wouldn't be 'worriting' herself 'now that the fun and games have started out here. I don't suppose it is necessary to say so but you mustn't bother yourself too much – it's not good for you – and I only hope you can muster up sufficient courage to present a cheerful countenance in spite of all your fears and forebodings inside.'[5]

Despite the feigned indifference, the population was having to come to grips with the scale of the catastrophe unfolding. Marjorie wrote: 'I certainly thought [the Dutch] would be able to hold out a little longer than five days.' The only thing that distracted her was the arrival of the first refugee children. 'We hope we will be lucky enough to get a nice one, and have prepared all sorts of things for its arrival here. It is rather fun really and gives [me] something else to think about.'[6]

No doubt Marjorie saw through Alfred's feigned nonchalance. She knew that he could be 'economical with the truth' if he felt it would reassure her. She had written touchingly to him during the Munich Crisis a year earlier: 'Remember you do not belong entirely to yourself now. You belong to me as well! Please let me know how you are when you can, & don't tell fibs, see?!!!'[7]

Generous by nature, Alfred considered the German nation had been misled. While he regretted the need to return to war, he was confident that the allies would take up where they left off in 1918 and defeat Germany.

GERMAN AND FRENCH TACTICS

Sadly, it was the allied soldiers who were misled. The AASF, located at airfields around Reims, were thought to enjoy a strong defensive position. To the north east lay the fortifications of the Maginot Line. Due north, their positions appeared to be protected by the Ardennes, a beautiful wilderness of mountains and steep valleys, covered in deep forest, through which ran only narrow, twisting roads. The French calculated that such rough terrain would deter any attack from the north, so much so that the fortifications of the Maginot Line ended at the point where the French, Luxembourg and Belgian borders meet.

The French Commander in Chief, General Maurice Gamelin, assumed that these

Camouflaged 3-inch anti-aircraft guns near Reims, March 1940.
Wikimedia Commons – IWM, F 3307

obstacles left German commanders with only one option – a thrust through Holland and Belgium circumventing the Maginot Line and the difficult terrain of the Ardennes. His plan was to counter the expected German attack by advancing into Belgium.

Gamelin's plan was repeatedly criticised by his commanders who pointed out that an attack in Belgium could be a diversion. If the main attack came through the Ardennes the Allied forces would be unable to oppose it as no preparations had been made to extricate them from Belgium to counter such a move. Importantly for the AASF the development of Allied strategy was exclusively in the hands of the French. The British, recognising they were the smaller partner in the alliance, agreed to the French proposals.[8]

ALLIED INTELLIGENCE FAILURES

It was a tragic miscalculation, compounded by the fact that intelligence supported the criticisms made by Gamelin's commanders. The Belgian authorities had received intelligence reports throughout the winter of 1939–40 indicating that German forces were concentrating along the Belgian and Luxembourg frontiers. The deductions drawn by Belgian Intelligence convinced them that the plan was to attack through the Ardennes and then swing west to the English Channel to cut off the Allied field armies in Belgium and north-eastern France. They also correctly anticipated that the Germans would try to land airborne and glider troops behind the Allied lines to break open Belgian fortifications. The warnings were not heeded by either the French or British.

Then, in March 1940, Swiss intelligence detected six or seven Panzer Divisions together with several motorised divisions on the German–Luxembourg–Belgian border. French intelligence also knew, through aerial reconnaissance, that the Germans had constructed pontoon bridges halfway over the Our River on the Luxembourg–German border.

Other reports indicated massive troop movements along the German frontier, French aerial reconnaissance sighting a 100 km column of German armour moving towards the Luxembourg border. The French military attaché in the Swiss capital, Bern, warned of a German assault on the Meuse at Sedan, even predicting the date – some time between 8 and 10 May.[9]

With hindsight it seems incredible that, despite the accumulated weight of intelligence, Gamelin's confidence in his strategy was unshaken.

GERMAN STRATEGY

Hitler and his generals proved to be masters of high risk, unconventional tactics. Von Rundstedt, commanding Army Group A, planned to launch his main attack through the supposedly impenetrable Ardennes.[10] His Chief of Staff, General Manstein, had devised a high risk strategy that brazenly set aside conventional military wisdom. The 'Manstein Plan' envisaged an armoured assault through the Ardennes, concentrating XIX Army Corps and most of the Panzer divisions at Sedan. Rather than breaking out and heading south for Paris, these forces were to sweep to the west, cutting off the British and French in Belgium. It was a massive gamble exacerbated by a further unconventional tactic – the Panzer divisions would execute their swift and deep strategic penetration towards the English Channel without waiting for the main body of infantry divisions.

Tragically, Gamelin, considered one of the best commanding generals in Europe, respected even among the Wehrmacht, ignored the doubts of his own commanders and walked straight into the trap.

The Manstein Plan was the genesis of the 1940 *blitzkrieg*. Its dependence on the deployment of armour without infantry support was considered perilous bordering on foolhardy. The German General Staff doubted such an operation could work. Even Hitler had his doubts.[11]

GERMANY STRIKES

Eventually Hitler was persuaded and ordered his generals to throw everything into a massive double offensive. In the early hours of 10 May 1940 Von Rundstedt attacked south through the Ardennes while General von Beck, commanding Army Group B, attacked Holland in the west. Terror tactics of bombing combined with airborne and glider troops ensured that strongpoints were overwhelmed and bridges captured intact. Bombing damaged key railway junctions and drove panic stricken refugees into trying to escape, blocking the roads.[12] Germany achieved total surprise.

The small Dutch Air Force was quickly overwhelmed but initially its Army put up strong resistance. While the Wehrmacht seized all the strategically vital bridges in and around Rotterdam, completely sidestepping the Dutch system of defence by flooding, a separate Luftwaffe operation to seize the Dutch seat of government in the Hague ended in complete failure, costing heavy casualties in both men and transport aircraft – 50 per cent of the Luftwaffe's transport fleet was lost. Moreover, the airborne operation resulted in a 50 per cent casualty rate, or 4,000 men.[13]

The news was reported in the UK and Marjorie, like everyone else, was amazed at the success of the Dutch air defences. 'Just fancy Holland bringing one hundred Nazi planes down! And Germany losing about 200 altogether yesterday!' But wary that the news might be embellished she added '(If that is true of course!)'[14]

However, in Belgium the Luftwaffe quickly succeeded in gaining control of the air. Despite this, the German Army was confronted by sophisticated fixed defences controlling access to the key bridges over the Meuse. Once again, they deployed unorthodox tactics, landing glider troops in the early hours of 10 May and overwhelming the strongest Belgian defences. Shocked by this, the Belgian High Command withdrew its forces five days earlier than planned.[15]

ALLIED RESPONSE

The Allies responded to Beck's move into Holland by implementing Gamelin's plan and advanced into Belgium to confront the German attack. To their horror they discovered that expected strongpoints and prepared trenches did not exist. Such was the speed of the German advance that the Allies found themselves forced to man an unprepared line of defence.

The Allies' problems were compounded by the discovery that von Rundstedt's advance guard had simply driven through the supposedly 'suicidal' narrow valleys of the Ardennes and swept down on the ill-prepared French defences. The Belgian Army just did not have sufficient anti-tank capability to block the staggering number of German tanks facing them and quickly withdrew behind the Meuse.

The German advance involved more than 41,000 vehicles. This huge armada had been allocated only four routes through the Ardennes and their biggest problem was congestion caused by the sheer number of troops trying to force their way along the poor road network. They were wide open to French air attacks but these never materialised. The French High

German Panzers move through the Ardennes, May 1940. The Allies assumed the dense forest would prevent invasion from this direction.
Wikimedia Commons – Bundesarchiv, 101I-382-0248-33A

Command were reluctant to challenge the Luftwaffe so close to the German border, another missed opportunity.[16]

ATTACK ON THE AASF

In the early hours of 10 May the Advanced Air Strike Force headquarters at Reims were caught up in the surprise. Simultaneous with the invasion of Holland and Belgium, the Luftwaffe attacked the military aerodromes around Reims, the raids 'continuing spasmodically throughout the day. All gun stations of this unit were in action'. The targets were the military airfields but, early on, one bomb fell on a house close to the American Hospital, killing three of the occupants.[17]

The scale of the attack was vividly captured by Gunner Alan Rayment in the 53rd's sister regiment, 73 HAA, at Épernay:

On the 10th May, I was one of the first to be on the gunsite just before sunrise. In the distance, on the horizon, as day broke, there appeared hordes of planes flying parallel to our site. It could have been a huge cloud of locusts filling the skyline. Unfortunately, this was war for real, these planes were part of 1,500 assigned by the Germans, including many Junkers 87 dive bombers, to blast away any obstacles in the way of the Panzer armour divisions.[18]

53RD FIRST ACTIONS

The initial attack was ambitious and ferocious, with five aerodromes attacked simultaneously – Rouvres, Celles-lès-Condé, Mourmelon, Bétheniville and Berry-au-Bac – all defended by the 53rd.

Such was the level of surprise that the flight crews of No. 12 Squadron, based at Berry-au-Bac, were still asleep in their lodgings 3 km away when Junkers aircraft heavily bombed the airfield.[19]

158th Battery was the first in action, the AA log recording in the early hours of 10 May:

Time under	Enemy aircraft	Remarks
04.46–05.28	3 Dornier 215 2,500'	04.28 Planes probably hostile, heard in south. No warning received.

Immediately more aircraft arrived, and over the next forty-five minutes, thirty-one aircraft appeared in nine waves of between five and nine planes, many of them as low as between 600–1200 metres. On at least one occasion 'the machine gunners returned our fire'.

The Regiment's first successful strike was noted at 4.47: 'Two hits' with the comments: '2 rounds very close, and Bren gunners report smoke and flames seen'.

Taking stock in a brief lull after these attacks the Battery commander's remarks note that in all probability only nine planes were involved in the attack 'but they were breaking formation continuously and reforming so that it is impossible to be certain. No warning was received... At the beginning light was bad, targets approaching and receding in all directions – Bren gunners did magnificent work, and consider the guns extremely satisfactory. Shooting was <u>very</u> good… The behaviour of all personnel was excellent, under fire for the first time. Bren Gun detachment did a very good job – Dornier 215s returning fire continuously.'

Dornier 215s, c.1940. Wikimedia Commons – Bundesarchiv, 101I-342-0603-25

But there was to be no let up. Within minutes of making this entry, at 5.55, a Heinkel III bomber was sighted at 3,800 metres. Eight rounds were fired, the first two recorded as 'possible hit'. However, firing had to be stopped as an unidentified fighter came into sight. The two planes disappeared 'Fighter firing, and sitting on the tail of the He III.' It was a baptism of fire for men who had not seen combat before.

Any respite was short. That evening at 18.45 two Junkers 88s were sighted by 157 Battery. 'Both appeared to be shot down by A.A. fire, diving vertically. One crashed in wood N. of position and burned fiercely.'

The toll on the civilian population was immediate. Despite the intensity of the bombing, refugees began to fill the roads. Alfred mentioned in his letter of 10 May that Belgian civilians were already passing by, 'their faces full of despondency'.[20] Many years later, Alfred noted in the margin of his copy of Charles Gardner's AASF: 'It was the most pathetic sight I saw [in] the whole of the war.' The book, full of his marginalia, is now in the Imperial War Museum Special Collections.

Within three days Marjorie reported that refugees 'are already arriving by the boatload' and the family were thinking of taking in two refugee children. 'Two would be company for each other and probably not much more trouble … We must do something to help.'[21]

At 5.40 the next morning the Luftwaffe returned, '5 hostile' aircraft spotted attacking Juvigny airfield at low level. They were possibly decoys to draw away the Hurricanes from the airfield as five minutes later sixteen Dornier 17s approached along the Chalons–Juvigny road flying virtually at ground level 'in low level formation of six, seven, three'. The planes then 'hedge hopped' to the south edge of the aerodrome. 'There they rose to [15–30 metres] and methodically bombed the whole aerodrome.'

During the initial attack the battery fired shrapnel rounds but the low level of the aircraft meant that guns were trained below their safety arc and firing had to cease. Once over the airfield, with the exception of its northern edge, the aircraft were out of sight of the battery whose problems were exacerbated by the intense pall of smoke. Shrapnel firing was tried on individual targets but 'the noise was so terrific (sixty bombs approximately being dropped) that no fixes or orders could be heard by guns'.

The Dorniers then turned their attention to 157 Battery, 'raking the gun position up and down by machine gun fire two or three times. [There was] an incessant stream of bullets over the position throughout the whole of the engagement.'

The Battery Bren gunners engaged the aircraft but to little effect. Such close-range fire forced the men operating the guns and siting instruments to take cover and one man was hit.

As suddenly as the action started it was over: 'Planes then flew off fast at low level out of the north end of the valley.'

All the warnings about the potency of modern air power had been dramatically demonstrated. In just fifteen minutes, between 5.45 and 6.00, immense damage had been caused. Allied aircraft caught on the ground at Juvigny were destroyed or damaged by incendiary bombs and machine-gun fire. The petrol dump was ablaze and the airfield left pitted by high explosive craters.[22]

142 Squadron Fairey Battles destroyed at Berry-au-Bac by Luftwaffe attacks, 10–15 May 1940. Note the abandoned vehicles littering the airfield. © worldwarphotos

Some years later, in an understatement so typical of him, Alfred recorded: 'I remember going through Chalons when it was being bombed. I had 5 tons of ammo on my lorry and had to jump into a ditch when things got a bit hot.'[23]

Further attacks continued throughout the morning and afternoon with heavy bombardment of the aerodromes defended by the 53rd. In 1940, however, bombing was very inaccurate. Six bombs were dropped on Chateau Polignac, the AASF headquarters, but missed, albeit by only 90 metres. More bombs fell to the south and east of the 157 battery gun position, probably intended for Chalons and Épernay. The day's AA Log entry ends with the resigned observation: 'Lack of Allied fighters throughout.'

In truth, that wasn't fair. By 6.30 AASF squadrons reported bringing down several enemy aircraft and 73 Squadron had lost two Hurricanes, 'crew safe'.[24]

UNREALITY ON THE HOME FRONT

Back home, an air of unreality prevailed. Despite the disastrous military set-back in northern France the population seemed oblivious to the possibility that the British army faced defeat. Widespread complaints followed the cancellation of the Whitsun Bank Holiday.

Marjorie grew increasingly anxious and it was probably a good thing she had no idea of the dangers facing Alfred and his comrades. 'I wonder where you are today and what you are doing … May God always bless you and bring you safely home at the end.'[25]

Censorship constrained the media's freedom to report events. The country was completely unaware of the catastrophe unfolding as German forces swept through the Low Countries and northern France, so much so that Marjorie wrote on 12 May: 'I'm thankful that so far Germany isn't making much headway worth speaking of in Holland or Belgium.'

Marjorie's underlining betrays her apprehension. 'In the 6 o'clock news [it was reported] that several towns in France had recently been bombed and one sounds very much like … yours.'[26]

The following day she was overjoyed when she received Alfred's letters dated 8 and 10 May. However, ominously, the post also included a 'whizz bang', date stamped 11 May, the day after hostilities had started. While the 'whizz bang' served its purpose, perversely, it increased her apprehension. 'There is nothing I hate to see more than whizz bangs. They tell you nothing except you are alive and kicking when you sent it.' While these postcards brought reassuring news, the recipients did not know the reason why post was restricted and ended up speculating. 'You may be on the move again and are not allowed to write a letter. Is that the case with this one? Oh, I hope not!'

The reality was that the Luftwaffe already controlled the air space and the airfields around Reims where the AASF squadrons were deployed were suffering relentless attacks.

The aerodromes at Vraux and Mourmelon were severely damaged, the village of Bétheniville, adjacent to Alfred's gun station, Wilfred II, was bombed on 13 May and on the 14th 158th Battery headquarters was hit. The target was the railway bridge over the River Aisne but this remained intact. However, by unfortunate timing a French troop train was standing in the station. This was hit, with many casualties.[27]

The air raids continued until 15 May.

SCALE OF LUFTWAFFE ATTACKS

The 53rd's three batteries were located in a line running from Guigincourt (158) north of Reims to Villers-Marmery (157), with Cernay-lès-Reims (159) in the middle, just east of Reims. The distance between the 158th in the north and 157th in the south is little more than 40 km. Unfortunately, many of the gun station AA logs are missing. For example, only one log remains for 14 May, that of 158/Squeak II.[28] The surviving logs reveal relentless bombing, especially in the early morning between 5.00 and 8.00.

For example, on 10 May, the morning of the initial surprise attack, Squeak I sighted thirty-five aircraft in fourteen waves between 4.36 and 6.00. Two days later Wilfred II recorded at 7.00 a formation of twenty aircraft in a series of Vs in line astern, so many that the battery was unable to identify the types of bomber involved. 'Reims-Champagne aerodrome and Reims appear to have been heavily bombed.'

Between 10 and 15 May the batteries each record anything between two and seven waves of aircraft between 5.30 and 8.00, varying from seventeen bombers to as many as the fifty-two sighted by Wilfred I on 13 May. In one hour between 5.32 and 6.32 seven waves of bombers were sighted by the battery. At 5.59 33 Heinkel and Dornier bombers appeared. 'Before targets came into range Dorniers flew west and Heinkels flew east over position.' The formation scattered, 'one Heinkel on fire, hit by a Hurricane'.

The raids increased in numbers over 14 and 15 May, with large numbers of bombers attacking in the afternoon as well as early morning. Squeak II, the only battery whose log survives for the 14th, records twenty-four aircraft in two waves in the early morning with four more groups totalling thirty-one aircraft in two hours between 11.43 and 13.53.

The attacks reached a climax on 15 May. Only the AA logs for 159/Wilfred I and II survive and even these are incomplete. Alfred's battery, Wilfred II, recorded seven waves totalling thirty aircraft in the morning and a further forty-four aircraft in five waves in two and a half hours in the middle of the day.

The AA log required a note of the number of rounds fired in each action. In the last four actions recorded that day the battery commander noted across the column: 'it is impossible to accurately say how many rounds were fired at each engagement but 107 rounds were fired in all'.

AA logs ran for twenty-four hours from 18.00 to the same time the following day. Each engagement is numbered sequentially. Only the last page of 159/Wilfred II's log remains for 15 May. This reveals that the battery was engaged a staggering forty-six times over the twenty-four hours. Between 13.25 and 18.53 the battery engaged eight formations totalling forty-five bombers, the largest consisting of twenty-one aircraft in 'close V formation, line astern'.[29]

It is not possible accurately to calculate the number of bombers involved in raids on the airfields defended by the Regiment but, on the remaining evidence, they must have numbered hundreds.

LIMITATIONS OF 3-INCH ANTI-AIRCRAFT GUNS

The aerial onslaught by the latest German bombers was met by the gunners of the 53rd, equipped with 3-inch anti-aircraft guns. The battery logs record their bravery, but the odds were stacked heavily in favour of the Luftwaffe aircrews. The World War I 3-inch heavy guns were inappropriate for the role assigned to them: their maximum range was less than 14,000 metres, so they were useless against high-flying aircraft; and firing single shells weighing 7.3 kg, they were ineffective against fast low-flying aircraft. What was needed was quick-firing light anti-aircraft guns, and twelve AA Brigade lacked this capability.

On 24 December 1939 the AASF headquarters had recommended to the Air Ministry that the 3-inch guns should be replaced with 3.7-inch guns, 'if possible immediately'; if this was not possible, then additional instruments were needed which could be fitted to the 3-inch guns. By the time the German offensive began only one light anti-aircraft battery had joined the brigade.

Events proved the recommendation to be chillingly accurate. When 12 AA Brigade came to analyse the performance of the anti-aircraft guns at their disposal, the diarist observed on 15 May that 'the 3.7 and 44 mm [guns] were most successful, particularly the former who by their superior range were enabled to break up high flying hostile formations and inflict damage… Where hostile aircraft were in range the 3-inch guns achieved good results but the great majority were out of range for the 3-inch [guns].'[30]

GERMAN BREAKTHROUGH, ALLIED CONFUSION

The thrust by Army Group A through the Ardennes in the early hours of 10 May initially fell behind schedule as huge traffic jams built up.

On 11 May, Gamelin ordered reinforcements to the Meuse sector but the French lacked a sense of urgency, believing the build-up of German divisions would be correspondingly slow. While the French high command was aware of the strength of German tank and infantry formations their confidence in their own fortifications and artillery superiority turned out to be misplaced.

However, the commanders of the French 1st Army Group to the west, advancing into Belgium to confront German Army Group B, recognised the threat presented by defeat at Sedan. They urged the destruction of the Meuse bridges.

Late in the afternoon of 12 May, while the Luftwaffe was pounding 53 HAA and the airfields around Reims they were defending, German advance forces reached the Meuse line. Three major bridgeheads were needed to enable each of the three armies constituting Army Group A to cross the river – Dinant, Monthermé and, the most southerly, Sedan, within an hour's drive of the Battalion HQ at Reims.

Under cover of darkness in the early hours of 13 May, three Panzer divisions were able to position themselves at their designated crossing points in and around Sedan. However, with most of his artillery stuck in the Ardennes traffic jams, Guderian's plan now depended on the Luftwaffe. They did not fail him. From 8 am on 13 May the French forces defending Dinant were subjected to eight hours of relentless carpet and dive bombing. It was the heaviest air bombardment the world had seen to date. The morale of the French defenders was shattered.

Such was the confusion on the Allied side, however, that it was not until 3 o'clock the same afternoon that 12 AA Brigade received unconfirmed reports that the Germans were in force near Sedan and Mezieres but 'the lack of any definite information was a feature'. The reports emanated from the AASF headquarters who, in turn, had received them from 'HQ BAFF which did not seem to be in the picture as regards operations on the ground'.[31]

To circumvent the heavily defended Meuse bridges the Germans constructed pontoon bridges and during the night of 13–14 May their forces successfully crossed the river.[32]

German troops under fire, crossing the River Meuse, May 1940.
© warfarehistory.com (copyright pending)

AASF LOSSES

On the morning of 14 May the BAFF responded with all the resources available to them. The entire force of serviceable bombers, including the ill-suited Fairey Battles of the AASF, was employed in an effort to destroy the bridges.

No aircraft were lost during the morning raids but when they returned later in the day they were met by Luftwaffe fighters.[33] The ferocity of the air battle is captured by a signal to AASF headquarters from one of the Air Wings:

To PANTHER[34]
From CRYSTAL

Following as requested by telephone … 14/5
HQ AASF Intelligence summary report period 1200 to 2000 hrs 14/5

57 Battles and Blenheims of AASF escorted by all available fighters attacked bridges across Meuse from west of Sedan to Mouzon, the bridge at Douzy, and the road from Bouillon via Givelle to Sedan. 32 aircraft returned, rest lost chiefly from fire from ground …

Our fighters have shot down 3 ME.109, 4 JU.87, 1 HE.111 definite, and 2 JU.87 awaiting confirmation.

Our Battles have shot down 2 ME.109, and our AA has shot down 1 DO.17

Fairey Battle of 103 Squadron crash landed after being hit on approach to Mouzon Bridge during the raids on the Meuse bridges in the Sedan area, 14 May 1940. The figures are curious German soldiers inspecting the wreckage. Between 10–15 May 103 Squadron lost nine aircraft with thirteen crew killed and two POWs.
© David Fell

The AASF had lost twenty-four bombers against thirteen enemy aircraft shot down. It was a terrible price to pay for a relatively modest result – two pontoon bridges destroyed, a third pontoon bridge and a 'permanent bridge' in Mouzon damaged by direct hits.[35] 'No higher rate of loss in an operation of comparable size has even been experienced by the Royal Air Force.'[36]

Charles Gardner wrote in his diary:

Monday, May 13th to Wednesday, May 15
Two days of unending raids on both sides. The Germans are through all right… The work of the Battle squadrons is beyond praise. The courage of those boys, outnumbered, attacked by hordes of fighters and in slow aeroplanes – they have been going at those German lines of supply the whole time. We don't get any details of casualties now but I imagine that many more of our friends have gone.[37]

Gardner was right. The aircrew of the AASF had suffered grievous losses. When Germany attacked on 10 May the ten bomber squadrons making up the AASF had 135 serviceable bombers. Two, later three, Hurricane squadrons supported them. The losses among the bomber force were appalling. By 12 May the AASF had been reduced to seventy-two serviceable bombers.[38]

The terrible fact was that the possibility of this level of losses had been anticipated by the head of Bomber Command, Air Marshal Portal, two days before the German attack. In a chillingly prescient memo he wrote to the Chief of Air Staff: 'I am convinced that the proposed employment of [the Blenheims] is fundamentally unsound, and that if it is persisted in it is likely to have disastrous consequences on the future of the war in the air … the area concerned would be literally swarming with enemy fighters and we should be lucky to avoid crippling losses.'[39]

Overall, the French Air Force and the AASF lost 44 per cent of their combined bomber fleet. The outcome of this Herculean effort? – the Allied air forces were unable to prevent the German forces achieving the first objective of the Manstein plan: Army Group A had broken through the Meuse defences. Bearing in mind the formidable French defences and difficulty of the terrain it was a stunning military achievement.

DUTCH FORCES OVERWHELMED

North west of the Ardennes the valiant spirit of the Dutch troops was broken on 14 May when they saw the effect of German bombing on Rotterdam. The entire historic city centre was destroyed, 900 people killed and 85,000 made homeless. Göring immediately threatened to destroy Utrecht. Faced with the prospect of every city being destroyed, the Dutch Army, still largely intact and suffering only half the casualties of its enemy, surrendered the following day.

It should not be forgotten that this was the Battle of France. By May 1940 the BEF numbered around 450,000 men. The French government had mobilised around one third of the male population, of which around 2.24 million were in the north.[40] They suffered grievously.

One incident will suffice as an example. On 14 May the Record Book for AASF HQ Operations Room noted:

10.25

Report rec'd from G/Capt KIRBY that 6 enemy dive bombers have just attacked a FRENCH troop train in Guignicourt station – killing or wounding hundreds of men.[41]

12 AA BRIGADE CONSIDERS WITHDRAWAL

Back in Reims, 12th Anti Aircraft Brigade was forced to consider withdrawing with the AASF to the area around Troyes, 125 km to the south. The Brigade war diary reeks of exasperation: 'Repeated efforts had been made in the past few months to obtain a plan for such an event from the RAF without success and now the plan was being decided at the last moment.'[42]

ENDNOTES

1   NA, WO 167/617.

2   AAL 10.05.1940.

3   ML 10.05.1940.

4   ibid.

5   AAL 10.05.1940.

6   ML 15.05.1940.

7   ML 03.10.1938.

8   Blatt, p. 312.

9   Bond, pp.36–46.

10 Brian Bond, Britain, *France and Belgium, 1939–1940*, Brassy's, 1990, pp. 32–33

11 Melvin, pp. 148–55.

12 Harman pp. 26–29.

13 Hooton, pp. 50–52.

14 ML 11.05.1940.

15 Dunstan, pp. 32–54.

16 Evans, p. 50.

17 NA, WO 167/617.

18 bbc.co.uk/history/ww2peopleswar (June 2015).

19 Flt Lt. G. Purslow, www.bbc.co.uk/history/ww2peopleswar (visited 16.01.16).

20 AAL, 10.05.1940.

21 ML 13.05.1940.

22 NA, AA log 157 battery, 10/11.05.1940, WO 167/617.

23 Gardner, p. 244, AAL marginal comment.

24 NA, AIR 24/21.

25 ML 13.05.1940.

26 ML 11.05.1940.

27 NA, WO 167/617.

28 53rd HAA consisted of three batteries with eight guns each, a total of twenty-four. In early 1940 these were divided into two gun stations, i.e. six in all, although there is one AA log for Squeak III. There should be six AA logs per day. The largest number is four logs, on 12 May, and there is only one for 14 May. However, bearing in mind the dramatic events that followed it is remarkable that any logs have come down to us.

29 NA, WO 167/617, appendix, AA logs.

30 NA WO/167/443//182.

31 ibid.

32 Hooton, pp. 64–5.

33 Richards, p. 120.

34 Panther was the code name for AASF headquarters. Crystal was an unidentified Air Wing. Gardner, p. 248.

35 NA, AIR 24/24.

36 Richards, p.120.

37 Gardner, p. 160.

38 Richards, p. 119.

39 Richards, pp. 109–10.

40 Dear & Foot, p. 323.

41 NA, AIR 24/21.

42 NA, WO/167/443/182.

6

SCRAM!

Contrary to expectations, von Rundstedt's Army Group A did not sweep south towards Paris but swung west to cut off the French and British forces in Flanders. Rather than crossing the Aisne behind which most, but not all, of the AASF were located, the Germans merely used the river to protect their southern flank while pressing west to the English Channel.[1]

Suddenly Alfred and his colleagues found themselves less than three hours from the German forces but ignorant of their intention. It is extraordinary, therefore, that on the day Germany attacked he found time to write a long four-page letter to Marjorie feigning lack of concern. Clearly he was writing under the constraints of censorship but he only mentions once that 'the fun and games have started'.[2] It was a good she didn't know the real situation. The Expeditionary Force comprised almost all of Britain's combat-ready troops. 'The realisation that it was trapped with its back to the sea and had little hope of breaking out was staggering.'[3]

PLANS FOR WITHDRAWAL

The AASF bases straddled the Aisne and were threatened by the German breakthrough. Fortunately the force had somewhere to go. Presciently, as it turned out, the RAF had undertaken an extensive scheme of airfield construction and a number of grass landing strips were almost ready south of Champagne around Troyes. A withdrawal area would put both the Aisne and the Marne between the AASF and Germans forces.

However, the AASF had been reduced to a static body as, located behind the Maginot Line, it was regarded as well protected. As a result it had been starved of transport resources and was six hundred vehicles short of its official complement. It was pure good fortune that the German advance did not cripple the Force.

On the morning of 14 May, four days after Germany's surprise attack, 12 AA Brigade called a meeting of commanding officers. They were briefed 'on the possibility of a move of the AASF from the Reims to the Troyes area in the event of the threat to the French defences becoming too acute'. Details were given to Lt. Col. Krohn of the airfields that 53 HAA would be defending in the new location.

Despite the heavy losses incurred by the RAF and the ferocity of the air raids, commanders still did not grasp the extreme danger facing them and their men. The 53rd's War Diary noted that 'it is important to point out that all details were given [at the meeting] as provisional, and the impression conveyed that the move was by no means certain to take place'.

EMERGENCY MOVEMENT ORDERS

Krohn returned to the 53rd's Reims HQ and, at a meeting of his battery commanders, issued orders for the batteries to prepare to move at short notice. Gun stations were provisionally assigned to airfields in the Troyes area. One officer from each battery was to report to the Commanding Officer at 4.00 am the following morning to accompany him on a reconnaissance of the new area allotted to the Regiment.[4]

Despite this apparent sense of urgency, the reality still hadn't struck commanders. That evening, at 9.20 pm, the 53rd's Emergency Movement Order was issued. Unbeknown to the AASF, General Heinz Guderian, the commander of the German XIX Armeekorps, ignoring orders to halt and dig in, swung his Panzer divisions west. They were now within 125 km of the 53rd's position, a mere two hours driving.[5]

General Heinz Guderian, commander of German XIX Armeekorps. An early exponent of mobile warfare, his tactics overwhelmed the French forces and BEF in 1940.
Wikimedia Commons – Bundesarchiv, 101I-769-0229-15A

The level of incompetence within the AASF was culpable, the senior command blissfully ignorant of their precarious position. However, in less than twenty-four hours 12 AA Brigade had drawn up detailed plans to move the 53rd and 73rd HAA Regiments, together with their searchlight units, to the Troyes area. This was to be done in two orderly phases: Phase I, units north of the Marne (158 Battery), Phase II units south of the Marne.

The Brigade staff frantically organising the withdrawal faced two problems – first, the immobility of the 3-inch guns, which had been lowered into gun pits with their wheels removed and, second, the shortage of transport, especially towing vehicles.[6] However, while the Brigade had been badly caught out, their ability to react decisively to a disastrous situation was impressive.

Two orders were issued, the first by 12 AA Brigade and, acting on this, the 53rd's Emergency Movement Order. The former consisted of five typed pages with a circulation of 25 recipients. The opening paragraph stated dryly:

INFORMATION

1. It may be necessary to withdraw the AASF from the REIMS area to the TROYES area.

INTENTION

2. To withdraw 12 AA Bde to protect AASF aerodromes in the TROYES area[7]

The Order was completely free of errors or corrections. The stenographers must have been brilliant; there is not the slightest hint of haste or panic.

Before the guns could be moved they would have to be lifted out of the gun pits, which had taken so long to build, and reassembled as mobile units. Furthermore, the Regiment suffered from a severe shortage of Scammell towing vehicles, so much so that the adjacent Regiment, 73 HAA, located further south, had been deprived of all its towing vehicles and a proportion of its 3-tonners to facilitate stage 1 of the 53rd's move. Alfred later lamented: 'If only we had been mobile – the role in which we had been trained by the T.A.'[8]

The Brigade Order set out the sequence of moves and the priorities to be assigned; personnel first, followed by 3.7-inch and 40 mm Bofors guns, instruments, 3-inch guns and searchlight equipment with the oldest equipment, Type H 3-inch guns, the last to be moved. The Order was extraordinarily prescriptive. Understandably, batteries and their sections were directed to specific locations but the order went into details of routes to be taken, including villages to be avoided, the rations and fuel to be carried.

It is only towards the end of the document that the Brigade acknowledges that its units might have to escape in a hurry. Paragraph 17 addresses what should be done to equipment and stores which might have to abandoned: RDF[9] sets to be destroyed 'as laid down in standing orders for GL mark I equipment forwarded under this office S/15 of 16 Mar 40', breech blocks and instruments to be removed from guns and evacuated, ammunition abandoned and full petrol cans to be split open and spilt. 'This will not be done in the vicinity of buildings.'

If the Brigade's reaction seems sclerotic, the 53rd's Emergency Movement Order does convey some sense of urgency. The Brigade Order required the Regiment to be ready to move at six hours notice. Krohn decided to instruct his unit to be prepared to move at two hours notice. A footnote sets out the action to be taken if guns had to be abandoned. 'In the event of there being no time even for this, Guns will be blown up as described verbally.'[10] In addition, light machine guns were to be mounted on all vehicles during the move.

Crucially, however, there was a variation in the Order issued by 12 AA Brigade. A specific note instructed that should guns have to be abandoned 'breech mechanisms will be carried away and any sights, fuse setters and receiving dials destroyed'. There is no explanation as to why the Order differed from the instructions issued by the Brigade. Surely it was standard practice to remove instruments along with breech mechanisms? It was a change which would come back to haunt the Regiment.

BUREAUCRACY

Despite the urgency of the situation, the level of bureaucracy that continued to be maintained is staggering. Although the German main force was only two hours away, and reports that parachute troops, disguised as workmen, had been dropped, the Brigade and Regimental paperwork was still churned out. The 53rd's Emergency Movement Order was typed, timed, dated and signed by the CO and twelve copies distributed, 'copies 10, 11, 12 spare at RHQ'. One interpretation is that this was evidence of discipline remaining intact. The alternative view is of a command structure totally unaware of their dire situation and struggling to keep pace with developments.

Buried in paragraph 9, Brigade Order No. 1 stated:

NOTIFICATION OF MOVE
(a) the issue of the word 'SCRAM' from Bde HQ will be the order to carry out Part
    I of the move.

The Brigade issuing the words 'SCRAM TWO' would instigate Part II of the move.

The war correspondents attached to the AASF appear to have had a much better understanding of the dangerous situation. The BBC's Charles Gardner wrote in his diary for 15 May that 'the German push seems to be developing rapidly. We are all under an hour's notice to leave.' He reported that all the roads were guarded and machine guns and anti-tank nests controlled the bridges. Ominously, the main French air force base at Reims Champagne airport had not been bombed for two days. '[The Germans'] are obviously planning to use it themselves.'[11]

Air raids continued throughout daylight of 15 May and the Brigade's guns were constantly in action. The ferocity of the raids was illustrated when thirty aircraft bombed Reims. Three were shot down by the Brigade's batteries and two by fighters.

FEIGNED CALM IN THE STORM

On 15 May, in the middle of all this fury Alfred was still able to write to Marjorie, another letter once again feigning calm lack of concern. He mentions, but only in passing, that he had been 'sent for at about 9 [pm] and told to get all my things together and pack off to the gun station'. He also confirmed an apparently lighthearted enquiry made by Marjorie in a recent letter: 'You are right in your guess that we are wearing our tin hats more now but it is as much for keeping the sun off as for anything else as our side-hats are useless for the job – and the sun is terribly strong and hot. Most of the time I walk about in my shirt sleeves trying to find a shady spot!' At this point he probably sensed that his description of indolent sunny days might not be credible and adds: 'when I'm not working of course!'

However, while describing his previous day's activity of collecting and loading coal he quietly slips in a low key warning: 'I don't know how long I shall be here [back at the battery] but probably not more than a couple of days or so & as there is a possibility of being pretty busy for a while I might not be able to find time to write for three or four days, so if a lapse of letters occurs you mustn't start getting unduly worried and anxious.'

After describing the suntan he had acquired and the fact that Holland had surrendered he urged Marjorie: 'Keep your pecker up my Love, and keep smiling. If we can out here (and we do!) then I'm sure you must be able to at home!'[12] So despite the apprehension he must have felt, Alfred's concern is to reassure Marjorie that everything is fine and there is nothing for her to worry about.

CRISIS

Although Alfred tried to project casual nonchalance, the situation was rapidly deteriorating. As an ordinary gunner he wasn't to know that earlier on the evening of 15 May, at 6.00 pm, the French Mission voiced the opinion to Brigade HQ that there could be a thrust at Reims as it was a centre of communications. The Brigade immediately warned all units to be ready to move at short notice. Between 8.30 and 11.30 pm reports reached Brigade HQ of German armour approaching Reims. While these were unconfirmed they were alarming – 'AFVs [armoured fighting vehicles] at Liart, 75 km to the north; AFVs at Montcornet'. Montcornet was within 50 km of Reims.

Brigade HQ tried to remain objective, the War Diary noting that the continued reports of enemy progress were 'doubtful [but] alarming'. Throughout the evening, however, the Brigade's superiors at the AASF, 'were still out of touch with the ground situation'.

Finally, at 11.30 pm the AASF activated Part I of the evacuation plan. Despite the lack of hard information it seemed clear that the Strike Force was in a perilous position, which was getting more dangerous by the minute. The orderly plans, which envisaged withdrawal in two parts twenty-four hours apart, were now clearly irrelevant. Two hours later, in the early hours of the 16th, AASF HQ activated Part II.[13]

THE 53RD ENGULFED IN CHAOS

At 4.00 am on 15 May the reconnaissance group of five officers, led by the CO, had set off for Troyes. Despite the early start, progress was slow as 'the roads were crowded with refugees moving in a general southerly direction'.[14] Unknown to the reconnaissance party, the situation at the 53rd's positions around Reims was fast deteriorating.

The return journey to the Regiment's headquarters in the city must have been equally slow and a shock awaited them when they finally reached Épernay, still half an hour from Reims.

The bridge over the River Marne on the northern side of the town was heavily barricaded and passage across forbidden. To compound their problems, the party discovered that the Reims–Épernay road had been bombed and all traffic was being diverted. The group did the logical thing and drove to the Regiment's No. 4 CCS (Command & Control Station) only to discover that it was in the process of being evacuated.

Lt. Col. Krohn phoned his HQ in an attempt to find out what was happening. Once again he was in for an unpleasant surprise. The adjutant had been urgently summoned to Brigade headquarters and was not in.

The situation was now extremely serious but the Regiment's Commanding Officer was completely in the dark and away from his communications centre. He had to get back to his own HQ at Reims as quickly as possible but the diversion meant the reconnaissance party had to travel via Louvois, a distance of over 60 km, double the distance of the direct route. 'Progress was pitifully slow. There was a virtually unending stream of traffic moving south, refugees on foot, on bicycle, in car or horse drawn cart, intermixed with heavy RAF lorry convoys.'[15]

It was not until 3.00 am[16] on 16 May that Krohn finally managed to make it back to the 53rd's headquarters. He and his reconnaissance party had been continuously on the move for almost twenty-four hours.

It must have been a shattering moment when they entered the building. Instead of a full complement of Regimental headquarters personnel, they were met by the adjutant and a dispatch rider who had stayed to await Krohn's arrival. His entire headquarters staff had left for Anglure, over 100 km south on the road to Troyes.

As Krohn was still struggling to make his way back to Reims, it fell to 2nd Lt. Charles Moore[17] to rush back to Regimental HQ and implement the withdrawal. The regimental war diary paints a picture of chaos. Worst of all, there was no time to follow his commanding officer's orders to destroy the guns. It must have been a very nervous Adjutant, therefore, who greeted his commanding officer in the shell of an empty HQ.

He reported that at half past midnight on the 16th, having been urgently summoned to Brigade HQ, he had received verbal orders from the Staff Captain 'to complete [the] move of the Regiment forthwith in one stage, and not in three stages, as laid down in 12 AA Bde Operations Order No.1 of 14.5.40, which meant that 16 out of 24 guns would be left behind'.[18]

One of the duties of the Adjutant was to write up the War Diary. It is hardly surprising, therefore, that his entry is so detailed. As one of the most junior officers in the Regiment it had fallen to 2nd Lt. Moore to order the immediate evacuation of the Regiment, necessitating the loss of most of their guns.

GUNS ABANDONED

It is a long tradition and point of honour that artillery regiments never abandon their guns. Only two days beforehand, Lt. Col. Krohn had anticipated such a disastrous situation, setting out explicit orders that 'in the event of guns having to be abandoned breech mechanisms will be carried away and any sights, fuse setters and receiving dials destroyed. In the event of there being no time even for this Guns will be blown up'.[19]

Rumours reaching Brigade HQ had filtered through to 53 HAA. 'Alarmist reports' had been received of enemy formations close to 158 Battery's positions north of the Aisne: Panzer tanks and parachute troops in the Guignicourt area and Panzers at Montcornet, less than 40 km away.

At forty minutes past midnight on 16 May 2nd Lt. Moore was able to reach 158 and 159 Batteries by phone and order them to 'move in toto forthwith in accordance with 12 Bde's verbal instructions'. However, a dispatch rider (DR) had to be sent to 157 Battery HQ 'as

German Panzer IV, France 1940. Wikimedia Commons – Bundesarchiv, 101I-055-1599-31

telephone lines were known to be down'. By 1.30 am, when Moore tried contact with 12 Brigade to report progress and seek further instructions, he was unable to get through as the phone lines had been disconnected.[20]

EVACUATION OF 158 BATTERY

The 158 Battery gun sites straddled the River Aisne and were the most northerly of the 53rd's positions. It was the battery closest to the advancing German units and therefore the one in greatest peril. Squeak I was south of the river at Aguilcourt while Squeak II and III were north of the Aisne at Juvincourt-et-Damary, and Guignicourt. Both were 30 km north of Reims, about an hour's drive for heavy towing vehicles. The only route to Reims was via the road bridge at Berry-au-Bac.

Major White, commanding 158 Battery, could not have known of the latest situation and the proximity of German troops to his gun stations. On receiving the code word 'SCRAM', he immediately passed on the order to get out to his three gun stations and began the operation to move the Battery HQ. Fortunately, following the initial warning from Brigade HQ, 158 Battery had started to move its RDF equipment and towing vehicles were positioned at Juvincourt gun stations in anticipation of an urgent move. That was as far as the carefully worked out Brigade Order No.1 had progressed. It is little surprise, therefore, that the War Diary gives the impression of pandemonium ensuing when the order to 'SCRAM' was issued at half past midnight.

Although the Regiment's precious Scammell towing vehicles were already in position, White discovered that the guns could not be moved before 2.30 am. He, therefore, gave orders that only personnel and instruments should leave. The towing vehicles could have been sent to Squeak III but their guns, still in the gun pits, were not yet mobile as they were not scheduled to move in Part 1. The Scammells were therefore diverted to Regimental HQ in Reims. This meant that they had to contend with the chaos of roads clogged with refugees. While evacuating personnel and instruments first was in accordance with the priorities set out in Krohn's Emergency Movement Order, it meant that the only battery in a position to withdraw its guns failed to do so.

WITHDRAWAL OF 157 AND 159 BATTERIES

It took Major White an hour and a half to reach Regimental Headquarters where he found

Krohn who had also just arrived. The CO immediately grasped the situation and ordered Capt. Garland, who had accompanied White, to divert the three Scammells to 159 Battery, Alfred's unit. White was ordered to get over to 159 Battery headquarters and warn them that these vehicles were on their way. One Scammell was already held in reserve at 159 Battery HQ. This vehicle plus the other three Scammells were to proceed immediately to remove the four guns from the 159th's gun stations. However, these were nearly 30 km apart, at La Neuvillete on the northern outskirts of Reims (where Alfred was located) and Hauviné east of the city.

In the depths of the night the race was now on to remove as many of the Regiment's guns as possible. In the dark, and with communications down, chaos reigned. On receipt of the order to 'SCRAM' the officer commanding Pip III gun station was unsure whether or not the two Parts set out in the Emergency Move Orders would operate. With no phone connection to the Regiment's headquarters, at 2.30 am he decided he would have to travel to Reims to obtain clarity. Valuable time was lost as a result as 'considerable difficulty was experienced on the road due to convoys and considerable numbers of evacuees, fires and traffic accidents'. When he finally arrived he was told by Krohn and Moore to 'get out as quickly as possible as enemy armoured vehicles were only a few miles away north – possibly on the Aisne Canal'.

How long it took him to make his way back through the traffic jams is not recorded but on reaching the Battery HQ he immediately repeated the Colonel's orders to his colleagues commanding the 157th's gun stations at Aubérive and Juvigny, the latter 30 km to the south. 'Transport was limited and guns not ready for the road'.[21] Two guns were hastily towed out from Pip III but the four guns positioned at Aubérive and Juvigny had to be abandoned. These were not scheduled to move in Part 1 of the move to Troyes so were not ready to be hooked up, even though towing vehicles were available. The best that could be done in the time available was to load the instruments and, with them, the gun crews.[22]

PIP III was ready to move, transport having been delivered to them, but the Battery Diary noted despairingly:

p.m. 15/5/40.
Remainder of transport spread over B.H.Q., PIP I & II [Reims, Aubérive and Juvigny] who were in position to take instruments and personnel only, in the case

of PIP I and instruments only in the case of PIP II. B.H.Q. took valuable stores and personnel.[23]

Despite the urgent dispatch of towing vehicles to the 159 gun stations, only three guns were moved. The fourth had to be abandoned as it proved impossible to fit the wheels in time.

The 158 Battery gunners at Aguilcourt faced considerable difficulties. In the early hours of the morning the petrol dump at La Malmaison aerodrome 'went up in flames'.[24] With no fuel and earlier warnings of tanks and parachutists in the vicinity, the gun station commander, 2nd Lt. Hughes, felt he had no option but to give the order to move and leave the guns. Similarly, the two guns at Aguilcourt II were abandoned, the gun crews escaping with only the instruments.

Alfred, who had returned to 159 Battery based around Cernay les Reims, wrote later in the margin of his copy of Gardner's book:

> We were given the one command 'SCRAM' and 'scram' we did within one hour of the order at 3.00 am Jerry was only a matter of a few miles away and we were defenceless against land attack. We had no vehicles – no, I believe we had two to tow the whole Regts. guns, 24 in all. It broke our hearts to have to destroy the guns & leave.[25]

In actual fact, the guns were not destroyed. That Alfred's memory is incorrect on this point is hardly surprising. Instead of the organised move that was planned, the regiment found itself forced into a chaotic escape in the dark. It must have been traumatic.

Charles Gardner was told to prepare to move at an hour's notice. He had picked up a rumour that the AASF might also have to withdraw. He wrote in his diary: 'What chaos that'll be.'[26] It was a prescient observation. Looking back many years later Alfred concurred: 'What chaos it was.'[27]

TROYES

In the early hours of 16 May, the convoys of vehicles constituting the 53rd's three Batteries made their way independently to their new gun positions north of Troyes, 157 to Droupt-Sainte-Marie, 158 to Queudes and 159 to Fontvannes. Once again, they were widely separated, the distance between 157 Battery, the most northerly, and 159 Battery, just to the west of Troyes, was over 60 km.

While the adjutant finally set out for the Troyes area at 4.15 am, Krohn headed back to check that the 157 and 159 gun stations south of the Aisne had been vacated.

SHORTAGE OF TRANSPORT

The chronic shortage of vehicles across the RAF and anti-aircraft units of AASF had been badly exposed. The 122 AA Brigade war diary noted later that the availability 'of transport was inadequate for mobile operations, units being on Base and Forward Establishment, it was extremely difficult to arrange for the move of units and extensive improvisation was necessary. This lack of transport [was] a serious check on the withdrawal operations.'[28]

The shortage of transport was so acute that a number of men had to escape on foot. The 158th Battery Diary noted: 'personnel marched south and were picked up later'.

Gunner Roy Harvey was one of those who had the misfortune to find that there was no room for him on the transport. He later recounted how 'we were individually told that if we were awoken by somebody calling out 'SCRAM' we were to immediately get up (we were in our uniforms) pick up our side kit and mess tins and literally scram into the woods adjoining our gunsite which we did pronto. This was obviously to avoid a probable attack on our guns. However, this did not happen, but our Colonel drove up under the trees in his jeep. He said, 'The Germans have broken through with their Panzer troops, from this second onwards each and everyone of you must proceed on foot southwards across fields and rivers until I get further south and hopefully find a rendezvous … Don't travel in a bunch or crowd, as obviously the Germans would soon spot you, go in twos or threes at the most.'[29]

Harvey and another gunner who he only knew as Jack ('a great guy … reliable and tough') lay low until 10 o'clock in the morning. They set off

with several packets of iron rations which we spread and skilfully we pounded across ploughed fields, etc. We had previously run out of ammunition and did not have rifles. Within an hour I spotted a dot in the clear blue sky above a spinney some way ahead. I knew it was a German and thought very quickly when we were about 30 paces from a haystack, the only cover of any sort around. 'Dash for the haystacks, Jack' I said, which we did. When a few yards from the objective, and both of us out of breath, I yelled out, 'spread-eagle yourself as you run into the stack Jack, do not crouch down in a heap'. The seconds were passing and the German fighter plane was very near, the pilot fired the machine gun, and the bullets crashed into the ground about a foot from our bodies. If we had piled in a heap on approaching the haystack we would not have been here today.[30]

Ironically, the Brigade commander, Brigadier W.T.O. Crewdson, had identified additional towing vehicles in the early hours. At 4.15 am he had arrived at Chouilly, close to Épernay, to find the 73rd HAA headquarters personnel preparing to leave. Amazingly the telephone lines were still intact. Presumably Crewdson snatched some rest as it was not until 9.00 am that he put through a call to Anti-Aircraft GHQ. There Lt. Col. Jacobs Larkcots revealed that they had spare towing vehicles. These were probably among three hundred lorries held by the French, apparently unallocated, which were 'borrowed' by the AASF.[31]

Failures in the command structure and communications breakdown meant that the extra towing vehicles, which the 53rd so desperately needed, were in fact available but they were unaware of this. Larkcots agreed to immediately dispatch 20 to help 12 Brigade but by then it was too late for these vehicles to play a part in the withdrawal from the Reims area.

THE DESPERATION OF REFUGEES

Charles Gardner and several other war correspondents had been ordered to get out at 4.00 in the morning. 'The whole AASF is on the run – though heaven knows where to.' They set out 'in the trail of the refugees for Paris. The sight of these poor people, with their pitiful little handcarts and broken down motor-cars trying to save something at least of a home life which they may never get again, drove me to a queer mixture of feeling – half tears – half anger.' He arrived in Paris to find the British Embassy 'in a flap burning all its papers … everyone was preparing to evacuate'.[32]

Alfred confessed that he had 'wept inwardly' at the plight of the refugees, their only means of transport 'from cars down to carts, prams, fairy cycles and the very poor on foot just carrying a sack full of bare necessities'. He bemoaned the fact that he was virtually powerless to help them. 'I will spare you the details of them as it is too sad a topic but I have driven over 40 or 50 miles at a stretch on the wrong side of the road overtaking them – and not so much as ten yards separating each little lot on average. However far it stretched over all the roads they must have been travelling on I don't know but it must have run into hundreds.' The only blessing for the refugees was the fine weather. 'Few of them have any means of shelter against rain, although they must get footsore and weary trudging along the hot dusty roads.'[33]

Refugees fleeing south, May 1940, 'footsore and weary, trudging along the hot dusty roads'.
Wikimedia Commons – IWM, F 4505

War has many unexpected consequences. While northern France was crammed with refugees, one of Alfred's Belgian clients, Marcel Dens, was in London on business when the German attack took place. He had been married only twelve months but found himself cut off and unable to return to his wife who was still in Brussels.[34]

It took Roy Harvey and his companion several days on foot to meet up with the Regiment. 'We joined the hundreds of refugees fleeing south. They were very frightened but friendly.

All modes of transport from old prams, wheelbarrows, farm carts, one of which we were invited to join. I remember one old car being towed by a cow as petrol was nil. Old people and disabled folk trying their best to keep going, lots of young children and babies crying.'

Harvey and his mate set off with a reasonable supply of 'iron rations' but were forced to find other food. On several occasions sympathetic farming folk offered them fruit, biscuits and eggs. The high point came when a farming family provided 'a most wonderful chicken casserole with all the right herbs, etc and several glasses of local red wine. We were even allowed to choose the chicken we would like to have for dinner.' Eventually, however, they only managed to survive by eating raw swede scrounged from the fields.

Despite their desperate situation the refugees were extraordinarily generous and 'we were given morsels of bread and oranges'. Their reception from French soldiers, on the other hand, was very different. The two British gunners encountered great hostility, on one occasion a column of French soldiers shouting profane insults at them which drew the comment from Harvey: 'Not exactly friendly. Makes one wonder where they learnt their English!'

Eventually the two lost gunners decided that they couldn't stay with the refugees as 'the Germans decided to strike the refugees column, lots wounded and killed'.[35] It was a desperate escape.

DISAPPEARANCE OF 53 HAA

Charles Gardner did not discover the whereabouts of the AASF until 22 May. 'We gather that the evacuation of Reims was unbelievably chaotic. Even the efficient gunners had to leave their guns behind (having first removed the breech blocks).'[36]

The extent of confusion is indicated when the Chief of the Air Staff, Air Marshall Sir Cyril Newall, reported to the War Cabinet on 27 May that the AASF 'had been operating in the Arras area'.[37] This was incorrect. The AASF had never been in the Arras area. His mistake shows the strains under which everyone from the most senior officers to the lowliest gunners were operating.

In all of this chaos, Krohn's character and leadership stand out. The War Diary entries reveal the burden that the young Adjutant, Moore, must have felt in the absence of his commanding officer. Others, such as the commander of Pip III, were unsure of themselves and failed to take the initiative, wasting valuable time turning to headquarters to seek clarity when he should have known what to do. The code word 'SCRAM' was explicit: get out! It must have been a huge relief, therefore, when the CO finally returned in the early hours of 16 May. Krohn quickly grasped the severity of the situation facing the Regiment, especially with its three batteries dispersed over a large area. He immediately restored some semblance of order and direction. There is no greater compliment to his leadership and courage that, when the rest of the Regiment had left for the temporary refuge of Troyes, he stayed behind to contact outlying batteries immediately north of the city and to the south east.

The chaos afflicting the 53rd also affected the senior command at British Air Forces in France (BAFF), the unified command for all RAF units in France. BAFF had no idea what was going on. The 12 AA Brigade war diary entry for 15 May, i.e. after the event, analysing the chaotic withdrawal, drew the conclusion that 'the air of uncertainty due to the lack of information caused by lack of liaison between RAF and French formations. There was no local source of information and any reports received emanated from BAFF and & were too vague and out of date to be of any real value.'

Unbeknown to the Strike Force, Guderian, commander of XIX Armeekorps and Rommel, commanding the 7th Panzer Division, had decided that the Aisne would form a natural protective barrier for their left flank wile they swept west leaving Reims alone.

Gardner wrote subsequently:

It was later on that evening [14 May] that we were told the German advance had reached within 20 miles of us … Actually, it turned out that the enemy, having got so near Reims in the westward push from Sedan, turned north in a scythe-like movement, and made for the Channel ports. The AASF took the decision to leave late on the night of Wednesday 15 May, but Reims itself remained in Allied hands for nearly another month.

Alfred had no illusions about the Wehrmacht's strategy to swing west and head to the Channel ports: 'That saved us.'[38] Only two of the 53rd's gun stations were in the line of the German's sweep to the west. The scramble to withdraw had been completely unnecessary but the AASF had escaped to fight another day.

ENDNOTES

1   Richards, p.125.
2   AAL 10.05.1940.
3   Gelb, p.3.
4   NA, WO 167/617.
5   Evans, pp. 70–72.
6   NA, WO/167/443/182.
7   NA, WO 167/617, appendix .
8   Gardner, p.244, AAL marginal comment.
9   Range and Direction Finding equipment. This was a Gun Laying system, initially developed at Bawdsey, Suffolk to assist aiming anti-aircraft guns and searchlights.
10 NA, WO 167/617, appendix.
11 Gardner, p. 162.
12 AAL 15.05.1940.
13 NA, WO 167/443/182.
14 NA, WO 167/617.
15 ibid.
16 The War Diary states that 'the C.O. arrived back eventually at R.H.Q. at approximately 15.00 hrs'. This must be a mistake and the time has clearly been altered. The amended time does not tie in with the preceding events noted and timed in the diary.
17 Charles Moore, 11th Earl of Drogheda KG, KBE (1910–1989). In 1940 he was styled Viscount Moore, succeeding to the title on the death of his father in 1957. (wikipedia.org/wiki/Charles_Moore, visited June 2015).
18 NA, WO 167/617.
19 NA, WO 167/617, 53 HAA Emergency Movement Order, 14 May 1940.
20 NA, WO 167/617.
21 ibid.
22 ibid.
23 NA, WO 167/637.
24 NA, WO 167/617.
25 Gardner, p. 167, AAL margin comment.
26 Gardener, p.162.
27 Gardener, p. 162, AAL margin comment.
28 NA WO/167/443//182.
29 deardad blog (visited 11.11.2015).
30 ibid.

31   Richards, p. 120.

32   Gardner, p. 164.

33   AAL 20.05.1940.

34   AAL 13.05.1940.

35   deardad-lettershome.blogspot.co.uk (June 2015).

36   Gardner, p. 167.

37   NA, CAB/65/7/36 (visited 10.04.16).

38   Gardner p. 183 and AAL margin comment.

7
TEMPORARY RESPITE – TROYES

Despite initial discomforts and the bad weather, over the preceding five months the 53rd had settled into life at their dispositions around Reims. Alfred referred in his letters to 'our café'. It was also possible to get away, temporarily, from the rigours of wartime army life in the armchairs and hot baths at Sandes. Most evenings the cinemas of Épernay showed English films and he had befriended locals who gave him meals and mended his clothing. The uncertainty of the Phoney War was compensated by simple comforts and the confidence that whatever the German forces threw at them the British Army and the RAF would prevail.

The suddenness and violence of the German bombing smashed these illusions. After five exhausting days in action the Advanced Air Strike Force had no option but to make an ignominious withdrawal. In the words of Charles Gardner they were 'on the run'.[1] Gardner later wrote that it was 'an unbelievable five days when the AASF, after an autumn and a winter of preparation, were bombed out of house and home'.[2] It must have been a traumatic shock for the troops.

With the safe arrival of the 53rd in the Troyes area the relief in the war diary entry is palpable:

> Villacerf nr Troyes, 17.5.40
> On the morning of 17.5.40 the AASF woke up in the Troyes area. It was not woken up by air raid warnings.

THE AASF GOES MISSING
Such was the speed of their withdrawal, however, that it seemed as though the squadrons and their anti-aircraft support had disappeared. Sometime between 17 and 19 May, Gardner noted in his diary: 'No one knows where the AASF is – or what's happened to its people. I

did a broadcast from PTT which was used in the 9 o' clock news but I wasn't allowed to hint at the evacuation of the AASF. Apparently, the Germans think we are still there and are still bombing our ex-aerodromes.' The confusion was such that the AASF themselves speculated whether anyone knew where they were. Commenting on Gardner's diary entry Alfred wrote later: 'we wondered a bit'.[3]

It took Gardner, still in Paris, another five days to discover the whereabouts of the Strike Force, noting in his diary on 22 May: 'After everybody's been hanging around this town getting depressed-er and depressed-er, we have at last found out where the remains of the AASF have beaten it to. As I write this, the place is so secret that I can't even put it down here but it's about the same distance from Paris as Reims is, though not so near the actual front.'[4]

Ironically, the reverse was true for the troops of 53 HAA. While they knew exactly where they were located, they had no idea of developments elsewhere as wireless sets had yet to be erected and no newspapers were available.

The British people might have been prevented by the censor from knowing the whereabouts of the AASF but there was one person who did find out. Using the agreed code, Alfred wrote to Marjorie on 19 May, the first letters of each paragraph revealing that he had moved to Troyes:

The worst of all this …
Rupert will be coming as well with his lorry …
One of the chief advantages …
You will probably be thinking that a calamity has befallen us …
Each day now I suppose must be treated as a critical one …
Sunday being a 'day of rest'…[5]

However, there would have been a delay in the letter reaching England and Alfred realised that the family at home would be worried. He was especially concerned about his mother. 'I do hope she isn't worrying too much, poor dear; it must be a trial to keep on wondering what we are doing and where we are. But I think she can rest assured – as can you all – that we are quite capable of looking after ourselves and taking care!'[6] The last sentence must have been for Marjorie's benefit as much as anyone else.

If the Regiment was relieved to have escaped the advancing German forces they still faced formidable problems. Their new locations left them close to defenceless 'and yet no enemy raiders pursued the AASF to Troyes'.[7]

12 AA BRIGADE TAKES STOCK

The entire Brigade must have been exhausted but the CO, Brigadier Crewdson, immediately gave instructions for a temporary gun park to be established at Morains, 60 km south of Reims. The guns which the 53rd and 73rd had managed to rescue were directed here.

During the day of 16 May a number of units passed through on their way to Troyes – several searchlight batteries from north of the Marne, the closest to German forces, a detachment of the Royal Army Service Corps and, importantly, the majority of the personnel of both the 53rd and 73rd plus their stores.[8]

Colonel Krohn finally arrived at the 53rd's new headquarters at Villacerf, the new Regimental HQ just north of Troyes, at 3 o' clock in the afternoon of 16 May. Despite being without sleep for thirty-six hours he immediately made arrangements to recover as many guns as possible together with the Regiment's abandoned stores. He also ensured that the six guns which had been brought out by the Regiment were readied for action.[9]

He was followed by units of the 53rd, which had been ordered to move to the new area in independent convoys. The 159 Battery HQ convoy, with Alfred aboard, arrived at their new location, the village of Fontvannes, 6 km west of Troyes at 4.00 pm. It had taken them ten hours to cover 140 km.

By 8.00 pm all 159 Battery personnel were accounted for and billeted in farmhouses around the village.[10] It must have been a mighty relief.

Gradually the gravity of 12 AA Brigade's situation became apparent. By 11.00 pm only fifteen guns out of a total of forty-eight had arrived. Late in the afternoon of the 17 May Krohn reported to the Brigade that he had not been able to evacuate the guns of 158 Battery. While he was arranging for all the other abandoned guns to be recovered, together with their stores and ammunition, the 158 Battery guns were a special concern. The Battery was positioned on either side of the River Aisne, close to Berry-au-Bac. With Von Rundstedt's Army Group A closing on the river the guns positioned north of the Aisne were now within 20 km of the last reported position of German troops.[11]

It was not until midday on 18 May, two days after the Brigade had evacuated their positions that the towing vehicles promised by Anti Aircraft GHQ arrived. The Brigade

Diary notes that ten were retained and ten returned, presumably because their own efforts had made the latter redundant.

The situation around Troyes was stabilising, particularly with the successful recovery of stores and guns by 73 HAA. Over the next twenty-four hours stores and ammunition were retrieved from the 53rd's gun positions together with the eleven remaining guns from 157 and 159 Batteries. Despite these successes 'there was still very little definite news of the situation and there was great uncertainty whether [the] AASF would move again or not'.[12]

Gardner observed that 'no one knew where the Germans were, and as a result, there was chaos on our side. At Troyes no one seemed coherent about the doings even of our own squadrons.' Hurricanes patrolling up to the limits of the BEF area had to land and refuel close to the front line. In one incident, a forward flight was about to land 'when they were violently waved away by a French mechanic on the ground. The Hurricanes opened up and went around again to see what the trouble was. They had a good look – and then saw a column of German tanks moving up the aerodrome road.'[13]

While the Brigade's units had largely reassembled, the haste of the move to Troyes meant that its effectiveness was severely impaired. Had the air raid sirens been sounded the 53rd, for one, would not have heard them as they were widely dispersed throughout the upper Seine Valley. 'Communications were bad, telephone lines nonexistent D.Rs [dispatch riders] were incessantly at work.' Having experienced such difficulties during the evacuation it is little surprise that few guns were ready for action. Alfred was acutely aware of their predicament: 'We went to Troyes but as we were minus our guns we weren't much use to the poor old RAF.'[14]

On top of this, and despite the trauma of the move from their previous positions around Reims, there were virtually no aircraft on the new aerodromes and 'no enemy raiders pursued the AASF to Troyes'. Convoys were able to move unmolested, their greatest impediment being the endless stream of unfortunate refugees who continued to move south. Reading between the lines, is there an inference that the 53rd considered that the evacuation had been ordered prematurely?[15]

RECOVERY OF ABANDONED GUNS

Over the next two days, armed patrols from 157 and 159 Batteries returned to the gun stations they had vacated to recover their heavy guns, ammunition and stores: 159 Battery sent two armed patrols of twenty men each and recovered their five abandoned guns,[16] and the 157th recovery operation was also successful.

However, 158 Battery occupied the most northerly of the 53rd's gun positions at Juvincourt, Guinecourt and Aguilcourt, either side of the River Aisne, 30 km north of Reims. During the evening of 15 May reports had reached Brigade HQ of enemy troops near the Aisne. It was, therefore, decided that the area around the 158th gun positions should be reconnoitered to assess whether or not they were accessible. A young officer, 2nd Lt. Ruddock, was instructed to lead a reconnaissance group to the 158 Battery area. They returned twenty-four hours later and reported that all the 158th's gun stations were accessible.

Ruddock's information was confirmed by Capt. Estlin, officer commanding the Royal Army Ordnance Corps (RAOC) workshops, who had also returned to the area to recover stores. Krohn immediately issued orders for 158 Battery to prepare parties to return to their old positions and recover their guns and stores. Clearly there were risks involved in this operation and, when Krohn reported his plans to the Brigade, Brigadier Crewdson directed that the Battery commander, Maj. White, should himself take charge of the evacuation.[17] To make up the requisite numbers, 2nd Lt. E. Snowdon of 159 Battery led one of the recovery parties.

White's plan was to set up a temporary Battery Headquarters at Ville-aux-Bois, just north of the River Aisne, close to the crossing at Berry-au-Bac. At 5 o'clock in the evening of 18 May two convoys set off, Ruddock leading a reconnaissance patrol of two NCOs and six men in two light cars and three motorcycles. The 'convoy proper' was made up of three officers, a warrant officer and six sergeants together with eighty-four men. Their transport was six trucks, including four heavy towing vehicles. The convoy was under orders not to cross the bridge at Berry-au-Bac until Ruddock had confirmed that all was clear at the gun stations north of the Aisne.

Maj. White followed two hours later. The route necessitated driving through Reims and, while there, White took the opportunity to stop at a French Divisional HQ and enquire about the 'tactical situation' north of Berry-au-Bac. A French captain 'was dubious' and suggested that White should enquire at Berry. White proceeded to Berry-au-Bac but had he received a warning and failed to realise the potential risks?

On arrival he met the CO of the 2nd Regiment of Chasseurs à Pied, charged with the defence of the bridges over the Aisne. The French officer was helpful but his reports

Scammel Pioneer heavy artillery tractor (illustrated vehicle is the heavy recovery variant). Four Scammels were in the convoy sent to recover the guns abandoned by 158 and 159 Batteries' guns. © Peter Ledger

indicated a hazardous situation north of the Aisne – four enemy tanks in villages just north and east of the crossing and machine gunfire. That afternoon his troops had fired anti-tank guns at a copse up the road where it was believed enemy tanks were sheltering. The French officer gave a succinct summary: 'it was dangerous to proceed to Squeak 2 [Juvincourt], risky to go to Squeak 1 [Aguilcourt] but thought we should be quite safe in going to Ville-aux-Bois and Squeak 3.'

White proceeded to Ville-aux-Bois[18] and met up with Ruddock. He had already decided that it was out of the question to send a reconnaissance patrol to the gun position at Aguilcourt but had sent recovery groups to the remaining gun stations to collect stores and guns. However, he already had a problem as one of the essential towing vehicles had broken down around 10 km south of Berry-au-Bac.

Working in the dark, loading was eventually completed and the convoy moved to an assembly point south of the Aisne. Here they were joined by the second convoy, which had successfully recovered two guns. The convoys were ordered to return to the Regiment's new base, the last vehicles leaving at 2.30 am. Ahead of them lay a drive of over 100 km in the dark.

By now it was clear to White that it was dangerous to remain north of the Aisne. He rendezvoused with Ruddock south of the Berry-au-Bac bridge. The precariousness of their position was confirmed when the young subaltern reported that he had heard a tank moving up the main road at 2.00 am. White ordered him to set up a sentry at the Cormicy–Aguilcourt crossroads on the road north to Berry and to turn back any of the Regiment's vehicles heading towards the river crossing.

White left for the Troyes area at 3.00 am. Four hours later, at 7.00 am, he reported to Krohn and recommended that no further efforts be made to recover either guns or stores from 158's gun stations as there were no French patrols in the area. It was also decided to recall Ruddock and his small group. Having submitted his report, White immediately turned round and made the four hour journey back to the crossroads where Ruddock and four men were still manning the check point south of Berry.[19] It must have been around 1 o'clock in the afternoon before they eventually rejoined the Regiment, eighteen hours after they had originally set off.

MISSING PATROL

What Major White had not realised was that a number of his men had yet to return. The 159 Battery war diary, a curiously dry document compared with the others in the Brigade and Regiment, has a chilling single line entry:

> 19.5.40   2/Lt. Snowdon and party not yet returned.

No further mention is made of the group. Did they return safely? Were they posted missing? What happened? The Diary remains silent. Surely the Battery was interested in the fate of their comrades?[20] The Brigade Diary, although also brief, does convey some of the drama:

> 19.5.40   09.00
> Reported that some parties who had been sent back to the REIMS area had not

returned. All later reported except 2 Lt. Snowdon, 6 men and REV HOBLING.

Fortunately, an appendix included in the 53rd's Diary contains a full report covering one and a half pages on the fate of Snowdon and his men. This was based on an eyewitness account given to Capt. Estlin of the RAOC.

At around 7.00 pm on the 19th, the day on which Snowdon was reported missing, Estlin stopped a British Army truck on the Reims–Épernay road. The vehicle had been looted by a group of refugees who were using it to escape south. Estlin took the vehicle, a Leyland lorry, and the refugees to the *Gendarmerie* at Épernay. There the man who appeared to be their leader recounted that at around 2.00 pm on the 18th between twelve and fifteen German infantry troops arrived in Amifontaine on bicycles. They were armed with rifles and revolvers but were a rag-tag bunch. They were poorly clothed and extremely hungry. They forced the inhabitants to hand over food, which they then ate, sitting on the pavement.

At around 6.00 pm on the 19th a British truck appeared with six or seven troops on board. The Germans fired two shots at it and then took the men prisoner. The British soldiers were clearly taken by surprise and didn't, or were unable to, return fire. The Mayor of Amifontaine was taken prisoner at the same time. Estlin noted the lorry's identification number and it was clear that this was one of the two lorries assigned to 2nd Lt. Snowdon.

Snowdon had been dispatched to the 158 Battery area with an NCO and twelve men in two lorries. However, to get to Amifonatine, Snowdon's group would have had to pass through the check point set up by 2nd Lt. Ruddock. Why hadn't the sentry prevented them from crossing the Aisne?

It transpired that whenever enemy aircraft were overhead Ruddock's sentry was ordered by French pickets to leave the main road and take cover. It was therefore assumed that Snowdon and his men passed the sentry post during one of these periods.[21]

The 53rd suffered a second blow that day: 'It must furthermore be reported that Captain J.C. Hobling, the regimental chaplain, is missing.' Hobling had been extremely anxious to assist in the operation to recover 158th's guns and, as none of the battery officers was available, it was agreed that he should travel to Nogent-sur-Seine, 50 km from the regiment's new positions at Troyes. There he was to collect two towing vehicles and escort them to Berry-au-Bac. In the event, Hobling failed to make contact with the towing vehicles, but did not report this to his commanding officer.

The regiment realised that the situation north of the Aisne was becoming dangerous and decided that the towing vehicles at Nogent should be brought back to headquarters rather than heading north beyond Berry-au-Bac. A dispatch rider was sent to tell Hobling but failed to find him. Just how Hobling came to be captured was unknown but it was assumed that, like Snowdon, he drove through the crossroads checkpoint without being challenged while the sentry was sheltering from enemy aircraft. He then must have crossed the Aisne, unaware of the risks in doing so, and run into an enemy patrol.

Both Snowdon and Hobling were desperately unlucky. The extent of their misfortune was revealed by the account given by the escaping refugees to Capt. Estlin. Between 10.00 and 11.00 on the 19th another British lorry went through Amifontaine but no Germans were about. At around 2.00 pm on the same day, two light lorries carrying German troops had again gone through the village but they did not appear to be armed.

It was at this point that the refugees decided it was time to get out. Snowdon's abandoned vehicle gave them the opportunity to escape. They climbed aboard the lorry at around 3.30 pm and drove south. They crossed the Aisne about an hour later and, although they had heard some gunfire, they had not seen any German troops.

The commandant of the Chasseurs à Pied guarding the Aisne crossing had indicated that the front line was very fluid on 18 and 19 May. It was the misfortune of both recovery parties that, by chance, they encountered enemy troops. But was Snowdon's party careless? Despite all the evidence and warnings that enemy troops were in the area, the refugees reported that their Bren Gun stand was mounted but the gun was not on it. They confirmed that the British troops did not return

'Our beloved Padre' Rev. Capt. Joseph Hobling, captured 19 May 1940. Tragically, Hobling died when the POW camp in which he was held, Stalag XVIII was bombed by Allied aircraft in late 1944.
© Ian Brown

fire. The Germans eventually left the village after dark, taking the Bren gun with them, but left the lorry.[22]

The capture of two officers and six men[23] must have been a big blow to the morale of the regiment. The 53rd's diary recorded that 'their loss is deeply regretted' and Lt. Col. Krohn referred to the loss of 'our beloved Padre, Capt. the Rev. Hobling'.[24] The news even reached Charles Gardner in Paris. Tragically, Hobling did not survive the war.

2nd Lt. Snowdon commanded Alfred's section, his signature frequently appearing at the end of letters censored by him. Alfred wrote later that among the captured men were 'some of my friends, including Winnie de Castle and "Scruffy Crombie".'[25]

REORGANISATION

Despite the trauma of the previous few days the Brigade had to move on but its plans were in shreds. The Operation Order issued in the heat of the air raids on 14 May assumed that seventeen of the 53rd's complement of guns would be deployed to defend five airfields in the Troyes area.[26] At 6.00 pm on 18 May the Brigade discovered that only four of the regiment's twenty-four guns could be put into action.

Brigadier Crewdson's fury on discovering this can be gauged from the Brigade Diary, which tersely reported: 'in 53 HAA Regt orders regarding guns which had to be abandoned ... had been somewhat exceeded. Although breech blocks had been removed according to op. order No.1 in most other cases dials had been smashed ... It was therefore unlikely that more than four guns of this Regt. could be put into action with any rapidity.'[27]

The Operation Order was crystal clear. If guns had to be abandoned 'breech blocks and instruments will be removed and evacuated'.[28] The fact that 158 Battery had been forced to abandon six guns was not the issue. 157 and 159 Batteries had followed Krohn's Movement Order but it seems he had misinterpreted Crewdson's instructions. The Brigade Diary did not mince words: the two batteries had exceeded orders. 53rd HAA were in deep trouble with the Brigade.

The 73rd HAA, on the other hand, based south of the 53rd, had achieved the objective of the withdrawal. It was completely intact with all its men, guns stores and ammunition.

53 HAA were to pay a heavy price for their mistake.

ENDNOTES

1   Gardner, p. 164.
2   ibid., p.168.
3   ibid., p. 166, and AAL marginal comment.
4   Gardner, pp. 166–7.
5   AAL 19.05.40.
6   AAL 20.05.1940.
7   NA, WO 167/617.
8   NA, WO 167/443/182.
9   NA, WO 167/617.
10 ibid.
11 NA, WO 167/617 and NA 167/443/182.
12 NA, WO 167/443/182.
13 Gardner, p. 186.
14 Gardner, p. 167, AAL margin comment.
15 NA, WO 167/617.
16 ibid.
17 ibid.
18 Ville-aux-au-Bois-les-Pontavert.
19 NA, WO 167/617, appendix.
20 The 159th battery war diary is typed whereas most of the others are handwritten in pencil. It is possible that parts or the entire original document were lost and the diary recreated when the Regiment had returned to England.
21 NA, WO 167/617.
22 NA, WO 167/617 and appendix, report 20.05.1940.
23 NA, WO 167/443/182.
24 NA, WO 167/617, appendix, Special Order, 21.06.1940.
25 Gardner, p. 144 and AAL margin comment.
26 at Gaye, Allemanche, St. Lucien Ferme, Echemines and Faux Villecerf.
27 NA, WO 167/443/182.
28 NA, WO 167/617, appendix, Brigade ops. order No.1, p.4.

8
REORGANISATION AND NANTES

Sunday 19 May 1940 had been disastrous for 12 AA Brigade. The 73rd was still intact but the 53rd was reduced to just four operational guns; in the chaos of the withdrawal six had been abandoned and the instruments for fourteen others had been deliberately damaged, rendering the guns ineffective. For the moment at least, the Regiment had virtually ceased to exist as a fighting force. There was still very little definite news and great uncertainty as to whether or not the AASF would remain in the Troyes area. This must have caused great concern within the Brigade as the move 'had revealed the extreme immobility of the AA defences'.

12 AA BRIGADE REORGANISED

Brigadier Crewdson's reaction to this apparently calamitous situation was decisive but severe. The loss of two officers and six men had been reported to him at 9.00 but he quickly moved on and by 10.30 he and his staff were discussing proposals to convert the Brigade into a mobile force. Crewdson had already given instructions for a new allotment of tasks 'in view of the state of guns of 53 Rgt'. These were produced and also discussed.[1]

Crewdson's proposals were quickly approved by the AASF and a conference of unit commanders was called at 4.00 am.

Lt. Col. Krohn must have approached the conference with apprehension. The Regiment's war diary succinctly described the situation: '53 HAA Regiment, through no fault of its own, had lost 6 out of its 24 guns. 73 HAA Regiment which occupied the southernmost positions in the Reims area was intact. 53 HAA Regiment must therefore suffer for the good of the whole AASF.'

It must have been a crushing moment for Krohn. His opinion wasn't sought. He was told that his Regiment was to be split, 'one battery [158] to be transferred complete, together with 4 guns and the most modern instruments in [the] possession of the Regiment'. And it didn't stop there. The 53rd was to be raided by transferring 181 officers and men together with forty-one vehicles to the 73rd so that all anti-aircraft units in the AASF could be brought up to a higher establishment level.[2]

The final blow then fell. The dejection of the Regimental diarist can be felt when he records: '53 HAA Regiment, shorn of 158 Bty, 8 officers and 173 O[ther] R[anks]s and the best part of its instruments and transport, was to proceed to NANTES for its defence, with 14 guns, none of which was effectively ready for action … RHQ, 157 and 159 Btys were to prepare for departure on 21.5.40.'

THE 53RD MOVE TO NANTES

The die was cast and, once again, however aggrieved the Regiment might have felt, they knuckled down and planned for their departure to Nantes on the Loire, 50 km from the Atlantic coast. Krohn immediately called a conference of his senior officers and an urgent message was sent recalling Maj. White, CO 158th Battery, who was still up in the Berry-au-Bac area. It must have been a shock to be told on his return that his battery had been transferred to 73 HAA while the rest of the Regiment was moving immediately to Nantes.

Simultaneously, one officer and seventy other ranks from the 7th Searchlight Battery were attached to the 53rd.[3]

The following day the 53rd's equipment was loaded on to rail freight wagons at Rouilly and Geraudot stations in the Troyes area, the Brigade diary noting that 'as usual the 3-inch guns were a great difficulty but fine work by subaltern officers succeeded in completing the task'. After the Brigade's overt criticism of the 53rd, was the diarist throwing a bone to the much reduced Regiment?

Throughout the day on 21 May 1940 the trains moving the Regiment's heavy equipment left for Nantes, the last departing at 10.00 pm. Road convoys left at the same time.

Once again, moving a large military unit across wartime France was painfully slow. Travelling south from the Troyes area and west of Paris, it took the Regiment two days to reach Nantes, a distance of around 500 km. The journey must have been exhausting. The trains carrying the guns and equipment arrived in the early hours of the morning of the 23rd and the road convoys during the course of the day.[4] The 53rd had been at Troyes for just five days.

NANTES

The Regiment now came under the command of the Nantes Base Sub-Area. It immediately set up headquarters at the Château de la Lombarderie and a camp was established in the grounds for the troops. The accommodation consisted of tents and marquees, the latter prized for being less claustrophobic and 'consequently we have more light, air and room and are not continually treading on one another's kit or persons!'

It does seem extraordinary that so many chateaux were readily available for occupation in France in 1940. The Chateau was set in a park full of fine trees, which clearly brought considerable pleasure to Alfred, revealing what was to become a lifelong love of trees and woodland landscape. 'Nearby are some glorious old oak, beech and pine trees… There are also some fine chestnuts.' However, the realist in him observed that it seemed a shame to clutter the landscape with 'such uninspiring and unnatural things as tents – but we are glad of their natural camouflage'.[5]

There was no respite for the Regiment. The two remaining batteries were immediately deployed either side of the River Loire flowing through the centre of the city. Three gun stations were posted north of the river, three to the south, all within 5 km of the city centre. Whether they were effective at this moment is a moot point as the guns were without instruments and the Regiment had been sent to Nantes so that its guns could be repaired in the RA workshops.

RETURN OF LEAVE PARTY

However, within twenty-four hours, the diminished 53rd received a much needed boost to its morale. The chaotic evacuation from the Reims area found one hundred men on leave in England. Alfred wrote to Marjorie that 'they were "lost" as far as we were concerned'.[6] After much delay, they rejoined the Regiment, the war diary noting with some surprise that the group 'included not only the 53 HAA leave party – 4 officers and 96 ORs – but the entire 12 HAA Bde leave party'.

The opening of hostilities and the move to the Troyes area had meant that these men had been unable to rejoin the Regiment. The pithy report in the war dairy makes no mention of the difficulties, which the group had to overcome in order to rejoin the Regiment.

The reality was chaos within the BEF. A.G. Shaw, a gunner in 157th Battery, recounted what happened in a letter to a friend:

On returning we found we could not get back to Reims as parts of the line had been bombed and smashed. Our luck – for as you will see we had the most extraordinary luck all the way – started at Cherbourg for the troop train immediately preceding ours was hit and there were many casualties. So we detrained and waited a few days, sleeping in the station at night and during the day visiting the cafés and other places and lounging on the shore (when we could get out).

Then we moved to Le Mans staying for some ten days in a barracks there. Day by day as the remnants of many regiments struggled in we waited, expecting every moment to be attached to an anti-tank or infantry unit and sent up north, for this happened to thousands including such branches as the RAOC and SC. Meanwhile, many afternoons were spent canoeing and bathing in the river – the Sarthe – just as we used to bathe and punt on the Granta!

It was a fantastic state of affairs for our Regiment was in action all [the] time we were there, we learnt afterwards, and it accounted for fifty or sixty planes in ten days. Apart from continual raid alarms (but no bombing) … we had a pleasant time. Hundreds of refugees passed through each day.

Next we moved to Nantes, where the whole of the stranded leave party were split up and attached to various units [of the 53rd].[7]

Shaw's account confirms the maxim that war is mostly boredom interspersed by occasional moments of extreme fear. It also illustrates the chaos that ensued when Germany launched its double strike through the Low Countries and the Ardennes. Despite all the intelligence indicating that massive German troop formations were assembling close to the French and Luxembourg borders the BEF did not cancel leave until the day before the German attack and the 53rd, with one hundred men absent back at home, found itself more than 15 per cent under strength just at the moment when they were needed to defend the AASF airfields.

CHAOTIC REORGANISATION

The arrival of the two leave parties reinforces the impression of chaos. It was a welcome boost to morale when the two groups arrived but many of the officers and men were in the wrong place and had to be reassigned. Some went to the two batteries now based in Nantes, the remainder needed to catch up either with 12 Brigade HQ or with 158 Battery who had moved to Tours, also on the Loire but 200 km east.

The 53rd's diary for the next five days records nothing other than a blur of men and officers moving between units. The reorganisation of the Regiment meant that the Motor Transport section was disbanded and Alfred and Rupert were redeployed to gun stations and 'a section completely new to us although of course we know all the personnel'.[8]

There appears to have been an element of opportunism involved as a number of personnel were switched from units at Tours to the 53rd – 2nd Lt. Lord Moynihan should have rejoined 158 Battery but was moved to the 157th, one officer and forty-three ORs from 7 Searchlight Battery were to be attached to the Regiment 'at least for the present'.

It was an encouraging moment when, on the 25 May, five officers and seventy-six other ranks arrived 'for re-equipment purposes'. This was E Battery, RA (Field) Base Depot, the unit assigned to repair the 53rd's guns and instruments. Four days later the repair unit departed, presumably having completed its work, 'apparently to be disbanded and return to No.1 [General Base Depot] D'.

Twenty-four hours later the war diary entry for 30 May consists of a single line: 'E Battery above now not to be disbanded'. The following day another single line entry noted: '3 officers and 27 ORs previously attached to 73 HAA return here once more'. So troops were being aimlessly moved from Nantes to Tours and back again. Nothing more eloquently illustrates the chaos that reigned at Brigade HQ.[9]

OPERATION DYNAMO, EVACUATION FROM DUNKIRK

However, this was nothing compared to developments 700 km to the north in the Pas de Calais. At the same time as the surprise arrival of the two leave parties on 24 May, German forces were sweeping west through Belgium and the north of France and making rapid progress towards the Channel. British forces were forced to evacuate Boulogne and were being shelled in Calais.

By chance, documents captured on the 24 May revealed that the German plan was to cut off the British forces from the sea. The situation was desperate. Churchill, Prime Minister for only fourteen days, and the commander of the BEF, General Lord Gort, realised that retreat to the Channel was the only option remaining. That evening, the order was issued for the evacuation by sea of as many soldiers as possible. Operation Dynamo, the code name

General Lord Gort, commander of the BEF and Air Vice Marshall Blount, commanding the Air Component. Gort was a controversial choice. A highly decorated officer, holder of the VC, DSO and Bar and MC, he did not enjoy the full support of his Corps commanders.
Wikimedia Commons – IWM, O 177

given to the Dunkirk evacuation, had begun.[10]

For the population at home the grim truth was dawning – the United Kingdom was in grave danger. Robert Angel wrote in his diary the day before Operation Dynamo was launched:

The position of the Allies, both England and France, is at the present moment in extreme danger and the outcome of the great battle which is proceeding is doubtful. Parliament has issued an order, taking full control of ALL persons, property, banks and all other resources. Any person or building may be commandeered as and when such are required. Industries, especially when engaged on war work, are to work 7 days a week and overtime when required. The Labour leaders are solidly behind the Govt. and trade unions also.[11]

Whether the troops in Nantes were aware of the disaster enfolding to the north is a moot point. While still at Troyes they were received no outside news and the move to Nantes does not seem to have improved matters. The entire Regiment, including the officers, seems to have been in the same boat. Where previously outside events had been recorded in the war diary, no mention is made of developments at Dunkirk, entries merely describing movements of personnel and refurbishing of the guns.

Amazingly, however, post continued to be accepted and Alfred was once again able to smuggle to Marjorie, right under the nose of the censor, details of his whereabouts:

> **N**o doubt you have discovered …
>
> **A**t the moment I among some of the lucky ones …
>
> **N**earby are some glorious old oak, beech and pine trees …
>
> **T**he roadside, likewise, is looking extremely beautiful …
>
> **E**vidently I have caused you not a little misapprehension …
>
> **S**o, at long last, …

The officer censoring the letter, Capt. A.R.V. Barker, deleted two words in the first sentence of the code: 'No doubt you have discovered from my last PC that I have been sent [redacted] [redacted] and my first impression of our present temporary position', but ironically he didn't spot the hidden scheme.[12]

Alfred wrote to Marjorie on 25 May that he may have given her information that 'we have been told since is "verboten". So in case the letter is torn up here [this] is to let you know all's well.' His concern was confirmed when he was interviewed by the censor officer, Capt. Barker. Whether Alfred sought the interview or was summoned is unclear but it was a friendly chat. At the same time the apparently trivial nature of his transgression illustrates the stress of wartime. Alfred explained: 'it all arose out of the fact that I had used the pronoun "we" instead of "I"'. Barker felt that correcting the letter was 'too complicated and suggested that it would be better to destroy it'.

Alfred knew he had had a narrow escape and was contrite. 'It just shows you how easy it is to slip up and that's the last thing I want to do.'[13]

LIFE AT NANTES

Once back at the battery life reverted to heavy manual duty. This time it was not 'all the digging and hut construction … as we are back to tent life again'. To Alfred's chagrin the work involved tree felling. 'A pity it had to be done as they were all fruit trees (cherries, apples and pears) of a fair size and age. They were all laden with fruit but mostly very immature.'

The reason was simple – to provide clear sight lines for the guns but the process will have been heavy-handed. No doubt the landowners were told the reason but they would not have had any choice. There was no question where Alfred's sympathies lay. 'The poor old girl that owns [the trees] seems somewhat perturbed but it's just got to be done for safety's sake.'[14] On this occasion Alfred used a euphemism to avoid spelling out the true reason, thus avoiding the censor's blue pen.

The tree felling was presumably due to 159 Battery becoming active once more. The war diary records that on 27 May '2nd Lt. P.E. Belson and 65 O.R.s occupy 159 bty. 3 gun position 5 km WNW of Nantes.' The following day 157th Battery similarly deployed 3 guns, east-south-east of Nantes.[15] The neutering of the 53rd was now fully apparent. Instead of their full complement of twenty-four guns defending airfields occupied by the AASF squadrons, they were reduced to providing anti-aircraft defence for Nantes with just six guns.

Nantes is over 600 km south-west of Dunkirk and the contrast between the circumstances of the 53rd and the disaster unfolding in Flanders could not have been more stark. Alfred reported that 'Life goes on here quite pleasantly and undisturbed' and that they were 'taking things easy'. In fact 'there's very little to be done'. Spit and polish had become things of the past 'until someone wakes up to the fact that we have time to do it'. In fact the work required by the army's insistence on smartly turned out troops never bothered Alfred. He realised it was part of the discipline needed to ensure an efficient fighting unit and only bemoaned that some of his comrades in Nantes took advantage of the relaxation 'to become slovenly again'.

All the same, the rapid escape from the Reims region and then Troyes meant that the troops did suffer privations. By the time the Regiment reached Nantes Alfred's 'only ambition was to enjoy a bath'. He had not had one for over two weeks.[16]

NEW ROUTINE

While life in Nantes may have settled into a routine not dissimilar to that in Épernay during the Phoney War, it was more rigorous. Alfred's elder brother, Alan, Rupert's twin, was in Kenya and had volunteered for the Kenya Defence Force. Marjorie told Alfred that, in a letter home, Alan moaned he had to get up 4.00 am so as to have a bath before the daily parade. His complaint wasn't so much the unsociable hour as the fact it was too early to expect his servant to run the water. Alfred was highly amused. 'I can well imagine him cursing and swearing at having to carry out such menial tasks as filling his own bath.' By contrast, 4.00 am reveille was late compared with army life in France. Even during routine manning the gunners were woken at 3.30 am. It meant that they never had an uninterrupted night's sleep.[17]

The weather was very hot and it was proving difficult to work in the middle of the day. The solution devised was to rise even earlier, carry out gun drills and then parade at 4.30 am for work details, and then work through until 12.30 when lunch was served, with breaks for breakfast, 'washing and shaving', and a half hour break at 10.45. After lunch the men were free to relax although this must have proved difficult as they were not allowed to leave the gun stations. A final work period from 6.30 to 7.45 ended the day.

Despite early doubts, Alfred found the new regime to his liking. Previously he had found it 'rather trying working with the sun just pouring down mercilessly'.

The relaxed atmosphere may have been influenced by the fact that 159 Battery was located 'among private plots of land'. The local inhabitants were able to walk past the guns and tents, and unsurprisingly the Battery was the centre of attention. Alfred commented to Marjorie that she might think he had become a 'pansy soldier' as he had been able to buy strawberries, which he had for tea. It was an extraordinary contrast with what was hitting 'the poor blighters in Flanders'.[18]

However inadequate the defences provided by the 53rd, albeit in its reduced state, their arrival provided some relief to Nantes, which had been without anti-aircraft defence 'for some weeks past. So far as warnings are concerned we are entirely dependent on French sources. The French themselves have a few machine gun stations, nothing more.' Communications with the French military had yet to be established.[19] The lack of confidence is palpable, especially as during the day, 3 June, three warnings were received of approaching aircraft.

By now, in Flanders, the encirclement of the British Expeditionary Force was complete. Boulogne and Calais had fallen and the desperate evacuation of the BEF from Dunkirk was in full swing. The war diary noted on 3 June that 'the BEF has largely been evacuated from the Flanders zone' and a day later: 'Evacuation from Flanders complete. 335,000 British and French troops evacuated to UK. 30,000 British casualties; also 1,000 guns and most [motor transport] lost.'

The scale of the disaster had clearly been briefed to the media and broadcast but, despite the perils facing the Regiment, the diarist shows not a flicker of emotion.

Operation Dynamo. The desperate evacuation of the BEF from Dunkirk is caught in the image of soldiers firing small arms at armoured Stuka bombers.
Wikimedia Commons – Australian War Memorial Database, 101171

But what did the men know? Alfred had complained to Marjorie that the one thing they lacked was news. They had been unable to set up a radio and received no newspapers. The hunger for hard information is illustrated when Alfred wrote on 20 May 'I understand one has been purchased today and I must try to get hold of it. Already the thousand and one rumours that we are bound to get have been allayed by its purchase and the fact that we have already got some news in 'black and white' does a lot to towards relieving the anxiety through its lack'.[20] Later the soldiers were reduced to what they could glean from local villagers and 'that's meagre and often doubtful'. The result was that they knew 'practically nothing that is going on'.[21]

WORRIES OF LIFE AT HOME

It was not until the 6.00 pm news on 3 June that Alfred learned of the Dunkirk evacuation. It was the first firm information he had received in three weeks and it came as a tremendous shock. He wrote to Marjorie that 'We certainly are passing through a grave and anxious time and I only hope it doesn't get you down too much.' He marvelled at Marjorie's grit and courage but admitted that 'we have definitely lost the first [round]' and bitterly regretted that 'the lesson has been bought in the loss of thousands of our brave men'. Despite this, his determination was undimmed: 'Never has there been a war such as this but now we fully realise what we are up against ... and what has to be done.' He likened Hitler's success in Flanders to Napoleon's march on Moscow: 'When he arrived back in France he couldn't exactly say he had returned victorious.'

He ends by urging Marjorie to 'take care of yourself and keep smiling and as cheerful as possible'.[22]

Underlying Alfred's concerns for Marjorie and 'the folks at home' was the knowledge of what ferocious bombing could do. He wished Marjorie was out of harm's way and dreaded the possibility of London being bombed. He realised it could happen, and advised Marjorie what to do. 'Now my darling, I don't want to put the wind up you or frighten you in any way' – but he had seen the results of bombing and he proceeded to dispense some advice: the benefits of 'proper' air-raid shelters to provide maximum protection 'apart from an unfortunate direct hit', 'failing that, a trench sufficiently deep to squat down in and no wider that two feet six ... or even a ditch'. He continued by breezily explaining that injury was caused by blast or concussion. 'I have seen chickens still alive and scratching about within six feet of ... a crater', which he took as proof that the nearer you are to the ground 'the greater the chance of coming away with simply a shaking. If a human being had been standing up in the same place as the chickens I don't suppose he would be alive to tell the tale.'

It's tempting to suggest that his advice had the opposite effect to that intended. At the same time, it is important to remember that Alfred and his colleagues were subjected to the terror of bombing when they were based around Épernay and he would have witnessed the dreadful results. In this context it is understandable that, while trying to give advice to Marjorie, he unintentionally erred on the dramatic side.

POSSIBILITY OF ANOTHER MOVE AND MORE CONFUSION

Despite his brave sentiments it was a desperately low moment. On 4 June Paris had been bombed, with 'a number of civilian casualties'[23] and the Regiment was still in France with the victorious German Army to the north. It didn't take a genius to work out that they would soon turn their attention to the rest of France.

With the BEF evacuated from Flanders it was more urgent than ever that gun sites were ready. Tours, just 200 kms upstream on the Loire, was bombed on 6 June[24] and an attack on Nantes must have been expected at any time. Unbeknown to Alfred and Rupert who were still busily cutting down trees – huge chestnuts, the work 'more interesting still, if a little more precarious' – the Regiment was told by telephone at 7.00 pm on 6 June to prepare to move at short notice 'in the direction of a Southern port'.

The speed of the German advance clearly instigated a rapid change of plans. Confusion reigned, or was it panic? Two reasons had been given for splitting the 53rd and moving the rump to Nantes: access to the artillery repair workshops, and the anti-aircraft defence of the city.

Immediately after noting the phone alert to prepare for a move the war diary states 'it was further learned that in fact the Regiment was still part of 12 AA Brigade and was only 'on loan' for [the] defence of Nantes'. It seems that this news was yet another surprise.

Only twenty-four hours before, on 6 June, at a conference at HQ Nantes Base Sub-Area, Krohn had been appointed Air Defence Commander of Nantes and given the news that one 3.7-inch battery and four Bofors guns would be arriving within forty-eight hours.

Although it is not recorded in the diary it would seem that the phone call from Brigade HQ had involved an argument. The reason quickly becomes apparent. The mystery destination was 'in the region of MARSEILLES almost 500 miles distant from NANTES'. The move from Troyes to Nantes had involved an exhausting forty-eight-hour journey, the men accommodated in cattle trucks. Marseille was nearly twice the distance.

The 53rd command appears to have found it difficult to understand these latest orders and the diarist must have been instructed to record:

> It may here be stated that the 3.7-inch Bty and the 4 Bofors guns above referred to are not now (at least for the time being) coming to Nantes. This very important Base will therefore be temporarily defenceless against Air Attack. (Its importance being all the greater since HAVRE and CHERBOURG have been bombed.)

The doubts of the 53rd's senior commanders about the wisdom of the move to Marseille are tangible.[25]

For the third time, the 53rd found itself forced move at short notice. And once again, despite the deteriorating military situation, the administrative machine moved efficiently into action. A conference of senior officers was immediately called and in little over 12 hours, on 7 June, movement Order 5/26/1 had been issued.

The following morning, at 6.00 am, Lt. Col. Krohn, the adjutant, and one officer from each of the two remaining batteries set off for Avignon by road en route to Salon-de-Provence, 50 km north-west of Marseille.[26]

ENDNOTES

1   NA, WO 167/617.
2   NA, WO 167/370 Appendix.
3   NA, WO 167/617.
4   ibid.
5   AAL 25.05.1940.
6   AAL 27.05.1940.
7   IWM, Documents.18817. Shaw papers (Letter 26.07.1940 written from Dulwich to P I de K Rainey, a friend at Haileybury and then Cambridge).
8   AAL 27.05.1940.
9   NA, WO 167/617.
10 Gilbert, pp. 649–50.
11 RJA 23.05.1940.
12 AAL 25.05.1940.
13 AAL 29.05.1940.
14 AAL 27.05.1940.
15 NA, WO 167/617.
16 AAL 30.05.1940.
17 AAL 29.05.1940.
18 AAL 02.06.1940.

19 NA, WO 167/617. The French 75mm anti-aircraft gun was old, based on a design of 1897. Despite this it was a remarkably effective weapon. By the 1930s, however, it was recognised that higher velocities were needed and a programme was instituted to retrofit new Schneider barrels. Construction of the Maginot Line starved the French Army of funds and by 1940 only 192 were in service. (*Encyclopedia of Weapons of World War II*, books.google.co.uk, visited 18.01.16).

20 AAL 20.05.1940.

21 AAL 30.05.1940.

22 AAL 03.06.1940.

23 NA, WO 167/617.

24 ibid.

25 Disappointingly, the 12 AA Brigade war diary pages between 01.06.1940 and 17.06 1940 are missing, so it is impossible to know the Brigade's perspective.

26 NA, WO 167/617.

9

MEANWHILE, ON THE HOME FRONT...

INFORMATION TREATED WITH SCEPTICISM

Back at home, the population received news from the BBC and newspapers. Marjorie recognised Churchill as more 'the bull-dog type' than Chamberlain, but she was also aware of his reputation for reckless haste: 'I hope he won't be too much of a dare-devil and get us into scrapes.'[1] She was sympathetic towards Chamberlain but acknowledged that Churchill was more fitted to be a wartime leader, writing to Alfred on 11 May: 'I think Churchill is far more of a fighter and will give the Germans no quarter.'[2] It is interesting that she used this phrase, as it was not typical of her. Churchill did not deliver his 'blood, toil, tears and sweat' speech to the House of Commons until two days after her letter so it is fair to deduce that it indicates the level of defiance that prevailed at home.

Winston Churchill, 1940. Appointed Prime Minister on 10 May, within days he was confronted by the realisation that the BEF, the bulk of the British Army, was encircled and ordered their evacuation from Dunkirk. Wikimedia Commons – IWM, H2646A

Marjorie had a healthy scepticism about news bulletins that were subject to censorship. Sympathising with Alfred over his lack of 'real and correct news', she commented, 'if there is any difference! … To get rumours only must be awful, and if I read that something dreadful has happened – or more so if I hear it – I always hope it is only a rumour until I'm fully convinced by "official confirmation".'[3]

For example, Marjorie was full of admiration for the fierce resistance of the Dutch forces but realised that official reports should be treated with care: 'Just fancy Holland bringing 100 Nazi planes down! And Germany losing about 200 altogether yesterday! (If that is true of course!).'[4] Paradoxically, the reports she read understated the success of the Dutch forces thus demonstrating the difficulties encountered by the government itself in obtaining accurate information. The actual numbers were ninety-six aircraft lost to Dutch anti-aircraft fire with 172 Junkers 52s destroyed or damaged.[5] All too often the authorities were in the dark themselves.

The Ministry of Information naively expected the media to be 'the shock absorbers' which shielded the British public from the grave reality confronting them. It turned out that many people shared Marjorie's scepticism. Opinion surveys secretly carried out by the Ministry revealed that the confidence of the public in the accuracy of news sources had been undermined. In early 1940, newspapers took matters into their own hands, *The Times* and others printing three communiqués side by side – British, French and German.[6]

MORALE AND RUMOUR

Charles Gardner observed that morale in the country was getting low. 'Despair was written on nearly all the faces in the streets. Practically everyone had a loved one or a friend in that hopeless battlefield, and the best that could be hoped for him was that he would be taken a prisoner of war. The country was facing the most disastrous loss in its history and was badly shaken up.'[7]

In the absence of confirmed news the rumour mill thrived, the atmosphere neatly encapsulated by the Rev. F.E. Jones, vicar of Wood Green, who recited a cautionary tale from his pulpit:

My aunt's charwoman's sister says
She heard a policeman on his beat

Say to a nursemaid down our street,

That he knew a man who had a friend

And could tell when the war would end.[8]

A casual encounter between Marjorie's father, Robert Angel, and a complete stranger on 30 May illustrates the point: 'Last night Pops met a man somewhere on a bus who told him he had seen crowds of worn-out and dirty troops – but still cheerful – coming up through Surrey from Flanders, the first to arrive back.'[9]

Gardner eloquently captures the moment when 'filtering up from our south coast came the first rumours of soldiers coming home. People spoke of boat-load after boat-load of troops landing at Dover. On railway stations one caught glimpses of packed trains hurtling along … Hopes began to rise again.'[10]

Exhausted troops at Dover, June 1940.
Wikimedia Commons – IWM, H 1647

The fact was that in an effort to maintain morale the full extent of the disaster unfolding in Flanders was kept from the British people for five days, by which time three quarters of the troops trapped in the Dunkirk pocket were safe. Between 26 and 30 May special trains were seen in the south and the Midlands, crammed with exhausted troops 'and yet the secret was kept'. Even some members of the government didn't know.

Part of the reason was that no journalists were at Dunkirk and the government received the 'willing and patriotic cooperation' of the press. Censorship did not need to be imposed; it was voluntarily accepted.[11]

It was not until 31 May that Marjorie 'heard on the wireless [that troops] had arrived at [Waterloo] and Mr Steele said he had seen them there and didn't know what the motley crowd was.'[12]

In fact Operation Dynamo, the Dunkirk evacuation, had started on 27 May, by which time 28,000 troops had already left France. By the time of Robert Angel's encounter with the mysterious stranger on the bus the evacuation was in full swing – in the following three days, and in the face of furious German air attacks, more than 150,000 men had been rescued from Dunkirk harbour and the adjacent beaches.[13]

ANGUISH OF FAMILIES AND FRIENDS

However, the families of the men in the AASF were completely in the dark as to their fate. They received news from the media of the German attack into Belgium and Holland and the enemy's alarming progress, but while the country was made aware of the 'headline' news, they knew nothing of the individual units in which their family members and friends were serving.

On the day Germany launched its attack, 10 May, Marjorie wrote, 'So at long last the war has really started', and while she recognised that 'we knew perfectly well it would' it was a shock all the same. Her expectation was that, with the inevitable opening of fighting, then at least the hostilities would be over quickly. She speculated that if the waiting had lasted for years it 'would only have sent the country bankrupt so that when it did eventually begin we couldn't have carried on'.[14]

Like everyone else, Marjorie had no idea of the fate the AASF. However, the secret code agreed between her and Alfred did put her in a privileged, if risky, position. If the 53rd did move then Marjorie knew the details, albeit after a delay as Alfred's letters took time to be delivered.[15]

On 12 May 1940 she speculated that the Regiment had been forced to move on somewhere. 'How I wish I knew what your new arrangements are … I'm sorry to be such a worry, love, but I'm naturally anxious to know all about you.' She then reassures herself, and Alfred: 'But anyway we have our own method of communication in the event of a move, haven't we?'

Understandably, Marjorie would have been very concerned about the whereabouts of Alfred and the 53rd. This is the only explanation for her writing so candidly. In doing so, however, she risked drawing attention to their code. Alfred was subject to military discipline and the consequences for both of them, if the authorities discovered they were breaking censorship regulations, does not bear thinking about.

How did those at home reconcile themselves to the increasingly alarming developments? In Marjorie's case, it was by turning to mundane, every day events, such as describing a visit to the local cobbler to collect a pair of shoes: 'I must tell you about the funniest bill I have [had] to pay – 'Squeaks removed – 3d.'[16]

Now, however, her letters invariably open with speculation about Alfred's whereabouts and what he was doing:

11 May – I wonder what sort of night you had last night – not one of unbroken sleep, I bet.

12 May – I guess you are not able to snooze this Sunday afternoon but have got to be 'up and at' something or other. How I wish I knew what your new arrangements are.

13 May – I wonder where you are today, and what you are doing.

Thirty-five letters follow, all in a similar vein, Marjorie expressing concern for Alfred's safety and then writing up to five pages of unexciting home news – of the family and friends, the possibility of housing a refugee child, first aid lectures, a blackbird singing, shopping trips and so on.

COMPLACENCY AND RESENTMENT

Despite the catastrophe facing the country, many people did not grasp the ramifications of military defeat. The Ministry of Information had been formed with the declaration of war in

1939 to promote the national cause. Initially it was relatively ineffective and the conscious campaign to galvanise the population had not swung into action.

As mentioned in Chapter 5, an immediate result of the German invasion of the Low Countries was the cancellation of the Whitsun holiday. Far from understanding that the British army in northern France was now in great danger and that sacrifices would have to be made at home, the loss of a public holiday brought complaints. Marjorie wrote indignantly: 'It makes my blood boil when I hear people grumbling about the Whitsun holiday being cancelled. I think that is the least a man at home can do for those who are risking their lives at war for them, and if they are not satisfied let them change places with them and not only do without holidays and Sundays and evenings and every comfort but be in constant danger as well. The silly girls seem to be the worst offenders!'[17]

Eight days later Marjorie was annoyed to find two men cleaning the windows of the next door neighbour's house. 'It does make me mad when I see strong hefty fellows here doing nothing to help their country … why can't they join up? Surely we could have dirty windows for a few months without any harm being done,' adding sarcastically, 'Maybe [window cleaning] is a "reserved occupation".'[18]

It is clear that, in mid-1940, divisions could have opened up across the nation and it was, therefore, vital that a coordinated campaign was launched to overcome this. Campaigns such as 'Saucepans for Spitfires' and 'Dig for Victory'[19] weren't launched until July 1940.

POLITICAL DIVISIONS SET ASIDE

Churchill was appointed Prime Minister on 10 May 1940, the day of the German attack. Chamberlain was forced to resign because Attlee and his colleagues in the Labour Party refused to serve in a National Government 'under the present Prime Minister,' i.e. Chamberlain. However, they confirmed that they were prepared to serve under a new prime minister.[20]

The paradox was that Churchill was an equally divisive figure. As Home Secretary in the Liberal Government in November 1910 he was demonised by the Labour Party for involving troops against rioting miners who were on strike at Tonypandy in the Rhondda Valley. 'For Liberals, Tonypandy represented the success of moderation. For Labour it became part of a myth of Churchill's aggressiveness.'[21]

Churchill was aware of his reputation, especially as it wasn't just the Labour Party who were critical of him. During the Tonypandy Riots the Conservative opposition accused him of a lack of ruthlessness. In his broadcast to the nation on 19 May, his first since being appointed Prime Minister, he was at pains to emphasise the inclusiveness of the National Government: 'Having received His Majesty's commission, I have formed an administration of men and women of every party and of almost every point of view. We have differed and quarrelled in the past; but now one bond unites us all – to wage war until victory is won.'[22]

Many people were equally suspicious of the Labour Party. Marjorie felt that one of Churchill's qualities was that he could 'stand the strains and hecklings from Attlee and his friends'.[23] Churchill's broadcast clearly struck the right note with her, writing 'Did you hear Churchill last night in the 9 o'clock news? He was very good, and I certainly feel he has the power in his character that we want now.'[24]

CONSEQUENCES OF INACCURATE REPORTING

Prior to 16 May the British media had concentrated on events in Holland and Belgium. Unbeknown to the British public this resulted in a distortion of the news, with reports initially suggesting that the Allies had the upper hand. The reason for this was simple: the French authorities had offered British journalists little or no co-operation. However, on 16 May there was a sudden falling off of news about the BEF, and on the 17th the midnight Home Service News broadcast revealed that the situation was deteriorating rapidly.[25]

What the media failed to report was that the German advance had not been held up by the supposedly impregnable Maginot Line; they had simply ignored the fixed defences and gone round them. Intelligence reports reached London indicating an imminent French withdrawal. If this occurred it exposed the BEF to great danger. Churchill immediately flew to Paris hoping that his personal influence would prevent this. To his dismay, he found the French High Command completely demoralised and without any plans to counter-attack.[26]

Marjorie sensed things were getting worse, writing on 16 May: 'I don't know how things are. We are just waiting for the 1 o'clock news now. It is certain that we are up against a very formidable enemy and will have to fight very hard to win ... But I can't believe that evil will defeat good in the end ... Oh well, wait and see, as usual! Let's talk about fish'[27] and continuing over the next four pages with news of friends and family.

Later in the letter Marjorie repeated the information gleaned from the BBC 1 o'clock news. Blithely unaware of the distorted information that was being broadcast she felt it was encouraging. 'We seem to be doing pretty well against the devils, and I bet the Germans won't like the RAF bombing their precious country.'

At the same time, reality was beginning to sink in. 'It is terrible, though, to think of the tremendous battle that is going on now. It just doesn't bear thinking about.'[28]

NEWS BECOMES MORE ACCURATE – BUT MORE ALARMING

Eventually, information released became more candid. By 22 May, knowing that the 53rd was based at Épernay, she was all too aware of the risks when she heard and read the reports of the German break through at Sedan. So it was with relief that she learned the German push south had stopped 'for the time being at any rate. May it get no further.'

As the situation deteriorated the Government appealed for people to invest in War Bonds. Alfred had told Marjorie that he felt they ought to do this and on 23 May she transferred £100, commenting 'I feel we must help the government all we can just now' even though a neighbour had observed 'if we win we have our money still safe, and if we lose it will be gone whenever it is!'[29]

The string of reverses became increasingly alarming and Marjorie admitted her spirits were 'rising and falling like a barometer'.[30] Boulogne fell on 25 May, Marjorie feeling guilty that she was determined not to worry 'so long as [the Germans] don't suddenly shoot off south, and then I will!'[31]

Apprehension was spreading across the country. Marjorie reported that she had never seen her church so full on Sunday and wondered 'if every other church in England, Scotland, Wales, Ireland, Canada, Australia and New Zealand [was] packed like it. Every available space that would hold a chair had one – right up to the altar rail.' The service opened with the National Anthem and the congregation, which overflowed into the vestry, included people she had never seen in church before. She went to church again in the evening, once more finding it packed, and each evening in the following week when the names of serving soldiers were read out, 'yours among them!' and prayers offered.

The inevitable began to dawn on Marjorie. The situation was deteriorating in France and Alfred had mentioned in his letter of 11 May that he might be too busy to write but would resort to field service post cards.[32] This was hardly surprising. The 53rd had more pressing priorities, the War Diary entry opening 'Heavy bombardment of aerodromes … All of our positions in action.'[33] Marjorie, however, could not know this and wrote in exasperation:

'What a world this is! Got a husband and immediately he is claimed by his King and Country and whisked off out of sight and now he can't even write to his missus!'

The continuing flow of bad news must have caused her great anxiety as she begins to reveal her emotions: 'If we are separated in body they can never separate us in spirit, can they love? And I practically always feel your presence is with me even if I can't see and feel you actually ... I believe that is one of the rewards of perfect love. Perhaps it is the same thing as though not seeing God we know his presence is with us. Well, whatever, it is it is a great comfort these days.'[34]

By 27 May Marjorie was commenting: 'we are certainly having a terrible time at [the Germans'] hands [but] I try my best not to think too much about it. I know that is a coward's way out but to let oneself get "down" would only ... make things worse.'[35]

Despite the constant flow of alarming news her morale was boosted by the arrival of mail from Alfred on 31 May, a letter and field service postcard, even though the 'whizz bang' and letter had been written eight and eleven days earlier.

Despite the stress of not knowing what had happened to Alfred and his comrades Marjorie's letter once again shows her stoic sense of humour. Army field service postcards set out prescribed information and all that the sender could do was delete those statements that weren't relevant. So the message contained in the 'whizz bang' of 23 May merely told Marjorie:

I am quite well.

I am being sent down to the base.

Letter follows at first opportunity

Marjorie commented that she was 'absolutely in the dark over the meaning of being sent down to base. What it actually is – or what it means ... Anyway, I am anxiously – but patiently – waiting your next letter.'

WAR GETS CLOSER

By now the fighting in France was no longer a distant war, out of sight somewhere abroad. Sitting in the back garden at Claygate, close to Epsom, Marjorie could hear the sound of distant gunfire, 'from the French coast I suppose. All last week – during the battle of

Boulogne – it was constant … it sounded horrible – especially as the huge convoy was constantly passing through the road to Dorking, it made war seem very real.'[36] To put this into context, Claygate is around 160 km as the crow flies from Dunkirk.

By 17 June the outlook was grim. The Dunkirk evacuation had ended two weeks beforehand, German troops occupied Paris on 14 June and on the evening of 16 June the French Prime Minister, Paul Reynaud, resigned. Marshal Pétain formed a new government 'whose sole aim was to negotiate an armistice'.[37]

But Marjorie still had no news of Alfred. She must have been overwhelmed by worry. She had received two 'whizz bangs' on 14 and 15 June but they were each over a week old. Clutching at straws she had checked the postmarks: 'I think the first was posted on the 8th and the last on the 10th … At least it means that you are still – or <u>were</u> still – in the land of the living and "quite well", for which I am very thankful.'

While the delayed news was reassuring it also served to increase her concerns. Why was Alfred restricted to sending the postcards? Was he too busy to write, the inference being that he was in action? Was he on the move again?[38]

By 18 June her anguish came to a head and she wrote despairingly:

> My darling precious Beloved,
>
> I didn't write yesterday – the first time I have missed since you went back in January – because I didn't know where we stood, or what was going to happen! Oh what a day it was! Every blessed thing that was awful seemed to happen [so] that in the end I began to wonder if I was having a nightmare! I thought that maybe – if France really had definitely given up fighting – the BEF that was [would be] able to leave France, just as they did over Belgium, and I hoped and hoped that you would be one of the lucky ones to escape. So in view of that fact, and the other awful thought that if you didn't get out, but were captured by the Germans instead, I decided it was useless to write, and I never for a moment thought that any more boats would take letters over. But this morning things looked a bit different in view of the French army continuing to fight so here I am just chancing to luck that you will get this.

In a classic understatement, typical of her, Marjorie wrote that 'isn't everything a pretty kettle of fish?' Then, in a mix of pathos and astonishing defiance she continued:

But whatever happens I hope and pray that you come out of it all safe and sound. To me, that and victory are the only big things that matter. Victory, because without that I very much doubt if we would ever be able to live a normal life together again. And without you nothing matters – I would rather be dead myself than to go on living without you, love.

Despite her distress, Marjorie was able to maintain a semblance of normality, telling her beloved Alfred all the gossip and news from home, beginning with: 'Well, now I will tell all that has happened here. Sunday evening [we] went to church and when we got home we were all talking at the gate, with life going on as usual.'

Four pages of inconsequential, but reassuringly normal, news followed. She ends by telling Alfred not to worry about her 'because I'm not a weeping willow really! At any rate not unless I get down in the dumps – which is very, very rarely, thank goodness.' The letter closes on a defiant note: 'I wonder if you will get this – or will it fall into a German's hands?!!! I hope not! If I thought it would I would have put a bit in to tell him what I thought of his tribe and precious Fuhrer!'[39]

It is no surprise that the letter is a rollercoaster of emotions. The most recent letters received by Marjorie from Alfred were three weeks out of date.[40]

The delay in receiving firm news was cruel but Marjorie, and millions like her, was only able to survive the uncertainty by developing extraordinary levels of stoicism. What Marjorie did not know, and could not know, was that twenty-four hours earlier, at 6.00 am on 17 June, a small British collier, the *Alma Dawson*, had slipped out of Marseille harbour with Alfred and the rump of the 53rd safely aboard. It would be a slow, hazardous journey but they were headed for Gibraltar.

ENDNOTES

1   ML 11.05.1940.

2   ibid.

3   ML 31.05.1940.

4   ML 11.05.1940.

5   Hooton, pp. 50–52.

6   Harman, pp. 268–9.

7   Gardner, p. 233.

8   RJA 23.09.1939, newspaper cutting.

9   ML 31.05.1940.

10   Gardner, p. 233.

11   Harman, p. 34.

12   ML 31.05.1940.

13   Thompson, p. 306.

14   ML 10.05.1940.

15   Until then letters had arrived within four to five days. Later in the war deliveries to troops were much slower. Raleigh Trevelyan, writing his diary at Anzio, noted on 1 April 1944: 'thirty letters arrived for me today from Algiers and some two months old'. Raleigh Trevelyan *The Fortress*, 1956, p. 47.

16   ML 10.05.1940 The bill was from a cobbler who corrected the soles of Marjorie's new shoes.

17   ibid.

18   ML 18.05.1940.

19   A campaign encouraging home food production. It included two cartoon characters, Doctor Carrot and Potato Pete.

20   Gilbert, p. 642.

21   Gilbert, pp. 210–21. The facts are that the Chief Constable of Glamorgan had appealed direct to the Army to send 400 troops. Churchill was not told until the troops were en route and ordered them to be halted, replacing them with 400 London policemen. Martin Gilbert's view is that throughout the disturbances Churchill was 'the conciliator withholding troops'.

22   churchill-society-london.org.uk (visited 11.01.15).

23   ML 11.05.1940.

24   ML 20.05.1940.

25   Hayward, cd41recordings.com (visited 10.01.15).

26   Gilbert, p. 647.

27   ML 16.05.1940. The reference to talking about fish is possibly a topical catch-phrase. Marjorie repeated it in her letter of 20.05.1940 and from time to time used it in conversation (per Angela Grant).

28   ML 16.05.1940.

29   ML 23.05.1940.

30   ibid.

31   ML 24.05.1940.

32   AAL 11.05.1940.

33   TNA, WO 167/617.

34   ML 26.05.1940.

35   ML 27.05.1940.

36   ML 31.05.1940.

37   Bullock, p. 587.

38   ML 15.06.1940.

39   ML 18.06.1940.

40   Numbers 57 and 58 dated 25 and 27 May, received on 3 June.

10
SALON-DE-PROVENCE AND ESCAPE

It seems that initially the men of the 53rd manning the gun stations around Nantes were blissfully unaware of developments. While the Regimental HQ was a flurry of activity, Alfred was writing to Marjorie on 6 June describing how 'in a boiling hot afternoon' he was sitting in the shade engaged in one of his 'most pleasant tasks – writing to you … I only wish you could be with me to enjoy the peace.'[1]

ON THE MOVE AGAIN

The economy of the Battery war diary endorses this, the entries for 2–5 June merely noting 'nothing to report'. The following day, the 6th, the battery commander returned from the Regimental HQ and called a meeting at midnight to advise that the 53rd was to move once again[2] and leave within forty-eight hours.[3]

Alfred quickly wrote to Marjorie on 7 June on the pretext that, with the mail becoming 'uncertain and various other contingencies, we never know when such opportunities [to write will arise] for a while … So my real reason for writing … is simply to reassure you that should you not hear at any time for a few days or even some time, then you mustn't worry unduly as to what we are doing.'[4]

Despite the alarming news of the German advance and the frantic activity needed to meet the Movement Order's schedule, Alfred's neat handwriting still manages to convey a semblance of order and calm. If he felt concern for his own and his comrades' safety there is no hint of it. Presumably the phrase 'other contingencies' was a clue that delays in receiving news would be due to the disastrous events unfolding in France. If so, as a gesture of reassurance, it was futile. Marjorie didn't receive the letter until after Alfred had been safely repatriated.

Once again, the Regimental administration swung into action and by 11.30 pm on 7 June Movement Orders had been issued to the Regiment. A freight train was assembled at the Gare de l'Etat that comprised thirteen *wagons couverts* for the men and stores and thirteen flat *wagons* for the guns and vehicles.[5] The *wagons couverts* were twin-axled wooden freight wagons. In theory if they were used to move personnel or livestock they were limited to a maximum of forty men or eight horses. When the doors were closed, the only ventilation was provided by eight folding louvres.[6]

The Regiment faced a long, perilous journey. The railway station and bridge at Saumur, 100 km east of Nantes, was bombed on the day before departure and Luftwaffe planes were sighted over Angers, the first main town on the route south.[7] A military train was a key target for attack from the air, so anti-aircraft protection was necessary. Light AA guns were mounted on the leading flat wagon and one in the middle of the train. Each flat also carried two Bren guns 'with 1,000 rounds in magazines'.

The train left Nantes at 4.35 pm on 9 June, more than an hour late, bristling with armour, with twenty officers and 460 men on board.[8]

RIGOURS OF A MILITARY TRAIN IN WARTIME

An exhausting journey lay ahead of them. As the *wagons couverts* also contained the 53rd's stores the men must have been very cramped together. Perhaps realising this, the Movement Order emphasised the need for sufficient supplies to keep the Regiment fed and watered. Four days' hard rations were to be carried together with water bottles, tea, sugar and milk along with petrol cookers 'and a cooks party detailed so that tea may be made quickly'.[9]

The Regiment boarded the train an hour before it finally departed. The heat was oppressive. What was planned as a thirty-six hour journey turned into a forty-eight hour ordeal.

The route was along the Loire valley via Angers and Tours, then south following the Rhone. Although Tours was only 200 km east of Nantes what should have been a routine two hour journey took nearly eight hours. The train was held up outside the city in the early hours of the morning 'for some time' as an air raid was in progress and didn't arrive at the main station in Tours until 2.00 am on 10 June.

The train then slowly made its way up the Loire valley, reaching Villefranche at 4.30 am, where tea and rations were distributed. It was held there for two hours. Maj. Chivers, the officer commanding the train, was eventually told by the Rail Traffic Officer at Villefranche that the next rest stop (*halte auberge*) would be Gilly-sur-Loire, 'approx. six hours run'. The advice reveals the wartime constraints under which the French railways were operating. The direct route from Villefranche to Gilly is only about 210 km. A six hour run meant an estimated arrival time of around 12 noon. In the event, the train took fourteen hours to reach Gilly.

At long last the troops received rations but the train was held for nearly three hours before finally departing at midnight.

The train crawled on through the night, stopping briefly at the village of Peyraud, whence it headed south down the Rhone valley, eventually reaching Le Teil. The 157 Battery war diary entry conveys a sense of relief: '11.6.40 08.30 arrived Le Teil – breakfast'. Routed on south via Avignon, the 53rd eventually reached its destination, Salon-de-Provence, at 2.00 pm on 11 June.[10]

Gunner Shaw gives another account in a letter written on his return to England, describing the journey as 'not comfortable for no food was provided and the train stopped only once on the way while nearly everyone had diarrhoea'.[11] While his account is short and to the point, it differs in several important details from the war diary. Either way, his version confirms that it was a gruelling journey, as does the war diary, noting that the train from Nantes which was due at 5.30 am finally arrived at 2.30 pm 'after an uncomfortable and tedious journey of 46 hours'.[12]

NO RESPITE FOR EXHAUSTED TROOPS

There was no rest for the exhausted troops. The men must have felt desperately weary but the guns and stores were rapidly off-loaded and transported to the French Air Force aerodromes at Salon and Le Vallon.

Gunner Raiment of the 73rd HAA gives an idea of the frantic activity required to establish the gun sites. On arrival at an airfield the gunners were immediately required to 'site the guns and control equipment, dig slit trenches, construct bivouacs using tarpaulin sheets off the ammunition lorries and chop sticks off trees to raise the tarpaulin sheets to resemble tents. The cooks were required to prepare field kitchens, and [one person] was to ensure his solid fuel boilers had hot water always on tap.'[13]

By 6.00 pm, just four hours after arriving, two 157 battery guns were ready for action, three 159 Battery guns ready 'by dusk' and by midnight the 53rd was almost fully operational with eleven guns manned. 157 battery were sited on the west side of Le Valon aerodrome with 'personnel under canvas', 159 Battery with three gun stations at Salon and the battery HQ temporarily located in a farmhouse near the aerodrome.[14]

53 HAA'S NEW TASK

The advance party had arrived on 9 June, before the main body of the Regiment had left Nantes. Travelling by road on a westerly route via Bordeaux and Toulouse and stopping for the night at Castelnaudary, it covered the 1,000 km journey in just over thirty hours.

A temporary Regimental HQ was set up in the Grand Hotel at Salon. During the afternoon Col. Krohn telephoned the RAF HQ nearby at Château Richebois, close to Salon. Bizarrely, having been ordered to move around 800 km due south, it was only when he spoke to Group Capt. Field, that he learned the details of the 53rd's mission – 'to provide AA protection for the Southern Force (known by the code name HADDOCK)'.

Field was the Commanding Officer of the curiously named Haddock Force. Wellington bombers, operating from England, would be serviced by 71 Wing based at Salon. The operations would be against Italy should it enter the war on the side of Germany.

Krohn was told that the 53rd, in addition to providing protection for Salon aerodrome, would also protect the base at Le Vallon, 30 km east of Salon, 'by dawn on the 12th'.

A flurry of activity followed. Field promised to lend RAF transport to assist with deploying the batteries and further transport was coming from the 73rd in the Vendôme area, over 700 km to the north-west. Presumably only a few vehicles could be spared as only six were dispatched, three 3 tonners, two of the valuable towing vehicles and a car, drawn from 158 battery. The small convoy was under the command of 2nd Lt. Ruddock who, on orders from 73 HAA 'was to be given plenty of public money [and] he was accordingly given 5,000 fcs (sic) from the Battery Imprest Account to cover the cost of maintenance of personnel and vehicles'.[15]

The need to move transport such enormous distances illustrates the extent to which the decision to bomb northern Italy stretched the British military assets remaining in France, south of the Seine. There is no doubt, however, that the additional manpower and vehicles facilitated the amazingly quick deployment of the 53rd's batteries.

Krohn immediately set off to reconnoitre gun positions and billets were identified. Later in the day of 10 June, No. 2 troop of 162 Light Anti-Aircraft Regiment arrived from

Vendôme, bringing with them Bofors guns. Two hours later Ruddock arrived with the vehicles deployed from 73 HAA.[16]

Unloading of the train was completed by 12.00 noon on 12 June. The anti-aircraft defence provided by the 53rd was made up of thirteen 3-inch guns organised in three batteries plus the troop assigned from 162 LAA, a section of the Royal Army Ordnance Corps, and a searchlight battery.[17] The additional vehicles provided by the 73rd were ordered back to Vendôme by 12 AA Brigade so it was a ragbag, under-resourced unit that defended the Haddock Force airfields.

LIFE AT SALON

Despite the frantic activity and the exhaustion he must have felt Alfred still found time to write to Marjorie. However, this time he did not use their code to tell her of his whereabouts. Perhaps, with the dramatic change of location, he thought things were getting too serious. He and Rupert were back cutting trees, one of which contained abandoned rooks' nests, which to his surprise, were lined with mud. They were so large that Alfred was able to sit in one when cutting away the two highest branches 'and that is the first bird's nest that I have ever sat in!'[18]

The greatest irritant facing the troops in their new location was a plague of flies, 'of which we seem to have more than our fair share. Why on earth they can't stay wherever they used to exist before our arrival I don't know but we just can't keep them out.' The problem was that it was intensely hot and there was virtually no shade except that provided by the Regiment's tents. To take advantage of the occasional cooling breeze it was necessary to roll up the sides, which allowed in swarms of the offending flies. Drastic measures were needed before the men could sleep at night and Alfred's tent organised a 'drive'. The sides of the tent were secured and the flies chased out through an open flap using 'towels, books and anything we could lay our hands on' then closing the flap before the flies could return. Alfred realised the whole exercise must have been a comical sight, writing: 'You would have laughed if you had seen us, but it meant a peaceful night.'[19]

There is little doubt, however, that the move to Salon took the Regiment away from the horrors being experienced in the north of France. After arriving in Provence, Gunner Shaw, with 157 battery, camped on 'an ancient seabed, now a rocky desert harbouring lizards, snakes and stinging insects. But not a mile away there was the most superb inland lake where I had the best bathe of my life. The water was 300 ft deep in places but the bed was always visible.'[20] While Shaw, and presumably his comrades, were enjoying a swim, to the north the German Army and the Luftwaffe were about to overwhelm the French forces.

POST AND NEWS DISRUPTED

Being on the move completely disrupted the Herculean efforts of the Forces Post Office to deliver mail to the troops. Even though Alfred had received no mail for over a week he considered himself fortunate to have received such a regular flow of letters and news from home. Several men had recently been transferred to the Regiment after being detached from their own units by illness. They had received no mail for four months. Having been sent to various locations for medical treatment 'the PO seems to have lost touch with them, poor blighters'.[21]

The speed of events, especially the sudden move to Salon, also meant there was little opportunity for Alfred to write home. Where previously he had managed to write one letter roughly every two days, between 9 and 21 June he only managed one letter and two 'whizz bangs', one of which was sent as the Regiment departed from Nantes. Alfred's only letter written from Salon was crammed with all manner of inconsequential news, partly as this did reflect the reality of much of day-to-day life in the Regiment, despite the war, and in part, presumably, to reassure Marjorie by describing every day events. If this was the case then circumstances again militated against him. Marjorie didn't receive the letter until 19 September, long after he was safely back in England. With hindsight, and bearing in mind the extreme difficulties that now prevailed, it is a tribute to the Army Postal Service that it was delivered at all.

A further problem caused by the dramatic move to Provence was that the sources of news organised by the troops were also disrupted. Three days after arriving in the Salon area Alfred was still without definite information. He eventually arranged for a young French lad to deliver 'the local rag but, like all French newspapers I have perused, it doesn't report very much'.

TENSIONS BETWEEN THE BRITISH AND FRENCH GOVERNMENTS

The Haddock Force mission exposed the tensions between the British and French governments. Britain had come to the aid of France under the terms of the Rhineland Pact, part of the series of Locarno Treaties (1925) signed by Germany, France, Belgium, Britain and Italy. Bizarrely in the light of subsequent events, the signatories agreed that if any of the first three states acted aggressively towards another, all other parties were to assist the country under attack.[22]

The purpose of sending the BEF to France, therefore, was to assist the French government in the face of German aggression. From a military perspective it was sensible to place British forces under French command. However, the BEF constituted the bulk of Britain's combat-ready troops. Norman Gelb succinctly summed up the crisis when he observed that 'The realisation that it was trapped with its back to the sea, and little hope of breaking out, was staggering.'[23]

Equipment could be replaced but manpower could not. Faced with this situation, French and British priorities suddenly diverged. While the French Prime Minister, Reynaud, appealed to Churchill for more aircraft to defend France, the British government considered it was imperative that as many men as possible should be evacuated. To achieve this the British political and military authorities began systematically to deceive the French and Belgian governments.[24]

Italy declared war on France and Britain on 10 June but, amazingly, the War Cabinet had received warning a month earlier via intercepts made by the secret code breakers at Bletchley Park. The Anglo-French Supreme War Council therefore agreed on 31 May that, if Italy entered the war on the side of Germany, industrial targets in north Italy should be bombed as soon as possible. In anticipation of this RAF 71 Wing dispatched an advance party to Salon on 3 June.[25]

The French Army, however, had successfully held their positions behind the Somme and Aisne rivers, delaying the German advance.[26] French fighters based near the Italian border had been sent north to assist the French forces resisting the German invaders. So despite the joint decision of the Supreme War Council, the division between French and British priorities came to the fore. The French government feared that raids on Italian cities would bring retaliation with bombs falling not on London, but on Marseille, Lyons and Paris.

The Air Ministry, however, had received the Supreme War Council's decision of 31 May and established plans for two bombing missions against northern Italian industrial targets. Long range Whitleys of Nos. 10, 51, 58, 77 and 102 Squadrons would refuel in the Channel

Islands and attack from there while the shorter range Wellingtons of 99 Squadron would fly to Salon, refuel and then continue to their targets.

ABSURD DEVELOPMENTS

The first detachment of Wellingtons reached Salon from their base in the UK at 3.30 pm on 11 June. While they were refuelling events descended into farce. Group Capt. Field at Chateau Richebois received a phone call from the nearest French Bomber Group saying that in no circumstances were Italian targets to be attacked. Field was still thinking this over when he received the executive order from the Air Ministry in London to dispatch the aircraft. A flurry of phone calls followed from the French authorities, each call from a successively higher level and each delivering the same message: operations against Italy were forbidden. On no account must his bombers be dispatched there.

Wellington bombers of 9 Squadron RAF. 99 Squadron RAF flew identical aircraft as part of Haddock Force. The Wellingtons landed at Salon-de-Provence for refuelling, prior to bombing Turin and Genoa. Farcical developments foiled their mission. Wikimedia Commons

Field ignored all this pressure, and a few minutes after midnight, the first Wellington began to taxi into position.

What Field did not know was that the French Chief of the Air Staff, General Vuillemin, had contacted the command of the British Air Forces in France asking for the operations against Italy to be cancelled. Air Marshall Barratt, commanding BAFF, phoned Maj.-Gen. Ismay, Churchill's chief staff officer. By chance, Ismay was in a meeting with Churchill and Prime Minister Reynaud at Tours in France.

Churchill recounted that 'there was a jarring interlude'. The Supreme War Council's decision that Italy should be bombed immediately on entering the war was of great importance to him. The French government's agreement that British heavy bombers should be moved to airfields near Marseille for this purpose meant 'all was now in readiness to strike. Scarcely had we sat down when Air Marshall Barratt … rang up Ismay on the telephone to say that the local authorities objected to the British bombers taking off … Reynaud, Weygand, Eden, Dill[27] and I left the table, and, after some parleying, Reynaud agreed that orders should be sent to the French authorities concerned that the bombers should not be stopped.'[28]

The orders percolated back through the layers of command on both sides. Vuillemin was firmly told that the French had officially agreed to the operation, the Whitleys were already on their way from the Channel Islands, so the Wellingtons must take off as arranged.

Vuillemin, in an act of flagrant disobedience, immediately ordered vehicles to be driven onto the airfield to prevent the bombers taking off. As the first Wellington taxied out, several French lorries appeared from beside the hangars and drove rapidly across the airfield, blocking the runway. Field had no choice but to abort the mission. He must have thought that he was living a nightmare.

Churchill was indignant: 'later that night Air Marshall Barratt reported that the French people near the airfields had dragged all kinds of carts and lorries on to them, and that it had been impossible for the aircraft to start on their mission.'[29]

As it was the Whitleys were equally unfortunate. Thirty-six aircraft had taken off from the Channel Islands but only thirteen reached Turin and Genoa, the rest experiencing heavy storms and severe icing conditions, which forced them to return to England.[30]

THE FALL OF FRANCE – ESCAPE BECOMES IMPERATIVE

The 53rd were blissfully ignorant of the shambles affecting the bombers they had been sent to defend. Fortunately, the Luftwaffe was still preoccupied with events in the north but alarming reports filtered through that the German advance had regained momentum.

On 15 June the war diary noted: 'Nothing to report but information was being received of considerable German advances and that Paris was in enemy hands.'

The Regiment's immediate concern was the severe shortage of transport. The rear party was still in Nantes and ordered to remain there 'until further orders by 12 AA Brigade'. At least nine more lorries were needed for the removal of personnel and essential stores. This was an unwelcome difficulty as the 53rd learned during the afternoon of the 16th that the base at Marseille 'was preparing to move'.

At midnight preparations were made for the possibility of 'sudden evacuation by sea' and at 5.00 am on the 17th Haddock Force was ordered to immediately embark at Marseille. 'It was learnt that France was contemplating asking Germany for terms.' Transport was so short that the 53rd had to borrow vehicles from the RAF.[31]

Within forty minutes the battery HQs were repeating the orders to the outlying gun stations and vehicles were assembled. A hint of panic emerges when, at 9.00 am, the batteries were ordered to move immediately and rendezvous at Marseille docks 'leaving stores and ammunition which cannot be transported on the vehicles available'.[32] Alfred described how '[we] did a quick bunk to Marseille (leaving the gun station within 50 minutes of the order,

British Army convoy, Cherbourg Docks, June 1940, a scene similar to that as the 53rd escaped from Marseille docks, most of the vehicles abandoned on the dockside. Wikimedia Commons – IWM, F 4847

all complete with guns and instruments).'[33] At Marseille, the previously friendly French population turned against the troops. 'We were spat upon by local women thinking we were deserting.'[34] It was an understandable reaction. With little news they were not to know that to the north, the Royal Navy in Operation Ariel had lifted 18,000 French troops from Bay of Biscay ports.[35]

The two batteries assembled from their gun stations and moved off in convoys, hauling their guns and carrying only personnel, instruments and essential stores. Their destination was Mole G in Marseille docks where, for protection, two Bofors guns had already been mounted on the quay and two loaded on to a small vessel, the *Alma Dawson*. There was heavy congestion on the roads and the convoys did not arrive until late in the afternoon.

It was little wonder that progress to the port was so slow. Gunner Shaw described how 'instructions were received to get out of the country by the quickest means and we joined a huge convoy making for the coast (there was no time to blow up the ammunition but we took the beer with us). On the way we heard from a dispatch rider that France had capitulated.'[36]

SS *ALMA DAWSON*[37]

The chaos of the situation is summed up when Alfred describes the Regiment arriving at the docks where 'we found that no one knew anything about us or expected us and that there was a strike on.'[38] Worse still, it was only then that the men discovered they had been allotted the *Alma Dawson*, a small British tramp steamer normally used for carrying iron ore and coal. Their hearts must have sunk. 'Decks and hold filthy, however this was the only accommodation available for approx. 600 men.'[39] The Regiment's war diary noted that the accommodation on the *Alma Dawson* was 'very bad and she was in a filthy condition, the decks and superstructure thickly coated with grime'.[40] Alfred was more succinct: the *Alma Dawson* was 'a dirty little 1500 ton collier.'[41]

To add to their concerns, Alfred relates that 'there were no naval vessels there and only two British cargo vessels and quite naturally neither of the skippers relished the idea of taking around 600 troops on board and out into the Mediterranean without escort because, you will remember, Italy was already agin [sic] us and that country wasn't so very far away!'[42]

The original plan had assigned two ships to the 53rd: the SS *Kultan* to carry all personnel, while the *Alma Dawson* was to be loaded with the guns, vehicles and stores. Group Capt.

Alma Dawson, 'a dirty little 1500 ton collier.' In fact Alma Dawson *was 3985 tons.* © wrecksite.eu

Field, still in command of Haddock Force, was concerned about congestion on the *Kultan* and advised Lt. Col. Krohn that around 400 men should be transferred to the *Alma Dawson*. Krohn, for his part, felt that this risked him losing control, so he requested that the entire Regiment should be on the *Alma Dawson* even though 'there would be a certain amount of overcrowding'.

Cramming 600 men aboard the small steamer meant that emergency equipment was completely inadequate. The lifeboats could only accommodate one hundred people, rafts a further fifty, and there were lifebelts for the crew only. 'Some 500 men were without any protection at all in the event of an emergency and would have to use the wooden ships fittings.' The cramped conditions were made worse as these fittings were laid out on the decks so they would be immediately available in an emergency.

PROBLEMS LOADING EQUIPMENT

Embarkation and loading of the guns and equipment started at 7.00 pm. It was then that the 53rd's real problems hit them. Krohn was told that 'the French refused to work the cranes on the quay'.[43] The 157 Battery diary was more blunt, recording that the dock workers were on strike and 'the French gave no assistance whatsoever'. The reason was simple. Whilst the French had welcomed the BEF on their arrival in the autumn of 1939, the British troops were now seen to be abandoning France.

Krohn was forced to advise Field that, without the quayside cranes, he would only be able to load the Bofors guns and light vehicles. Furthermore, he would have to 'render the 3-inch guns useless to the enemy by the removal of breeches, receiving dials and fuse setters'. The ship's derricks were used for heavier stores but the maximum load was only 2 tons. Krohn was promised the use of a floating crane but this would not arrive until the following morning. It, therefore, proved impossible to load the guns, vehicles and heavy equipment.

At 6.00 pm Krohn verbally gave the fateful order: 'remove breech rings, sights and fuse setters and abandon the guns'.[44]

Loading continued until around 10.00 pm when it had to stop as, with the black-out in force, artificial light was forbidden. The men settled down for the night as best they could on the filthy decks.

'SAIL AT FIRST LIGHT!'

Krohn had been told that an escort was being sent to take the *Alma Dawson* and other ships in convoy, 'probably to Gibraltar'. In the middle of the night, around 4.00 am, Krohn and the ship's master, Captain Townsend, were woken by a Royal Navy officer, Captain Noutar, with further bad news. Noutar told them that the *Alma Dawson* would have to sail at first light. The reason was that the escort would not be coming after all and they had to leave immediately. Noutar made one concession, agreeing that Krohn could have sufficient time for the two Bofors guns on the quay to be loaded.

The men were immediately roused and as many stores as possible loaded. Frantic activity ensued. There were no gangways and, although it was still dark, small stores and rations were either manhandled up the ship's ladder or hauled up by ropes. The ship's derricks were used to load the two remaining Bofors guns, ammunition, instruments and a lorry load of '1500 preserved rations', presumably tinned food. It was a difficult exercise with considerable risk of injury to both soldiers and ship's crew but loading continued until the last minute. It only stopped 'as the ship was casting off under the direct orders of the naval authorities'.[45]

At 6.00 am on 18 June 'the armed tramp *Alma Dawson* left harbour with the 53rd HAA and attached troops aboard. The quay was covered with abandoned stores and vehicles. Course was set for Gibraltar.'[46]

UNESCORTED CONVOY

The *Alma Dawson* was part of a small convoy of five ships, two of which carried civilian refugees and one with wounded. Despite the squalid conditions everyone aboard the *Alma Dawson* must have felt enormous relief.

However, there would also have been apprehension. Italy had just entered the war. Without a naval escort the convoy was exposed to attack from the air and sea – in particular, from Italian warships and Spanish patrol boats.

Spain was a neutral state, having avoided entering hostilities on either side. To reduce the risk of attack from Italian naval forces it was decided to hug the Spanish coastline, just outside what was known at the time as the '3-mile limit', 4.8 km. This was the limit in international law of a country's territorial waters. If approached by hostile ships the convoy could slip into neutral Spanish territorial waters but this could mean arrest and internment.

The Regimental war diary noted: 'Although the available defence against maritime attack was inadequate the A.A. protection of the ships was very formidable.' The four Bofors guns were mounted fore and aft along with fifteen machine guns. Anti-tank guns were mounted for use against submarines and, finally, the *Alma Dawson* also carried an 'antiquated 12 pounder mounted on the poop'.

The risks facing the small, unescorted, convoy are illustrated by an incident that occurred over Gibraltar on 30 June. By now the French colonies in North Africa were under the control of the Vichy French government, the authority established after the collapse of France and the signing of an armistice with Germany on 22 June 1940. Several French planes escaped and flew to Gibraltar. At 5.30 pm three more appeared, two landing safely but the third strayed into Spanish air space and was shot down, 'totally destroyed' by a Spanish machine gun post.[47] Technically Spain might have remained neutral but its territorial integrity was not to be messed with.

Progress was painfully slow and the convoy gradually became scattered. Only 65 km were covered by 12 noon on the first day. By dawn the next morning, 19 June, although the *Alma Dawson* was making 10 knots at best, only one vessel had kept up, the *Pencreep*, carrying refugees. The others were out of sight.

At 8.00 am, off Barcelona, a Spanish patrol boat was noticed moving slowly between the *Alma Dawson* and the coastline. 'It was very interested in us and tracked us across the bay.' Two passenger planes, 'of an obsolete Junkers type' were also sighted. As a precaution everyone on deck was ordered to keep below the ship's bulwarks.

This just added to the extreme discomfort of everyone on board. In addition to the filthy condition of the vessel, everywhere covered in coal dust, the sanitary arrangements were 'practically nil. We made our own.' Fortunately, the weather was warm and the sea calm and, unlike the French authorities in Marseille, the ship's officers and crew 'were extremely helpful and obliging'.

Cape Oropesa, Valencia, Cape Huertas (described, without amplification, as 'the danger area'), Cape de Gata all slipped by. But despite the painfully slow progress there was one huge bonus: 'no enemy activity'.

Then at 7.00 am on the 21st, three days after leaving Marseille, a patrolling RAF flying boat approached and circled the ship. It is difficult to imagine the relief felt by everyone on board. Here at last was a friendly aircraft. Gibraltar and safety were close at hand.

Later the same morning the flying boat returned and signals communication was established enabling information to be passed as to the nature of 'cargo' and 'passengers'. More patrolling aircraft were seen and at 1.15 in the afternoon a flying boat appeared signalling for details of the guns, ammunition and personnel on the ship. But still no naval escort arrived.[48]

Finally, the diary records in five brief words the moment everyone on the *Alma Dawson* must have been praying for:

21.6.40, 19.30 The Rock of Gibraltar sighted.

Just after 11.00 p.m. a Gibraltar pilot boarded. One wonders what he thought as he made his way to the bridge in the dark, scrambling over the men packed on the decks, covered in coal dust.

Two minutes before midnight the *Alma Dawson* dropped anchor off Gibraltar's South Mole. 'The Regiment was in British waters after a sea voyage of 730 miles without incident.'[49]

Restrained and factual to the last, but in its reference to 'British waters' the diary betrays the relief felt by the whole Regiment.

ENDNOTES

1   AAL 06.06.1940.

2   NA, WO/167/639.

3   157 Battery war diary, NA, WO/167/637.

4   AAL 07.06.1940.

5   NA, WO/167/617 Appendix.

6   Later in the war the wagons couverts became associated in France with the horrors of deportation (fr.wikipedia.org, visited 30.01.2016).

7   NA, WO/167/639.

8   157 battery had been told that the train must leave at 15.15., NA WO/167/638.

9   NA, WO/167/617.

10   NA, WO 167/637.

11   IWM Documents.18817.

12   NA, WO/167/617.

13   bbc.co.uk/history/ww2peopleswar/stories/96/a1994196 (visited 17.02.16).

14   NA, WO/167/617, WO167/637, WO 167/639.

15   NA, WO/167/638.

16   TNA, WO/167/617. N.B., there is a discrepancy between the war diaries of 53 HAA and 73 HAA. The 53rd diary states that 11 vehicles arrived. The 73rd diary specifies the vehicles sent, six in total.

17   NA, WO/167/617.

18   AAL 15.06.1940.

19   ibid.

20   Shaw papers.

21   AAL 15.06.1940.

22   britannica.com (visited 04.02.16).

23   Gelb, p. 3.

24   Harman, p. 16.

25   Richards, p. 145.

26   Alexander, in *War in History*, sagepub.com (visited 05.02.16).

27   General Maxime Weygand was the French Supreme Commander, succeeding Gamelin; Anthony Eden was Secretary of State for War; General Sir John Dill was Chief of the Imperial General Staff.

28   Churchill, p. 139.

29   ibid.

30   Richards, pp. 146–47.

31   NA, WO/167/617.

32   ibid.

33   AAL 11.07.1940.

34   Hewitt-Taylor papers.

35   Ellis & Butler, p.305.

36   Shaw papers. Prime Minister Reynaud resigned on 15 June 1940. His successor, Marshal Petain, broadcast to the nation in the early hours of 16 June, announcing his intention to seek an armistice with Germany. Gilbert, p. 663.

37   The ship was built in 1917 by Tyne Iron Shipbuilding as the SS *Whinfield*. In 1936 she was renamed *Alma Dawson* for F.S. Dawson & Co. She later struck a mine and sank on 24 November 1940 while on a voyage from Montreal to Ipswich (wrecksite.eu, visited 06.02.2016).

38   AAL 11.07.1940.

39   NA, WO/167/617.

40   NA WO/167/637.

41   AAL 11.07.1940.

42   ibid.

43   Krohn to Commander Royal Artillery, Gibraltar, 23.06.1940, NA, WO/167/617.

44   NA, WO 167/637.

45   Krohn to CRA. Gibraltar, 23.06.1940.

46   NA, WO 167/637, NA WO 167/617.

47   NA, WO 167/617.

48   NA, WO 167/637.

49   NA, WO 167/617.

11

GIBRALTAR AND HOME

Despite its commanding position at the entrance to the Mediterranean Gibraltar was a tiny oasis surrounded by hostile territory: neutral but distinctly unfriendly Spain to the north, Vichy French forces in north Africa, the Italian navy to the east, and the *Kriegsmarine* to the west in the Atlantic. For the men of the 53rd, however, Gibraltar represented not just safety and relief from the cramped conditions on the *Alma Dawson* but, just as important, comforting familiarity. The Regimental war diary describes arriving in 'British waters'. After nearly nine months in wartime France the men might not yet be home, but they were surrounded by reassuring signs of its proximity – red telephone kiosks, English street names, Post Office pillar boxes.

GIBRALTAR'S LIMITED AIR DEFENCES

Early the next morning, having spent the night at anchor, the *Alma Dawson* moved into the inner harbour and tied up at the Admiralty Mole. The men had endured a physically draining sea journey, but there was no let-up in discipline. Amazingly, considering the speed of the escape from Marseille, a typewriter and paper were available for Krohn to issue Disembarkation Orders. Neatly typed while he was still on board, they set out the sequence for disembarkation and tasks to be undertaken. The priority was to get the men off the ship followed by the Bofors guns 'with sufficient ammunition for immediate action'. If necessary these were to be instantly readied for action on the mole or the quay.

The arrival of the 53rd was an event of some consequence. Lt. Col. Krohn was met by the senior command of the locally based Royal Artillery – the Commander Brig. Lowe, Col. Learmont, and other officers of the garrison.[1] The real reason for such high level interest rapidly became clear. In June 1940 no fighters were based at Gibraltar and the government had yet to reinforce 'the Rock' and turn it into the fortress it later became. Krohn was told that the local garrison had only four 3.7-inch and four 3-inch heavy anti-aircraft guns and two light Bofors guns.[2] While reinforcements were on their way, when the 53rd limped into harbour one of Britain's most important strategic outposts was defended against air attack by the equivalent of two-thirds of a single heavy anti-aircraft regiment. It must have been a severe disappointment when the local command discovered from the returning flying boat the previous day that, in the scramble to leave Marseille, the Regiment had managed to rescue only four light Bofors guns.

Despite this, the arrival of a unit of battle-hardened anti-aircraft gunners was a welcome addition to the Gibraltar garrison. They were immediately deployed to various units: Regimental HQ, 157 and 159 Batteries to the Fortress Royal Artillery, the Bofors troop to the 10th AA Regiment, and other personnel to the Fortress Engineers and Royal Army Ordnance Corps.[3]

NORMALITY RETURNS AFTER A FASHION

The men were filthy after five days at sea on the collier but Krohn would not countenance troops under his command coming ashore as a rabble. 'Personnel on landing will be formed up in their proper units and will remain by their kits until further orders.' The only exceptions were those assigned to special duties. These included three unloading parties and special cleaning parties. The latter were required not to clean the ship itself but to remove rubbish left behind after the long sea voyage.[4]

Baths were provided, 'and every man [was] given a clean set of underclothes'.[5] It seems a miserly gesture after such hardship, particularly when the men had spent the day unloading the *Alma Dawson* but, in the circumstances, it must have been a real treat.

However, there was one important concession: the troops were, at long last, allowed to contact home by cable, telling their families where they were and that they were safe and well. Even better, Alfred received a message from Marjorie, and wrote to her on 24 June: 'I was terribly pleased to receive your cable and learn that both mine had reached you so that at least for the time being your fears would be allayed.' His letter is full of the excitement he felt on reaching the Rock. 'When we arrived – about 11.00 pm Saturday – there was a full moon (good old pal!) reflected in a most wizard yellow stream on the water and Gib itself looked like a fairyland with all its lights twinkling up the hillside.'[6] Curiously, Gibraltar was not enforcing a black-out. The contrast between the tension of the slow, gruelling voyage from Marseille and the relaxed atmosphere found here could not have been greater.

But uncertainty remained as to when the gunners would be allowed home. Brigadier Lowe made clear that the 53rd could not sail for England until the requested AA reinforcements had arrived.

LIFE ON THE ROCK

For the exhausted troops, after their hazardous escape from France, Gibraltar must have seemed like a sanctuary. Part of the Regiment, including 159 Battery, was accommodated at Europa Point Barracks – the officers housed at the Royal Artillery Mess, the remaining men at Windmill Hill Barracks.

In practice, apart from manning the Bofors guns, there was little for the new arrivals to do. Gibraltar provided a welcome respite: 'doing little else than a spot of marching. It was terribly hot and our khaki uniform didn't help matters. We had local leave every day if we wanted it and some of us had some delightful bathes off the rocks.'[7]

A VALEDICTORY ADDRESS

Before disembarking from the *Alma Dawson* Lt. Col. Krohn had issued a Special Order of the Day, which was circulated to the troops. Neatly typed over two pages, it is a testament to Krohn's consideration for his men. While it reads like a valedictory address, he caught the spirit of the moment when he made it clear that, despite the achievements of the Regiment, uncertain times lay ahead: 'The occasion of our landing at Gibraltar marks the end of the first phase of the war as the 53rd Heavy Anti-Aircraft Regiment, R.A. and attached troops are concerned.' His summary referred to the bitter winter months endured by the Regiment with 'the lowest temperatures experienced for over 100 years … THE CHEERFULNESS AND GOODWILL DISPLAYED BY ALL RANKS, NO MATTER HOW TRYING THE CIRCUMSTANCES, HAVE BEEN A CONSTANT SOURCE OF PRIDE AND ADMIRATION TO ME.'

The gunners had shot down between eight and ten enemy aircraft, and, Krohn wrote, 'double or treble that number probably never reached home. I say now, without fear of contradiction, that this can be considered a very creditable performance with the equipment in our possession and I heartily congratulate all ranks on their success.' Was this his first admission that the 53rd's 3-inch guns were not up to the task? Krohn goes on to describe the start of 'the war proper', the Regiment's withdrawal to Troyes, the temporary abandonment of fourteen guns, and the loss of an officer and six men who were captured. 'To these I extend the sympathy and good wishes of all ranks, and I trust, as do all of us, that they are at least being treated as human beings.'[8]

At Salon the Regiment had been ordered to withdraw 'at a few hours notice in a manner which was a credit to all concerned. The fact that the Regiment was forced to leave behind its guns for the second time, but on this occasion with no chance of recovery, has been to me, and all of us as gunners, a matter of the deepest regret.'

Was this a hint of Krohn's concern that he might face a court martial for breaking the gunners' code of never abandoning their guns? He softened the statement for the troops by adding:

> Our one satisfaction is that we have brought with us all essential instruments and parts of guns, thus rendering them useless to the enemy.
>
> What destiny may have in store for us I do not know, but I know that all ranks will want to be re-equipped with all possible speed, in order that we may once more be in a position to take our part.

He goes on to thank everyone under his command, careful not to omit any unit. To all ranks of the 53rd he wrote:

> of the 162nd Lt. AA Battery, Drivers of the Royal Army Service Corps. and RAF and to all ranks of the Workshops Section … attached to us, my very deep and sincere appreciation of the unswerving and loyal support I have always received. My one wish now is that I may continue to have the honour of commanding the Regiment and once again taking it into action.

However, Krohn does not end there, reserving his closing paragraph for a generous and moving tribute to the men of the ship:

> I wish also to express to Captain Townsend and the officers and crew of the S.S. ALMA DAWSON, the appreciation and thanks of all ranks for their kindness and help to us all during the voyage to GIBRALTAR. Few of us probably fully appreciate the responsibilities which Captain Townsend has had to accept in taking his ship with some 650 men on board unconvoyed through seas in which Hostile Submarines,

and over which Hostile Aircraft, may well have attacked at any moment. He and his men have truly lived up to the fine traditions of the Merchant Service.[9]

The Special Order gives an insight to the heavy responsibilities weighing on Krohn's shoulders – the loss of the Regiment's guns, the anxieties felt during the sea passage – but also his concern for the welfare of the men entrusted to him and his pride in them. It is the testament of a decent man.

DEFENDING THE DECISION TO ABANDON THE REGIMENT'S GUNS

Krohn still had to explain the reasons for withdrawing without recovering the guns of the Regiment entrusted to him. Two days after arriving in Gibraltar his report was delivered to Brigadier Lowe.

Krohn's opening paragraph hangs over the report like a dark cloud. The consequences for him were ominous if he could not provide a satisfactory justification: 'In accordance with instructions, I submit below details of the circumstances in which I abandoned 13 3-inch 20-cwt guns at Marseille on the morning of 18 June 1940.'

His report describes the anarchy in Marseille following the capitulation of the French government. Lack of leadership meant that the French dockers could refuse to work the cranes, and the possible solution, a floating crane, was prevented when in the middle of the night Krohn was advised by a senior naval officer, Capt. Noutar, that no naval escort was available. The Regiment's situation was now so serious that Noutar ordered him to 'put to sea at once'. Despite the perilous situation Krohn's focus was still on saving the guns, and he asked whether this would be possible. Noutar replied emphatically 'in the negative'. Krohn persisted, asking if at least he could be allowed to load the last two Bofors guns 'which I had put into action the night before'.

Krohn was pointing out that throughout all the chaos he had kept his commanding officer appraised of the reality – the dock workers' action risked his 3-inch guns falling into enemy hands – and despite orders to leave immediately he had persisted in trying to buy time to load the guns. When this was refused he had at least won sufficient delay to enable the loading of the last two light guns and the remaining instruments. This was only possible, however, as loading continued right up to the last minute.

'I am satisfied that had I been given another six hours I would, with the assistance of a floating crane which had been promised the night before, and the ship's derricks, have loaded all my 3-inch guns, the remainder of my stores, the bulk of the transport, as there was ample room in the ship's holds for the whole of these.' To emphasise the point he wrote: 'In this estimate I am supported by Captain Townsend.'[10] The records are silent on the outcome, but it is reasonable to assume that Lowe accepted Krohn's explanation.

With little activity to report, the war diary was reduced to noting the comings and goings in the harbour, and the weather. The battleship *Resolution* was already at anchor, and two of the navy's most powerful ships arrived on 26 June, the battleship HMS *Hood* and the aircraft carrier HMS *Ark Royal*. The battery commanders paid a courtesy visit to the *Hood*. Unbeknown to the diarist, they were part of Force H, which, controversially, attacked the French naval base at Mers-el-Kébir in Vichy-controlled Algeria.[11]

For the men of the 53rd the most important arrival was that of the *City of Cairo* on 27 June. It was their ticket home. On board was the 82nd HAA with sixteen of the latest 3.7-inch guns and 40,000 rounds of ammunition, together with four more Bofors. The

City of Cairo, 8000 tons, on which the 53rd HAA sailed from Gibraltar to Liverpool. Its sinking in November 1942 became famous for a rare moment of gallantry when the commander of U-boat U68, Karl-Friedrich Merten, provided the life-boats with the course to nearest land, parting with the words: 'Goodnight and sorry for sinking you'. © commons.wikimedia.org

cargo was so large that three days later working parties from 159 Battery had to be sent to the docks to assist with unloading ammunition.[12] The time needed to unload the *City of Cairo* reveals the difficulties facing Krohn in Marseille. It had been a heroic effort – lifting the vital breech rings and instruments, the four Bofors, a number of light vehicles and stores into the *Alma Dawson's* holds in the few hours available.

VOYAGE HOME – THE FINAL LEG

After what Alfred described as 'days of suspense' Brigadier Lowe was good to his word and the 53rd boarded the *City of Cairo* on 2 July 'and sailed almost immediately'.[13] The Regiment had been in Gibraltar for just nine days.

The *City of Cairo* was one of twenty-seven ships making up convoy HGY.[14] Vessels joining convoys for protection did so on the understanding that there were prescribed convoy routes. Thus, HG was the designation for convoys sailing from Gibraltar to Liverpool. The vessels were escorted by the Free French patrol ship *Président Houdouce* and the destroyer HMS *Witch*.[15] The voyage was painfully slow, needing ten days to complete a sea passage which takes a modern container vessel four days or less. The reason was twofold: the convoy was restricted to the speed of the slowest vessel, around 6 knots, and it had to deviate over 300 km west into the Atlantic to avoid detection by U-boats. 'We seemed to go half way across the Atlantic to avoid [them].'[16]

Once again, the Regiment had to endure being accommodated in the ships holds.[17] With nothing to do on board other than 'reading, chatting, sleeping or dozing' the voyage was tedious. Alfred was bored and seasick. 'Seasick, homesick and love-sick all rolled up in one. What a mixture!'

However, some troops were put to work. Gunner Hewitt-Taylor was assigned duties in the galleys, 'permanently washing up. The first time I had seen "sea-water" soap!'[18]

With little else to do and with the prospect of arriving back in the UK within forty-eight hours Alfred at long last felt able to write frankly to Marjorie, unburdening all the fears and apprehensions he had felt in the past few weeks. The greatest of these was that their exchange of letters and news had been interrupted. 'It [grieved] me no end to think of all the unnecessary worry and anxiety you must have suffered as to our whereabouts and safety.'[19]

Typically, however, Alfred felt that despite all the hardship he and his comrades had endured, 'compared with many others our lot hasn't been anything like it might have been;

at least we have bodies and souls intact and can hope to be with each other fairly soon – if only for a short time. (What a rotten husband you have got only to be able to come home "on loan" so to speak!).'[20]

Alfred and Marjorie had been separated for ten months, during which they had shared just a few precious days of leave in January. They had not seen each other for six months. Alfred, aware of the demands of the Army during wartime, realised that, on reaching Liverpool, he might not even be able to phone Marjorie. In a letter of 11 July he set out 'a brief summary of what we have been up to'. His description of the escape from Salon is economic, but vividly captures the tensions and hardships experienced by the troops:

> At Salon we received orders to quit as best we could and did a quick bunk to Marseille (leaving the gun station within 50 minutes of the order, all complete with guns and instruments). Arrived at the docks we found that no one knew anything about us or expected us and that there was a strike on. There were no naval vessels there and only two British cargo vessels and quite naturally neither of the skippers relished the idea of taking around 600 troops on board and out into the Mediterranean without escort because, you will remember, Italy was already agin [sic] us and that country wasn't so very far away! However our colonel talked one of the skippers into it and we sailed at dawn on 18th June in a dirty little 1500 ton collier, the 'Alma Dawson'. It was indeed fortunate for us that it was very fine and very warm because there was literally no accommodation for us. The holds were thick with coal dust so we couldn't go below deck at all and spent the whole time on what deck space there was. Going flat out in a calm sea the little old tub could only creep along at 10 knots maximum and as we had no escort and dare not risk putting out to sea in so slow a boat we crawled all round the coast of Spain on the three mile limit line – so we could hop into neutral waters if necessary and run the risk of being interned. It took us the best part of 5 days to make Gib and mighty glad we were to see it.[21]

Convoy HGY arrived at Liverpool a day later, on 12 July. The Regiment had been in France almost exactly nine months. Over that time most men had enjoyed one brief home leave, so perhaps they might have expected to be issued with rail warrants allowing them to travel home. Instead, the gunners were put on a train to London, and sent to Osterley Park, the grounds of which had been requisitioned by the War Office as a Home Guard training establishment. But as far as the 53rd were concerned, they were home.

ENDNOTES

1   NA, WO 167/617.

2   ibid.

3   NA, WO 167/617, appendix F.

4   ibid.

5   NA, WO 167/637.

6   AAL 24.06.1940.

7   AAL 11.07.1940.

8   NA – WO 167/617, appendix G.

9   ibid.

10 NA, WO 167/617, appendix C.

11 The Marine Nationale was the second most powerful European naval force after the Royal Navy. Eleven vessels were at anchor at Mers-el-Kébir, including four battleships. Churchill, still reeling from Dunkirk and stung by Vichy French collaboration, determined that the fleet represented an unacceptable threat and ordered an ultimatum: join Britain, sail to the Caribbean to put the force out of use, or scuttle the vessels. Admiral Gensoul refused and Force H attacked: 1,300 French sailors and marines died. The attack remains controversial but it decisively demonstrated to the world, and Roosevelt in particular, Churchill's determination to continue the war with Germany at all costs, even without allies if need be. (Bell, *France and Britain, 1940–1994*, pp. 19–20).

12 NA, WO 167/639.

13 Alfred's letter to Marjorie from the *City of Cairo* is dated Thursday 11 July 1940. He states that the vessel sailed on 'Tuesday of last week'.

14 NA, ADM 199/2185/39

15 naval-history.net (visited 24.04.16) Force H sailed the same day to Mers-el-Kébir, where they eventually bombarded the French fleet.

16 Hewitt-Taylor papers.

17 ibid.

18 ibid.

19 AAL 11.07.1940.

20 ibid.

21 ibid.

12

POSTSCRIPT

OPERATION ARIEL

The evacuation of Allied troops from Dunkirk, Operation Dynamo, had ended on 4 June 1940. While the bulk of the fighting troops in the BEF had been rescued, 150,000 troops, including the 73rd, had been cut off, still south of the Seine, and were threatened by German forces advancing southwest. A plan was hastily drawn up to evacuate as many as possible from ports in western France. Between 15 and 25 June around 192,000 troops, including French personnel, were successfully repatriated to the UK.[1]

158 BATTERY AND 12 AA BRIGADE

The Regiment that finally made it back to Liverpool on 12 July 1940 was the rump of the 53rd Heavy Anti-Aircraft that had left for France in October 1939. After the chaotic withdrawal from the Reims area, 158 Battery had been detached and transferred to 73 HAA, commanded by Lt. Col. A.L. Wood. What had happened to them?

German troops had broken through at the Marne and the 73rd, including 158 Battery, along with the units still remaining in the AASF, were directed to evacuation points stretching from Brest to La Rochelle.

If 157 and 159 Batteries, by now near Marseille, had experienced hardship and the fear brought on by uncertainty, 158 Battery were to suffer an even more traumatic time.

A week after the 53rd had departed for Nantes, 12 AA Brigade was still unsure of the situation to their north. 'The enemy position north of the Aisne is still in doubt … 73rd Regt. will send out patrols to find out the exact position.'[2] The state of ignorance is indicated by the information the patrols were required to gather. Where is the enemy? Where are the French? Do we hold the Marne and the Aisne, and what is the state of the bridges?[3]

In the event, the patrols, one of which was led by 2nd Lt. Ruddock of 158 Battery, gained valuable information from the French forces still in position to the north, on the extent of the German advance. Most precious of all, the French had captured a German GHQ staff officer who was carrying a copy of the 'plan of attack, Divisions in the line with numbers and front, and events proved it to be genuine. The "Spear Head" of the attack was led by 8 Panzer Divisions with ABBEVILLE, AMIENS and ARRAS as their objectives: the attack then proceeded north along the coast'.[4] The patrol report was signed by Lt. Col. A.L. Wood, commanding 73 HAA on 25 May, the day before the Dunkirk evacuation started. Presumably this information merely reinforced the wisdom of organising Operation Dynamo.

On 3 June the Advanced Air Striking Force withdrew 300 km west to the Vendôme area, between Le Mans and Orléans. The expanded 73rd had to move its guns by road, the journey taking thirty-six hours as the state of their wheels restricted their speed to 10 mph.[5]

INADEQUATE FACILITIES

The AASF were to provide defence for the six squadrons making up 75 and 76 Wings of the RAF. Finding sufficient aerodromes for such a large number of aircraft at short notice was a problem. Three of the allotted grass strips were not ready, and the rest provided insufficient cover for aircraft and vehicles. Worst of all, a shortage of telephone cables meant that dedicated lines could not be laid. The command system was compelled to use either the civilian network, which in 1940 lacked automatic dialling systems, or dispatch riders. Fortunately, there was little hostile air activity.

Accommodation was equally problematic. One location considered was Muides, a village with a peacetime population of around 600 people. However, this had been swelled by some 250 refugees, friends and relatives of the homeowners. As they had not been placed there under any scheme, the RAF advance reconnaissance team speculated that they could be evicted, although conceding that 'this might be difficult'.[6] Such are the terrible realities of war.

LOSS OF CONTROL LEADS TO CHAOS

Control of events was now slipping from the AASF. The 73rd's move to Vendôme coincided with orders for the 53rd to move to Salon. The hasty decision to transfer forty-one vehicles from the 53rd to the 73rd now meant that the former was short of transport. Hurriedly, eleven vehicles were sent south, led by 2nd Lt. Ruddock of 158 Battery, a journey over poor roads of around 750 km. The convoy arrived three days later on 10 June, only to be recalled thirty-six hours later. They got back to Vendôme, having completed an exhausting round trip of 1,500 km, to be told that 12 AA Brigade was withdrawing to the Nantes-Angers area, 250 km west.[7] With the collapse of France the Brigade's organisation was being stretched to the limit.

COMMUNICATIONS BREAKDOWN

The deteriorating military situation meant that communications were increasingly difficult, so much so that the Air Ministry was not sure of the whereabouts of the AASF. On 10 June Sir Cyril Newall, Chief of the Air Staff, advised the War Cabinet chaired by Churchill that 'few reports [have] been received'.[8] It was an extraordinary admission. The RAF squadrons assigned to the AASF had been decimated in their attempts to destroy the Meuse bridges, so much so that four squadrons had been disbanded and their remaining aircraft reassigned.[9] However, six squadrons remained but the Chief of the Air Staff had no idea where they were located.

The guns of the 73rd began to move during the night of 13–14 June. 158 Battery had been ordered to move to Tours, but the promised train was not available. 'There were no wagons and the line was blocked.' Maj. White had no alternative but to continue by road. Thirty hours later his reconnaissance party arrived at Nantes, only to discover 'clear evidence of an imminent complete withdrawal of all the British Forces'.[10] He had lost contact with his gun

Stores being destroyed at a Royal Army Service Corps depot, June 1940. Wikimedia Commons – IWM, F 4756

Motorcycles abandoned by the British Army near Le Mans, 13 June 1940. The equipment left behind during Operation Ariel was staggering, e.g. 322 guns, 32,000 tons of ammunition, over 4,700 vehicles and 500 motorcycles. Even more equipment was abandoned after Dunkirk.
Wikimedia Commons – IWM, F 4841

convoys. The last two sections did not reach the rendezvous until 3.00 am on the 16th. It had taken them nearly forty-eight hours.

The situation was becoming chaotic, and communications with units in the Brigade had completely broken down. The Brigade commander, Brig. Crewdson, had made his way to AASF headquarters at Angers where he was informed that the bombers were being withdrawn to England and that 12 Brigade was now under the command of the British Air Forces in France.

OVERTAKEN BY EVENTS

The Brigade's original task was being overtaken by events. In addition to providing air defence of Nantes aerodrome, they were now to provide air defence for St-Nazaire, Rennes and Brest. The situation was becoming a farce. Rennes is 110 km north of Nantes, and Brest further still, 350 km away on the Breton peninsula. The new tasks were completely unrealistic.

Despite this, Crewdson began to implement the new dispositions. In the early hours of the 16th 158 Battery was ordered to move to St-Brevin-les-Pins, 60 km west of Nantes, opposite St-Nazaire on the south bank of the Loire. Two sections were in position by 2.00 pm.

THE *LANCASTRIA* DISASTER

An hour later, the remainder of 158 Battery along with the 73rd HAA were ordered to St-Nazaire, where they boarded HMT *Lancastria*, a 16,000-ton Cunard liner which had arrived earlier in the day.[11] In all eight officers and 350 other ranks from 12 AA Brigade boarded, the majority of the unit being sent north to Brest.[12]

By mid-afternoon the *Lancastria* had also embarked an unknown number of civilian refugees and troops from both the Army and the RAF; estimates of the numbers range from 4,000 to 9,000. Just before 4.00 pm the ship was attacked by Junkers dive-bombers, and sank in minutes. Fewer than 2,500 survived. Those missing included thirty-eight men from 12 AA Brigade, twenty-six of them Alfred's comrades in 158 Battery.[13] The Battery diarist needed just fifteen words to record Britain's greatest maritime disaster: 'this ship was severely bombed while still in the harbour and sank in 15 minutes'.

DISCIPLINE MAINTAINED

Earlier in the day an even larger liner, the 20,000 ton *Oronsay*, had been struck by bombs and badly damaged.[14] With the final collapse of France the chances of escape seemed to be fading. It would be understandable if panic had broken out among the few units remaining, but discipline was maintained.

At 2.15 pm, before the *Lancastria* had been hit, all units south of the Loire were ordered to La Rochelle, 200 km south. Maj. White gave orders for the breeches and instruments to be removed 'but for the guns to be left in position'.

Seven hours later White, seven officers, and the men of the two gun sections were safely embarked on two small ships, both of them colliers. Orders were received to smash the instruments, and 'All battery records, literature and stationery were burned at the Quayside'.

Both colliers were crammed with men: around 1,200 RAF personnel were on board, along with the senior command of both 12 AA Brigade and 73 HAA. In the finest traditions of the British Army, Brig. Crewdson and Lt. Col. Wood were in the last group to leave. Also

The desperate state of overcrowding on the evacuation vessels is illustrated by this image of Guinean, *a general cargo ship, 17 June 1940 off Sainte-Nazaire. Similar overcrowding was experienced by the 53rd HAA on the* Alma Dawson. Wikimedia Commons

on board were 2nd Lt. Ruddock and the drivers he had led to Salon.[15] Bearing in mind all that he had been through, his was a charmed life.

AASF SQUADRONS

An indication of the stress under which the bomber and fighter crews had been operating is captured by an Operations Room diary entry for 15 June. At 5.00 am Wing Commander Walters reported that Nos. 1 and 242 Squadrons were 'very tired and badly in need of servicing'. By now Operation Ariel was in full swing. Nos. 1 and 242[16] were Hurricane squadrons assigned to provide air cover for Nantes and St-Nazaire, the most important evacuation ports. The Luftwaffe, completely dominating the skies over France, was determined to prevent more Allied evacuations after what, for Germany, was the Dunkirk debacle.[17] Despite this, Walters considered that the two squadrons were so exhausted that they could not be sent into action.[18]

Just after 9.00 am all bombing and reconnaissance operations scheduled for the 15th were cancelled and the Battle squadrons ordered to return to England. This is the last timed and dated entry in the AASF operations room diary, followed by the statement: 'The last two days have only been entered sketchily.' It is an evocative illustration of the stress under which the RAF had been operating.

The five fighter squadrons remained to provide air cover for the evacuation ports on the Atlantic coast and finally returned to England on 17 June.

AASF headquarters moved to Brest and were reduced to a skeleton staff organising the evacuation of RAF and Army personnel. The HQ staff finally escaped at 5.00 pm on 17 June on board one of the last ships to leave Brest. The following day, its task complete, the AASF was reconstituted as No. 1 Bomber Group.

The AASF had lost 229 aircraft, almost a quarter of the staggering losses suffered by the RAF in May and June 1940. Despite this, Denis Richards judged that they were not in vain. Even heavier losses had been inflicted on the Luftwaffe: over the same two months it had lost 1,428 aircraft[19] against the RAF's loss of 959, and important lessons had been learned which were to be vital in winning the Battle of Britain.[20]

POWS HOBLING AND SNOWDON

The Rev. Capt. J.C. Hobling, the (53rd's chaplain), 2nd Lt. Snowdon, and the six men captured while attempting to recover guns on 19 May 1940 spent the next five years in prisoner-of-war camps. Tragically, both Hobling and Snowdon died just as they were about to be liberated. Hobling died on 14 December 1944 when the prisoner of war camp in which he was held, Stalag XVIII, near Wolfsberg, Austria, was bombed by the US Air Force.[21] One of over one hundred Army chaplains who died in the war,[22] he is buried in the Commonwealth War Graves cemetery at Klagenfurt in Austria. He was thirty-six years old.[23]

Snowdon died in May 1945 and is buried in the Commonwealth War Graves cemetery at Clichy on the northern edge of Paris.[24]

53RD HEAVY ANTI-AIRCRAFT REGIMENT

On its return to England the Regiment reverted to the Home Forces Command. In May 1942 it was moved to the Far East and formed part of 1 Indian Anti-Aircraft Brigade.[25]

Lt. Col. V.R. Krohn and Capt. Kenneth Estlin were both mentioned in dispatches in

July 1940. Both citations were made by Brig. Crewdson.[26] The dispatch stated that 'when evacuating Marseille [Krohn's] initiative, energy and resource resulted in the salvage of much valuable equipment'.[27] This was slightly curious. There is no doubt as to Krohn's energy and initiative, but the citation overlooks the fact that as the *Alma Dawson* pulled away the quay was littered with abandoned stores, vehicles, and the 53rd's guns. Krohn was promoted to brigadier in 1941.

Estlin was commended both for his engineering skills and for his bravery in 'leading several recovery parties into areas occupied by the enemy to salvage instruments and vehicles which were thought to be lost'.[28] He escaped from La Rochelle on the same vessel as Crewdson and Ruddock.

Following the Regiment's safe return to the UK, Gunner R.L. Hewitt-Taylor was selected for officer training. After three months intensive training he was posted to 60th HAA. The Regiment landed in Normandy on D Day + 6 and saw action all the way through to Germany in 1945. He was demobilised in 1946 with the rank of Acting Lieutenant Colonel.

THE FINANCIAL COST OF THE WAR

In May 1940 Marjorie had speculated that the war could bankrupt the country. Little did she know how prescient she was. In September 1939 the Chancellor of the Exchequer, Sir John Simon, brought out a revised war budget. Robert Angel succinctly summarised the financial sacrifice the country was called upon to make: 'The total outlay for the war will be 2,000 millions, which is 700 millions more than when he introduced the budget in April last. The present extra taxation is 107 million. The income tax will go up to 7/6 in the £, or 2/- higher than in April (5/-) or 1/6 more than at the end of the last war. The £502 millions will be met by a loan.' Taxes on beer, spirits, wine and tobacco were all increased and allowances reduced.[29]

These were desperate measures. The anticipated cost of £2.0 billion is the equivalent of £1.2 trillion in 2017. The gravity of the situation facing the country could not be more starkly illustrated. The war would continue for another five years, and while it ended in the unconditional surrender of Germany it left Britain exhausted and financially bankrupt. The Government was left needing massive loans from its North American allies, the United States and Canada, to pay for reconstruction. The Anglo-American Loan Agreement, as it was called, was not paid off until 2006.[30]

RUPERT LEDGER

Alfred's brother, Rupert, was selected for officer training in September 1940. He was commissioned three months later and posted to 54 HAA. A number of postings around the UK followed until 4 June 1943 when he joined No. 1 Composite Anti-Aircraft Demonstration Battery, which was sent to the United States two weeks later.

The Battery arrived in New York on 10 July after a fourteen-day crossing.

Rupert spent the next twelve months in the USA and Canada, returning to the UK in July 1944, where he remained for the rest of the war. He was promoted to captain and was demobilised in December 1945.[31]

ALFRED AND MARJORIE

While still a gunner with the 53rd HAA Alfred moved frequently. Between July 1940 and January 1941 envelopes addressed to him by Marjorie show him located at five different locations in London and the south of England. He was selected for officer training on 18 April 1941 and posted to the Officer Cadet Training Group at Shrivenham. On 6 September 1941 he was appointed 2nd Lieutenant.

Alfred training two women in the Auxiliary Territorial Service, 1942. © Angela Grant

He was posted to the north midlands, moving five times between units and locations. It must have been an unsettling life. The constant moving ended in June 1942 with is final posting to 543/159 (M) Heavy Anti-Aircraft Regiment in Derby.[32] He was eventually promoted to captain and finally released from service on 5 January 1946.

After all the stresses of life during war, and despite continuing hardships suffered by the entire population in its immediate aftermath, Alfred and Marjorie picked up their life together. Their son John was born in 1943 while Alfred was still serving in the Army and their daughter Angela in 1945.

Alfred returned to his job in the City, and over the next forty years enjoyed a successful career in the insurance industry. He and Marjorie continued to live in Surrey until 1982, when they moved to the West Country. Alfred died on 3 November 1993, Marjorie on 15 September 1997.

Alfred and Marjorie enjoying retirement c. *1985.* © Angela Grant

Soon after Alfred was sent to France in October 1939, Marjorie had written to him: 'Just three months since we were married! What a lot has happened since then. We have certainly had a tempestuous beginning but let's hope our married life will have a more peaceful ending.'[33]

When Marjorie wrote those words she had no inkling of what lay ahead. Happily, her wish was realised.

ENDNOTES

1 Ellis & Butler, p. 305.
2 NA, WO 167/370 Appendix.
3 NA, WO 167/370 Appendix Z1, artillery patrols.
4 NA, WO 167/370 Appendix 4, officers' patrols 73 HAA.
5 NA, WO 167/638.
6 NA, AIR 24/21.
7 NA, 167/370, Appendix.
8 NA, CAB/65/7/55.
9 Richards, p. 120.
10 NA, WO 167/638.
11 The *Lancastria* had been requisitioned in May 1940 as a troopship and designated 'His Majesty's Transport': wikipedia.org/wiki/RMS_Lancastria (visited 16.04.16).
12 NA, WO 167/370.
13 ibid.
14 Sebag-Montefiore, pp. 487ff.
15 NA, WO 167/638; NA WO 167/370.
16 242 Squadron was manned by Canadians.
17 Richards, pp. 147–49.
18 NA, AIR 24/21.
19 Murray, p. 40.
20 Richards, p. 150.
21 There are three references to Hobling's death: Gardner, p. 144; AAL marginal note; stalag18a.org. The latter is correct.
22 ww2talk.com/forums/topic/24224-army-chaplainspadres (visited 17.04.16).

23   cwgc.org (visited 01.02.18).

24   cwgc.org (visited 16.04.16).

25   ra39-45.pwp.blueyonder.co.uk/haa (visited 24.04.16).

26   NA, WO 373/89/685; *London Gazette* 26.07.1940 and No. 5943.

27   NA, WO/373/89.

28   ibid.

29   RJA diary 28.09.1939.

30   news.bbc.co.uk 10.05.2006 (visited 08.01.2016). The loan was negotiated by John Maynard Keynes and totalled $3.75 billion, equivalent to $57 billion in 2015. Canada loaned US$1.19 billion, (in 2015 = US$18 billion).

31   Rupert Ledger Army Form B200B.

32   AAL Army Form B200B.

33   ML 01.10.1939.

BIBLIOGRAPHY

PRIMARY SOURCES

NATIONAL ARCHIVES

AIR 5/1343	Advanced Air Striking Force: operation reports and instructions, 1934–1940
AIR 24/21	Advanced Air Striking Force: Operations Record Books, 1939 Aug.–1940 June
AIR 35/51	Location of AASF: movement orders, 1940
ADM 199/2185/39	Convoy number HGY
CAB 65/7/55	War Cabinet Minutes: 10 June 1940
WO 167/370	12 Brigade Headquarters, 1939 Sept.–1940 Mar., June
WO 167/619	73 Heavy Anti-Aircraft (HAA) Regiment Royal Artillery, 1939 Aug.–1940 Feb., Apr., June
WO 167/617	53 Heavy Anti-Aircraft (HAA) Regiment Royal Artillery, 1939 Aug.–1940 June
WO 167/637	157 Heavy Anti-Aircraft (HAA) Battery Royal Artillery, 1939 Aug.–1940 June
WO 167/638	158 Heavy Anti-Aircraft (HAA) Battery Royal Artillery, 1939 Oct.–1940 June
WO 167.639	159 Heavy Anti-Aircraft (HAA) Battery Royal Artillery, 1939 Oct.–1940 June
WO 167/443	12 Anti-Aircraft Brigade Headquarters, Appendix
WO 373/89/685	Mentions in Despatches, 1940–1946

IMPERIAL WAR MUSEUM, LONDON

| Documents.18817 | Private papers of Lt. A. G. Shaw |
| Documents.26092 | Personal Papers of Maj. R. L. Hewitt-Taylor, RA |

LBY 11 / 907   Gardner, Charles, *A.A.S.F.* (Hutchison, 1940), Alfred Ledger's copy, annotated in the margins by him

SECONDARY SOURCES

Alexander, Martin, 'After Dunkirk: The French Army's Performance', in *War in History*, sagepub.com (visited 05.02.16)

Bell, Philip M.H., *The Origins of the Second World War in Europe* (Routledge, 2007)

Blatt, J., ed., *The French Defeat of 1940: Reassessments* (Providence, R.I.: Berghahn Books, 1997).

Buckley, J., *Monty's Men: the British Army and the Liberation of Europe*, (Yale University Press 2013)

Bond, B., *Britain, France and Belgium, 1939–1940* (Oxford: Brassey's, 1990),

Bullock, Alan, *Hitler, a Study in Tyranny* (Harmondsworth: Pelican, 1962)

Churchill, Winston, *The Second World War*, vol. 2 (Cassell, 2nd ed., 1950)

Craig Gordon, A., *Germany 1866–1946* (Oxford: Oxford University Press, 1978)

Dear, I. & Foot, M., *The Oxford Companion to World War II* (Oxford: Oxford University Press, 2001)

Deedes, William F., *Dear Bill: W. F. Deedes reports* (London: Pan Books, 1998)

Dunstan, S., *Fort Eben Emael: The Key to Hitler's victory in the West* (Oxford: Osprey, 2005)

Ellis, L.F. & Butler, J.R.M. (eds.), *The War in France and Flanders 1939–40, History of the Second World War United Kingdom Military Serie,* Naval & Military Press, 2004)

Evans, M.M., *The Fall of France: Act with Daring* (Oxford: Osprey, 2000)

Gardner, C., *A.A.S.F.* (Hutchison, 1940)

Gelb, N., *Dunkirk, The Incredible Escape* (London: Michael Joseph, 1990)

Gilbert, M., *Churchill, a Life* (London: BCA, 1992)

Gilbert, M. & Gott, R., *The Appeasers* (London: Weidenfeld & Nicolson, 1967)

Guderian, H. (trans. C. Fitzgibbon), *Panzer Leader*, (Futura Publications, 1974)

Harman, N., *Dunkirk the Necessary Myth* (Hodder & Stroughton, 1980)

Hooton, E.R., *Luftwaffe at War; Blitzkrieg in the West.* London: Chervron/Ian Allen, 2007)

Hayward, J., *Dunkirk and the battle of France & Flanders 1939–40* (cd41recordings.com, visited 10.01.15)

Kaufmann, J.E. and H.W., *Hitler's Blitzkrieg Campaigns: The Invasion and Defense of Western Europe* (Da Capo Press, 2002)

Keynes, J.M., *The Economic Consequences of the Peace* (London: Macmillan, 1919) www.luftwaffedata.co.uk

MacMahon, B., *History Ireland*, vol. 13 (historyireland.com 2005)

Melvin, M., *Manstein: Hitler's Most Controversial General* (London: Weidenfeld & Nicolson, 2010)

Murray, W., *Strategy for Defeat: the Luftwaffe 1933–1945* (Maxwell Air Force Base, Ala.: Air University Press, 1983)

Nicolson, H., *Peacemaking 1919, Being Reminiscences of the Paris Peace Conference* (Safety Harbor, Fla.: Simon Publications, 2001)

Nicolson, N., ed., *Harold Nicolson Diaries & Letters 1930–39* (London: Fontana, 1966)

Philpott, I.M., *The Royal Air Force*, vol. 2, *Rearmament 1930–39* (Pen & Sword Books)

Richards, D., *The Royal Air Force 1939–45,* vol. 1 (Stationery Office, 1953)

Routledge, N.W., *History of the Royal Regiment of Artillery – Anti-Aircraft Artillery 1914–55* (London: Brasseys, 1994).

Shirer, William L. *Twentieth Century Journey, Volume 2, The Nightmare Years: 1930–1940.* (Boston: Little Brown 1984).

Taylor, A.J.P., *English History, 1914–1945* (Oxford: Oxford University Press, 1965)

Thompson, J., *Dunkirk: Retreat to Victory* (Sidgwick & Jackson Ltd., London, 2011)

Trevelyan, R., *The Fortress* (Collins, London 1956)

Sebag-Montefiore, H., *Dunkirk: Fight to the Last Man* (London: Viking, 2006),

Murray, W., *Strategy for Defeat: the Luftwaffe 1933–1945* (Air University Press 1983) (www.ibiblio.org/hyperwar/AAF/AAF-Luftwaffe, visited 02.02.2017)

INTERNET

bbc.co.uk/history/ww2

britannica.com

churchill-society-london.org.uk

cwgc.org

deardad-lettershome.blogspot.co.uk

ww2today.com

iwm.org.uk

luftwaffedata.co.uk/wiki/index

nationalarchives.gov.uk

naval-history.net

news.bbc.co.uk

raf.mod.uk

ra39-45.pwp.blueyonder.co.uk

spartacus-educational.com

static.guim.uk/

ukpressonline.co.uk

ww2news.com

ww2talk.com

ww2today.com

wikipedia.org

wrecksite.eu

Abbreviations

AAL	Alfred Ledger to Marjorie Ledger
ML	Marjorie Ledger to Alfred Ledger
RJA	Robert Angel diary
NA	National Archives
IWM	Imperial War Museum